# Teach Yourself VISUALLY™

# iPad®
# 4th Edition

by Guy Hart-Davis

**Visual**
A Wiley Brand

## Teach Yourself VISUALLY™ iPad® 4th Edition

Published by
**John Wiley & Sons, Inc.**
10475 Crosspoint Boulevard
Indianapolis, IN 46256

www.wiley.com

Published simultaneously in Canada

Library of Congress Control Number: 2015954285

ISBN: 978-1-119-18863-6

Manufactured in the United States of America

10 9 8 7 6 5 4 3 2

## Trademark Acknowledgments

Wiley, the Wiley logo, Visual, the Visual logo, Teach Yourself VISUALLY, Read Less - Learn More and related trade dress are trademarks or registered trademarks of John Wiley & Sons, Inc. and/or its affiliates. iPad, iPad mini, iPad Air, and iPad Pro are trademarks or a registered trademark of Apple, Inc. All other trademarks are the property of their respective owners. John Wiley & Sons, Inc. is not associated with any product or vendor mentioned in this book. *Teach Yourself Visually™ iPad® 4th Edition* is an independent publication and has not been authorized, sponsored, or otherwise approved by Apple, Inc.

## Contact Us

For general information on our other products and services please contact our Customer Care Department within the U.S. at 877-762-2974, outside the U.S. at 317-572-3993 or fax 317-572-4002.

For technical support please visit www.wiley.com/techsupport.

**Sales** | Contact Wiley at (877) 762-2974 or /fax (317) 572-4002.

# Credits

**Acquisitions Editor**
Aaron Black

**Project Editor**
Lynn Northrup

**Technical Editor**
Galen Gruman

**Copy Editor**
Lynn Northrup

**Production Editor**
Barath Kumar Rajasekaran

**Manager, Content Development & Assembly**
Mary Beth Wakefield

**Vice President, Professional Technology Strategy**
Barry Pruett

## About the Author

**Guy Hart-Davis** is the author of *Teach Yourself VISUALLY iPhone S6; Teach Yourself VISUALLY Android Phones and Tablets, 2nd Edition; Teach Yourself VISUALLY Apple Watch; Teach Yourself VISUALLY Samsung Galaxy S6; Teach Yourself VISUALLY iMac, 3rd Edition; Teach Yourself VISUALLY MacBook Pro, 2nd Edition; Teach Yourself VISUALLY MacBook Air; iMac Portable Genius, 4th Edition;* and *iWork Portable Genius, 2nd Edition.*

## Author's Acknowledgments

My thanks go to the many people who turned my manuscript into the highly graphical book you are holding. In particular, I thank Aaron Black for asking me to write the book; Lynn Northrup for keeping me on track and skillfully editing the text; Galen Gruman for reviewing the book for technical accuracy and contributing helpful suggestions; and SPi Global for laying out the book.

# How to Use This Book

## Who This Book Is For

This book is for the reader who has never used this particular technology or software application. It is also for readers who want to expand their knowledge.

## The Conventions in This Book

### ① Steps

This book uses a step-by-step format to guide you easily through each task. **Numbered steps** are actions you must do; **bulleted steps** clarify a point, step, or optional feature; and **indented steps** give you the result.

### ② Notes

Notes give additional information — special conditions that may occur during an operation, a situation that you want to avoid, or a cross reference to a related area of the book.

### ③ Icons and Buttons

Icons and buttons show you exactly what you need to click to perform a step.

### ④ Tips

Tips offer additional information, including warnings and shortcuts.

### ⑤ Bold

**Bold** type shows command names, options, and text or numbers you must type.

### ⑥ Italics

*Italic* type introduces and defines a new term.

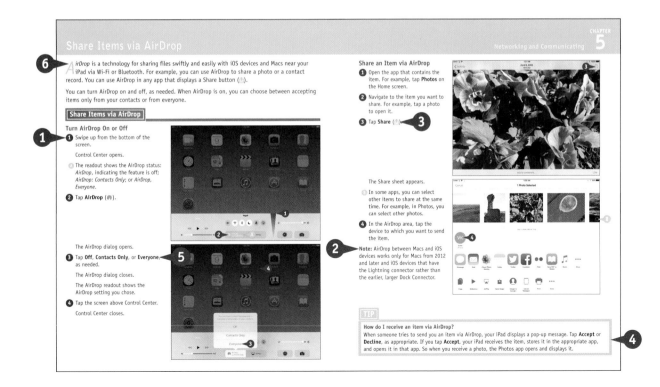

# Table of Contents

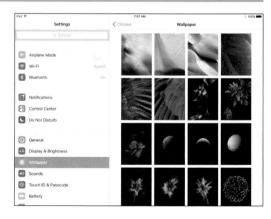

## Chapter 3   Working with Voice and Accessibility

## Chapter 4   Setting Up Communications

# Table of Contents

# Table of Contents

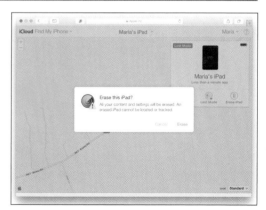

# CHAPTER 1

# Getting Started with Your iPad

The iPad is a series of powerful and extremely popular touch-screen tablet computers created by Apple. You can use an iPad either as a full-powered computing device on its own or as a companion device to your Mac or PC. In this chapter, you set up your iPad, sync data to it, and learn to use the user interface.

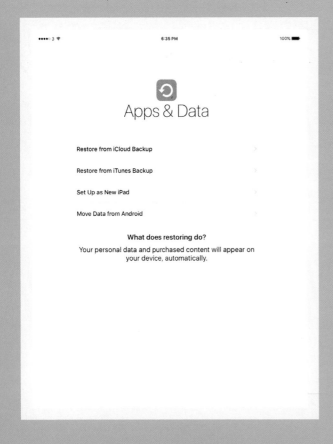

# Take a Look at the iPad Models

The Apple iPad is the most popular tablet computer on the market. Powerful, elegantly designed, and easy to use, the iPad can take over many of the tasks you normally perform on your desktop or laptop computer, such as surfing the web, exchanging e-mail messages, performing desktop publishing, and playing video games.

## Understand the Choice of iPad Models

The iPad comes in three sizes: iPad mini, iPad Air, and iPad Pro. As of this writing, the latest version of the iPad mini is the iPad mini 4; Apple still also sells the iPad mini 2, but not the iPad mini 3. The latest version of the iPad Air is the iPad Air 2; Apple still also sells the iPad Air, the first version. The latest version of the iPad Pro is the first version, which is called simply iPad Pro.

## Compare Screen Size and Device Size

iPad mini

The iPad mini 4 and iPad mini 2 have a 7.9-inch screen with 2048 × 1536 pixels at a resolution of 326 pixels per inch, or ppi. The iPad Air 2 and iPad Air have a 9.7-inch screen with 2048 × 1536 pixels at a resolution of 264 ppi. The iPad Pro has a 12.9-inch screen with 2732 × 2048 pixels at a resolution of 264 ppi. All of these screen measurements are diagonal.

Although the difference in diagonal measurements sounds small — less than 2 inches between the iPad mini and the iPad Air, and just over 3 inches between the iPad Air and the iPad Pro — the difference in screen size is dramatic. The iPad Air screen is one-and-a-half times as large as the iPad mini screen. The iPad Pro screen is one-and-three-quarter times as large as the iPad Air screen, and more than two-and-a-half times as large as the iPad mini screen.

iPad Air

The iPad mini measures 7.87 inches tall × 5.3 inches wide and weighs around three-quarters of a pound. The iPad Air measures 9.4 inches tall × 6.6 inches wide and weighs around 1 pound. The iPad Pro measures 12 inches tall × 8.68 inches wide and weighs 1.6 pounds.

iPad Pro

## iPad Storage Capacity

Apple offers the iPad Air 2 and the iPad mini 4 with three capacities: 16GB, 64GB, and 128GB. The iPad Air and the iPad mini 2 come in two capacities: 16GB and 32GB. The iPad Pro comes in two capacities: 32GB and 128GB.

Having more storage enables you to install more apps and carry more music, movies, and other files with you. The diagram shows examples of what you can fit on the iPad models.

Higher capacities command substantially higher prices, so you must decide how much you are prepared to spend. Generally speaking, higher-capacity devices get more use in the long run and are worth the extra cost.

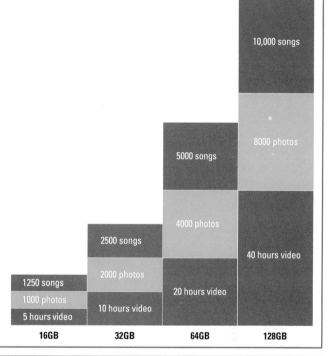

## Wi-Fi Only or Cellular and Wi-Fi

The iPad mini, iPad Air, and iPad Pro all come in Wi-Fi–only and cellular-and–Wi-Fi models.

With a Wi-Fi–only iPad, you can connect to the Internet only through wireless networks, such as those at your home or workplace, or wireless hotspots that are open to the public or to customers of the establishments that host them.

With a cellular-and–Wi-Fi iPad, you can connect both through the cellular network and through wireless networks, giving you Internet access no

matter where you go. This option costs more both in the purchase price of the iPad and in the cellular service fees with either a monthly or a pay-as-you-go plan.

continued ▶

The front of each iPad contains a touch screen that you use for most of your interaction with the device and its interface. The front of the iPad also contains a camera, located above the screen and sometimes called the "selfie camera," for taking self-portraits and for video chat. The rear of the iPad contains a higher-resolution camera capable of taking good-quality photos and videos.

Apart from being larger and designed for professional use, the iPad Pro has features and accessories that the iPad mini and iPad Air do not have, such as the Apple Pencil stylus and the Smart Keyboard.

## Touch Screen

Each iPad model has a touch screen that takes up most of the space on the front of the tablet. You use the touch screen to access everything on the iPad with your fingers and to view content. The iPad software uses gestures to scroll, rotate, and zoom in on objects on-screen.

All current iPad models have what Apple calls a Retina display, which has very high resolution. The original iPad mini has a lower-resolution display.

## Cameras

Each iPad has a camera on the front — the screen side — and another on the back.

The front camera is for FaceTime video calling and self-portraits. It can capture 1.2-megapixel photos and high-definition video at the 720p standard (meaning 720 vertical lines using progressive scan), which provides a good-quality video picture.

The back camera is for taking photos and videos of other subjects, much as you would use a stand-alone digital camera. The back camera on the iPad Air and on the iPad mini 2 can capture 5-megapixel photos and high-definition video at the 1080p standard. The back camera on the iPad mini 4, the iPad Air 2, and the iPad Pro can capture 8-megapixel photos. It can also capture slow-motion video at 120 frames per second and can take bursts of photos.

## Apple Pencil for iPad Pro

You can use your fingers on the touch screen to control the iPad Pro just as you can with the other iPad models, but the iPad Pro is also designed to use a custom stylus called the Apple Pencil. The Apple Pencil enables you to draw and make selections much more precisely than you can with a finger, giving you finer control over the documents you create and edit on the iPad Pro. The Apple Pencil and the iPad Pro screen are pressure sensitive, so you can draw lines of different thicknesses by varying the amount of pressure you apply.

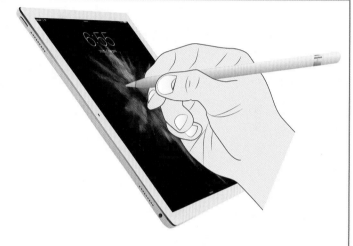

The Apple Pencil contains a rechargeable battery that you can charge by plugging the Apple Pencil into the iPad Pro.

## Smart Keyboard for iPad Pro

Like the iPad mini and iPad Air, the iPad Pro has an on-screen keyboard that you can use to enter text as needed. You can also connect a Bluetooth keyboard to the iPad Pro to enter text, as you can for any iPad.

But if you need to enter large amounts of text, you may prefer the Smart Keyboard, a custom keyboard that doubles as a cover for the iPad Pro. The Smart Keyboard connects to the iPad Pro via the Smart Connector interface on the side of the iPad Pro, which allows the Smart Keyboard not only to provide input to the iPad Pro, but also to draw power from it.

# Meet Your iPad's Controls

Your iPad has four hardware controls for essential actions: the Sleep/Wake button to control power, the Volume Up button and the Volume Down button for controlling audio volume, and the Home button below the screen.

If your iPad has cellular connectivity, it needs a SIM card. Some iPad models come with an Apple SIM that works with most carriers. Some carriers do not support the Apple SIM, so you must verify that your carrier does support it before you activate the iPad using the Apple SIM.

## Meet Your iPad's Controls

**1** Press and hold the **Sleep/Wake** button on top of the iPad for a couple of seconds.

The top of the iPad also contains:

**A** The microphone.

**B** The headphone socket.

As the iPad starts, the Apple logo appears on the screen.

**C** Above the iPad screen is the front-facing camera.

**D** Below the iPad screen is the Home button, which you press to display the Home screen.

At the bottom of the iPad are:

**E** The Lightning Connector.

**F** The speakers.

**2** Turn the iPad so that you can see its right side.

**3** On an iPad mini, move the side switch down, so that an orange dot appears, when you want to mute the iPad notifications, alerts, and sound effects. The iPad Air and iPad Pro do not have the side switch.

**Note:** You can configure the side switch to lock the screen rotation. To do so, tap **Settings** (⚙), tap **General** (⚙), and then tap **Lock Rotation** in the Use Side Switch To area.

**4** Press the Volume Up (+) button to increase the sound volume.

**Note:** When the Camera app is active, you can press the Volume Up (+) button to take a picture with the camera.

**5** Press the Volume Down (−) button to decrease the volume.

**6** When the lock screen appears, tap near the **slide to unlock** prompt, and then drag your finger to the right.

The iPad unlocks, and the Home screen appears.

---

**How do I insert a SIM card in my iPad?**

If you have a cellular iPad that does not yet contain a SIM card, get a suitable nano-SIM. Then insert the SIM removal tool or the straightened end of a paperclip in the SIM hole at the top of the left side of the iPad. Push the tool gently straight in until the tray pops out, and then pull the tray with your fingernails. Insert the SIM in the tray, and then push the tray in fully.

**What do I do if my carrier does not support the Apple SIM?**

If your carrier does not support the Apple SIM, get an approved SIM from the carrier and use it to activate your iPad. Do not activate your iPad using the Apple SIM, or you may not be able to use the iPad with that carrier in the future.

# Download, Install, and Set Up iTunes

To sync your iPad with your computer, you use Apple's iTunes application. iTunes comes preinstalled on every Mac but not on PCs; to get iTunes for Windows, you download it from the Apple website and then install it on your PC.

If you do not have a computer, or you do not want to sync your iPad with your computer, you can set up and sync your iPad using Apple's iCloud service, as described later in this chapter.

## Download, Install, and Set Up iTunes

① On your PC, open the web browser. This example uses Microsoft Edge, the browser that comes with Windows 10.

② Click the Address box, type **www. apple.com/itunes/download**, and then press **Enter**.

The Download iTunes web page appears.

③ Click the check boxes (☑ changes to ☐) if you do not want to receive e-mail from Apple.

④ Click **Download Now**.

⑤ When the download finishes, click **Run** in the pop-up panel that appears.

The iTunes installation begins, and the Welcome to iTunes dialog opens.

⑥ Click **Next**, and then follow the steps of the installer.

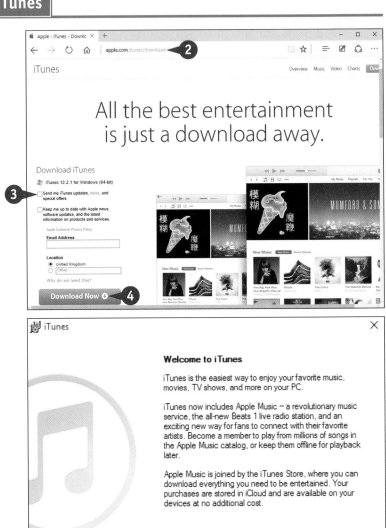

**Note:** You must accept the license agreement to install iTunes.

⑦ Click the **Add iTunes shortcut to my desktop** check box (☑ changes to ☐) unless you want this shortcut.

⑧ Click **Use iTunes as the default player for audio files** (☑ changes to ☐) if you do not want to use iTunes as the default audio player.

⑨ Click **Automatically Update iTunes and Other Apple Software** (☑ changes to ☐) if you do not want automatic updates.

⑩ Click **Install**.

When the installation finishes, the installer displays the Congratulations dialog.

⑪ Click **Open iTunes after the installer exits** (☑ changes to ☐) if you do not want iTunes to launch automatically when you close the installer.

⑫ Click **Finish**.

The installer closes.

Unless you chose not to open iTunes automatically, iTunes opens.

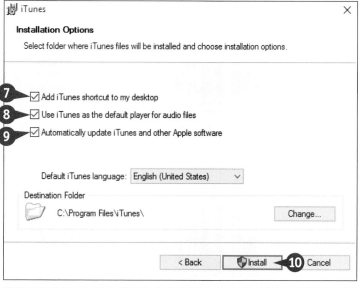

---

**TIPS**

**Should I allow Apple to install updates automatically on my PC?**

If this is your own PC, installing updates automatically is usually helpful. The updates may include fixes to bugs or vulnerabilities, new features, or both.

**How do I set up iTunes on a Mac?**

If you have not run iTunes already, click the **iTunes** icon (♫) that appears on the Dock by default. If the Dock contains no iTunes icon, click **Launchpad** (🚀) on the Dock, and then click **iTunes** (♫) on the Launchpad screen. The iTunes Setup Assistant launches. Follow the steps to set up iTunes.

# Begin Setup and Activate Your iPad

**B**efore you can use your iPad, you must set it up and activate. First, you choose your language, specify your country or region, connect to the Internet through either a Wi-Fi network or the cellular network, and choose whether to use Location Services. You then activate the iPad, registering it with the Apple servers. After this first stage of setup, you choose among setting up the iPad as a new iPad, restoring it from an iCloud backup, and restoring it from an iTunes backup.

## Begin Setup and Activate Your iPad

**1** Turn on the iPad by pressing and holding the Sleep/Wake button for a couple of seconds until the Apple logo appears.

**2** When the Hello screen appears, tap near the **slide to set up** prompt at the bottom and drag your finger to the right.

**3** On the Language screen, tap the language you want to use for the interface.

**4** On the Select Your Country or Region screen, tap your country.

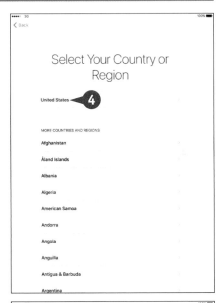

The Choose a Wi-Fi Network screen appears.

**5** Tap the wireless network you want to use.

**A** Tap **Choose Another Network** to connect to a network that does not broadcast its name.

**B** Tap **Use Cellular Connection** to connect to the Internet via the cellular network and set up your iPad. This button appears only on cellular-capable iPads.

**Note:** If the Connect to iTunes button appears, tap it to stop the setup process here. You can then continue as explained in the section "Set Up Your iPad Using iTunes," later in this chapter.

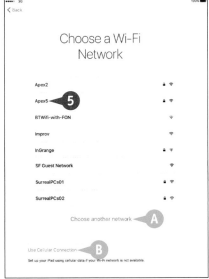

The Enter Password screen appears.

**6** Type the password.

**7** Tap **Join**.

Your iPad joins the wireless network and connects to the Internet.

The Location Services screen appears.

**8** Tap **Enable Location Services** or **Disable Location Services**, as needed.

**Note:** Enabling Location Services is usually helpful, because it lets apps such as Maps determine your exact location.

The Touch ID screen appears unless your iPad does not support Touch ID.

**9** Place your finger or thumb on the Home button and follow the prompts to scan your fingerprint or thumbprint.

The Complete screen appears.

**10** Tap **Continue**.

The Create a Passcode screen appears.

**11** Type a six-digit passcode, and then repeat it on the Re-Enter Your Passcode screen.

**Note:** You can tap **Passcode Options** to create a custom alphanumeric code or a four-digit code instead.

The Apps & Data screen appears.

**12** Tap the appropriate button:

**C** Tap **Set Up as New iPad** to set up your iPad from scratch using iCloud. See the next section, "Set Up Your iPad as New Using iCloud," for details.

**D** Tap **Restore from iCloud Backup** to set up your iPad using a backup stored in iCloud. See the later section, "Set Up Your iPad from an iCloud Backup," for details.

**E** Tap **Restore from iTunes Backup** to set up your iPad using a backup stored on your computer. See the later section, "Set Up Your iPad from iTunes," for details.

**F** Tap **Move Data from Android** to transfer data from an Android device. See the later section, "Switch from Android Using Move to iOS," for details.

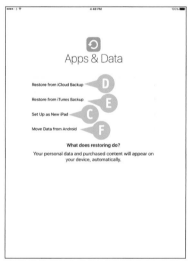

**TIP**

**Why does my network's name not appear on the Choose a Wi-Fi Network screen?**
If the network is within range of your iPad, the most likely reason is that the network does not broadcast its network name. Tap **Choose another network**. You can then type the network's name, choose the security type, enter the security information — such as a password — and connect to the network.

# Set Up Your iPad as New Using iCloud

If you want to set up and use your iPad without syncing it to your computer, you can set it up using Apple's iCloud online service. With this approach, you sync your data to your account on iCloud, from which you can access it using other iOS devices, a Mac or a Windows PC, or a web browser on any computer.

To set up a new iPad to use iCloud, follow the instructions in the previous section to begin setup, and then continue with the instructions in this section. If you have backed up your iPad to iCloud and want to restore it from that backup, turn to the next section instead.

## Set Up Your iPad as New Using iCloud

**1** Begin setup as explained in the previous section, "Begin Setup and Activate Your iPad."

**2** On the Apps & Data screen, tap **Set Up as New iPad**.

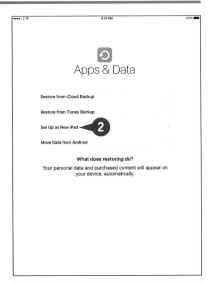

The Apple ID screen appears.

**A** If you do not yet have an Apple ID, tap **Don't have an Apple ID or forgot it?** and follow the screens that appear.

**3** Type your Apple ID.

**4** Type your password.

**Note:** If the Apple ID Security screen appears, prompting you to create new security questions, tap **Add Security Questions**, tap **Next**, and then create the questions.

**5** Tap **Next**.

The Terms and Conditions screen appears.

**6** Tap **Agree** in the lower-right corner of the screen if you want to proceed.

The Terms and Conditions dialog opens.

**7** Tap **Agree** in the Terms and Conditions dialog.

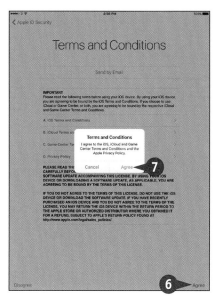

The Apple Pay screen appears.

**8** Tap **Next**.

**Note:** Tap **Next** on the Apple Pay screen even if you do not want to set up Apple Pay. On the next screen, you can skip setting up Apple Pay.

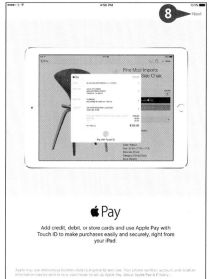

---

**TIP**

**What is Siri and should I enable it?**

Siri is Apple's voice-driven assistant, which enables you to interact with your iPhone by voice. Many people find Siri useful, but if you do not, you can turn Siri off at any time. See Chapter 3 for instructions on using and customizing Siri.

continued ▶

When you set up your iPad using iCloud, use an e-mail address that you intend to keep for the long term. This is especially important if you use the same e-mail address for the Apple ID that you use for the App Store; each app you buy is tied to that e-mail address, so if you change the address, you will need to authenticate again for each app update.

## Set Up Your iPad as New Using iCloud (continued)

The Add Card screen appears.

**9** Point the rear camera lens at your credit card or debit card.

The setup routine recognizes the card details.

**B** You can tap **Enter Card Details Manually** if the recognition fails or is inaccurate.

**C** You can tap **Set Up Later in Settings** to skip adding a card.

The Card Details screen appears.

**Note:** Correct the card details if necessary.

**10** Tap **Next** and follow the prompts to set up your card with Apple Pay.

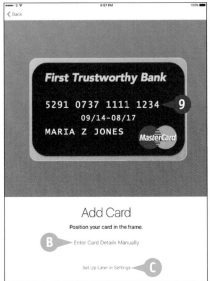

The iCloud Keychain screen appears.

**D** You can tap **Don't Restore Passwords** if you do not want to restore your passwords from iCloud to your iPhone.

**11** Tap **Use iCloud Security Code**.

The iCloud Security Code screen appears.

**12** Type your security code.

The iPhone verifies the security code with Apple's servers.

The Verification Code screen appears.

**13** Type the verification code sent to your trusted phone number.

The iPhone checks that the verification code is correct.

The Siri screen appears.

**14** Tap **Turn On Siri** or **Turn On Siri Later**, as appropriate.

**Note:** You can turn Siri on or off at any point after setup.

The Diagnostics screen appears.

**E** To learn which details the diagnostics and usage reports contain, tap **About Diagnostics & Privacy**.

**15** Tap **Send to Apple** or **Don't Send**, as appropriate.

The App Analytics screen appears.

**16** Tap **Share with App Developers** if you want to share usage statistics and crash data with the developers of the apps you use. Otherwise, tap **Don't Share**.

**17** Tap **Next**.

The Welcome to iPad screen appears.

**18** Tap **Get Started**.

The Home screen appears, and you can begin using your iPad.

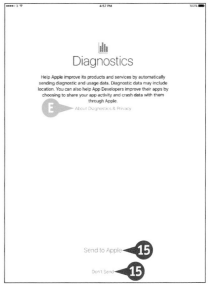

---

**TIP**

**What is iCloud Keychain?**
iCloud Keychain gives you an easy way to store your passwords and credit-card information securely on your iPad, other iOS devices, and Mac. Instead of having to remember the password for each website, or needing to look at a credit card so that you can enter its details, you can have iCloud Keychain automatically provide the details.

# Set Up Your iPad from an iCloud Backup

Instead of setting up your iPad as new using iCloud, you can set it up by restoring it from an iCloud backup of either another iPad or iOS device or the same iPad. For example, if you are upgrading to a new iPad, you can restore the backup of your previous iPad.

When you restore your iPad from an iCloud backup, you choose which backup to use. iOS automatically restores your settings, downloads your apps from the App Store, and then installs them on the iPad.

## Set Up Your iPad from an iCloud Backup

**1** Begin setup as explained in the section "Begin Setup and Activate Your iPad," earlier in this chapter.

**2** On the Apps & Data screen, tap **Restore from iCloud Backup**.

**Note:** On a cellular iPad, use a Wi-Fi network rather than the cellular network to restore your iPad from backup so as not to run through your data plan.

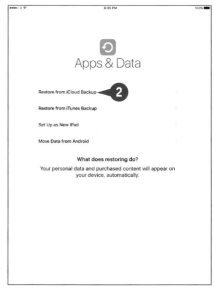

The iCloud Sign In screen appears.

**3** Type your Apple ID.

**4** Type your password.

**5** Tap **Next**.

The Terms and Conditions screen appears.

**6** Tap **Agree** in the lower-right corner of the screen.

The Terms and Conditions dialog opens.

**7** Tap **Agree** in the Terms and Conditions dialog.

iOS verifies your Apple ID.

The Choose Backup screen appears.

**8** Tap the backup you want to use.

**Ⓐ** If the backup you want to use does not appear, tap **Show all backups** to display other backups, and then tap the appropriate backup.

**Ⓑ** The Restore from iCloud screen appears while iOS restores the backup to your iPad.

After iOS completes the restoration, your iPad restarts.

The lock screen appears.

**9** Swipe to unlock your iPad, and follow any security prompts that appear. You can then start using the iPad.

TIP

**Which iPad backup should I use?**

Normally, it is best to use the most recent backup available for this iPad or for the iPad whose backups you are using. But sometimes you may find there is a problem with the latest backup. If this happens, try the previous backup.

# Set Up Your iPad Using iTunes

Instead of setting up your iPad using iCloud, as described in the previous two sections, you can set it up using iTunes. You can either restore an iTunes backup to the device or set up the iPad from scratch using iTunes.

When setting up your iPad for the first time, you can restore it from an iTunes backup of another iPad — for example, your previous iPad — or another iOS device. If you have already set up this iPad, you can restore it from its own backup.

## Set Up Your iPad Using iTunes

**1** Begin setup as explained in the section "Begin Setup and Activate Your iPad," earlier in this chapter.

**2** On the Apps & Data screen, tap **Restore from iTunes Backup**.

The Connect to iTunes screen appears.

**3** Connect your iPad to your computer via the USB cable.

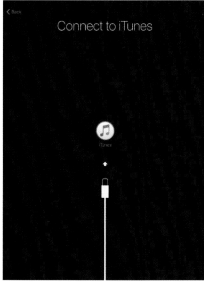

On your computer, iTunes opens or becomes active.

The Welcome to Your New iPad screen appears.

**4** Make sure the **Restore from this backup** radio button is selected (◉).

**5** Click the pop-up menu (▣), and select the appropriate iPad.

**6** Click **Continue**.

iTunes restores your iPad from the backup.

When the restore is complete, your iPad restarts.

The control screens for your iPad appear in the iTunes window.

You can now choose sync settings for the iPad as explained in the section "Choose Which Items to Sync from Your Computer," later in this chapter.

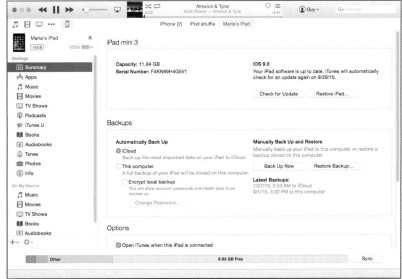

**How do I set up my iPad from scratch using iTunes?**

On the Apps & Data screen, tap **Restore from iTunes Backup**, and then connect your iPad to your computer via the USB cable. When the Welcome to Your New iPad screen appears in iTunes on your computer, click **Set up as new iPad** ( ⭕ changes to 🔘 ). Click **Continue**. On the Sync with iTunes screen that appears, click **Get Started**. The iPad control screens appear, and you can set up sync as described in the section "Choose Which Items to Sync from Your Computer," later in this chapter.

# Switch from Android Using Move to iOS

$I$f you have been using a phone that runs Google's Android operating system, you can take advantage of an app that Apple offers to help Android users move to iPhone or iPad. This app is called Move to iOS and is available for free from the Play Store on the Google Play service. As of this writing, the Move to iOS app works only for Android phones, not for Android tablets.

This section shows Android Lollipop, version 5.1, running on a Nexus 5 phone. Depending on the type of Android device you have, the screen will likely look somewhat different.

## Download and Install the Move to iOS App

First, download and install the Move to iOS app from the Play Store. Tap **Play Store** ( ) on either the Home screen or the Apps screen to launch the Play Store app. Tap the search box at the top of the screen, and type **Move to iOS**. Tap the **Move to iOS** search result to display the app's screen, and then tap **Install**.

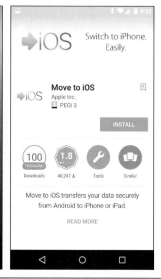

## Launch the Move to iOS App

Next, launch the Move to iOS app. If you still have the app's Play Store screen displayed, tap **Open** when the installation completes. If not, tap **Move to iOS** ( ) on the Home screen or on the Apps screen, depending on how your Android phone is configured.

When the Move to iOS screen appears, tap **Continue**. Accept the terms and conditions if you want to proceed. The Find Your Code screen then appears, prompting you to find your code on the iPhone — or, in your case, the iPad.

## Find Your Code and Connect the Devices

On your iPad, begin setup as explained in the section "Begin Setup and Activate Your iPad," earlier in this chapter. When you reach the Apps & Data screen, tap **Move Data from Android**. On the first Move from Android screen, tap **Continue**. The second Move from Android screen then appears, showing the code you should enter to connect your Android device to your iPad. Type the code on your Android device, and it connects to your iPad via Wi-Fi.

## Choose Which Data to Transfer

On the Transfer Data screen on your Android phone, tap to uncheck any item — **Google Account**, **Bookmarks**, **Messages**, or **Camera Roll** — you do not want to transfer to your iPad. Then tap **Next** to start the transfer, which may take several minutes.

When the Transfer Complete screen appears, tap **Done** to close the Move to iOS app.

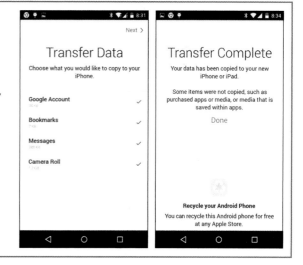

## Finish Setting Up Your iPad

On your iPad, the Transfer Complete screen appears. Tap **Continue Setting Up iPad** to display the Apple ID screen. You can then enter your Apple ID and password before proceeding with the rest of the setup routine. Go back to the section "Set Up Your iPad as New Using iCloud," earlier in this chapter, and start at step **3** in the list.

# Choose Which Items to Sync from Your Computer

After setting up your iPad, you can use the iPad control screens in iTunes to choose which items to sync from your computer. When setting your sync preferences, start on the Summary tab. Here, you can change the iPad's name, choose whether to back up the iPad to iCloud or to your computer, decide whether to encrypt the backup, and set general options for controlling syncing.

## Choose Which Items to Sync from Your Computer

### Connect Your iPad and Choose Options on the Summary Tab

1. Connect your iPad to your computer via the USB cable.

   The iTunes window appears.

2. If your iPad control screens do not automatically appear, click the iPad button (□) on the navigation bar at the top of the screen.

   **Note:** Your iPad appears in iTunes with either a default name or the name you have given it.

   The iPad control screens appear.

3. Click **Summary**.

   The Summary screen appears.

4. To change the name of your iPad, click the existing name, type the new name, and press Enter or Return.

5. In the Automatically Back Up area, click **iCloud** (○ changes to ◉) or **This computer** (○ changes to ◉) to specify where to back up your iPad.

6. If you choose to back up to this computer, click **Encrypt local backup** (☐ changes to ☑).

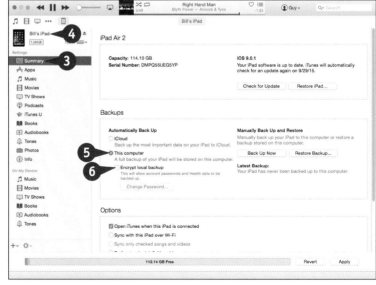

24

**7** In the Set Password dialog, type a password twice.

**8** On a Mac, click **Remember this password in my keychain** (☐ changes to ✓) if you want to save the password in your keychain.

**9** Click **Set Password**.

The Set Password dialog closes.

**10** Click **Open iTunes when this iPad is connected** (☐ changes to ✓) if you want iTunes to open automatically when you connect the iPad.

**11** Click **Sync only checked songs and videos** (☐ changes to ✓) if you want syncing to omit any song or video whose check box you have deselected (☐).

**12** Select **Convert higher bit rate songs to AAC** (☐ changes to ✓) if you want to compress high-quality song files to fit more on your iPad. In the pop-up menu, choose the bit rate.

**TIP**

**Should I back up my iPad to my computer or to iCloud?**

If you plan to use your iPad mostly with your computer, back up the iPad to the computer. iTunes stores a full backup, so you can restore all the data to your iPad, or to a replacement iPad, if necessary. You can also encrypt the backup; this enables you to back up and restore your passwords as well, which can save you time and effort. To keep your data safe, you must back up your computer as well. For example, you can use the Time Machine feature in OS X to back up a Mac.

Backing up your iPhone to iCloud enables you to access the backups from anywhere via the Internet, but make sure your iCloud account has enough storage to contain the backups. An iCloud backup stores less information than an iTunes backup.

continued ▶

# Choose Which Items to Sync from
# Your Computer (continued)

iTunes makes it easy to choose which items to sync to your iPad. By selecting the iPad in the navigation bar in iTunes and then clicking the appropriate item in the Settings area of the Source list, you can quickly choose which apps, music, movies, and other items to sync from your computer.

After choosing the items to sync, you click the Apply button to apply your changes or the Sync button to run the sync.

## Choose Which Items to Sync from Your Computer (continued)

### Choose Which Apps to Sync

**1** Click **Apps**.

**A** You can click the pop-up menu button (⊡) and choose how to sort the apps: Click **Sort by Name**, **Sort by Kind**, **Sort by Category**, **Sort by Date Added**, or **Sort by Size**, as needed.

**2** Click **Install** for each app you want to sync to the iPad (Install changes to Will Install).

**3** Scroll down the screen and click **Automatically install new apps** (☐ changes to ☑) if you want to sync new apps automatically. This is usually helpful.

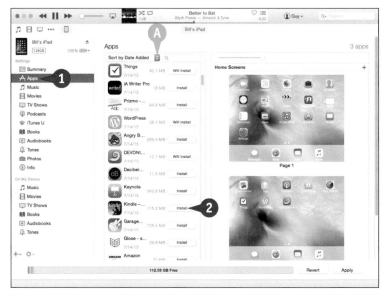

### Choose Which Music to Sync

**1** Click **Music**.

**2** Click **Sync Music** (☐ changes to ☑).

**3** To load a selection of music, click **Selected playlists, artists, albums, and genres** (◯ changes to ◉) instead of **Entire music library**.

**B** Click **Automatically fill free space with songs** (☐ changes to ☑) only if you want to put as much music as possible on your iPad.

**4** Click the check box (☐ changes to ☑) for each playlist, artist, genre, or album to include.

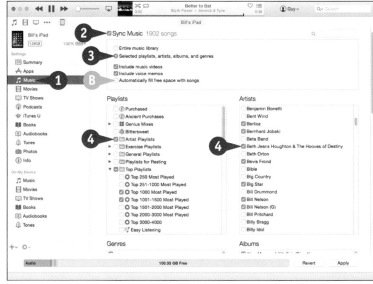

## Sync Photos

**1** Click **Photos**.

**2** Click **Sync Photos** (☐ changes to ☑).

**Note:** In Windows, click **Copy photos from** (☐ changes to ☑), and then choose the folder in the drop-down list.

**3** Click the pop-up menu button (⬍) and choose the source of the photos — for example, **Photos**.

**4** Choose which photos to sync. For example, click **Selected albums** (◯ changes to ◉), and then choose the albums to include.

## Apply Your Changes and Sync

**1** Click **Apply** or **Sync**.

**Note:** The Apply button appears when you have made changes to the times you will sync. Click **Apply** to apply the changes and sync them.

iTunes syncs the items to your iPad.

**C** The readout shows you the sync progress.

**D** If you need to stop the sync, click **Stop** (✕).

**2** When the sync finishes, disconnect your iPad.

---

### TIP

**How can I fit more content on my iPad?**

You cannot increase your iPad's storage capacity — with some other tablets, you can install a memory card — so the way to fit more content is to prune and compress the existing content.

Video and music files usually take the most space. For video, your only option is to remove files you do not need on your iPad. For music, click the **Convert higher bit rate songs** check box (☐ changes to ☑) on the Summary tab and choose a low bit rate, such as 128 Kbps, to reduce the size of music files while retaining acceptable audio quality.

# Sync Your iPad with Your Computer via Wi-Fi

Instead of syncing your iPad via the USB-to-Lightning cable, you can sync it wirelessly, or "over the air." To do so, you must connect both your computer and your iPad to the same network and enable wireless sync in iTunes. You can then have the iPad sync automatically when it is connected to a power source and to the same wireless network as the computer, and when iTunes is also running on your Mac or PC. You can also start a sync manually from the iPad even if it is not connected to a power source.

## Sync Your iPad with Your Computer via Wi-Fi

### Set Your iPad to Sync with iTunes via Wi-Fi

1 Connect your iPad to your computer with the USB cable.

The iTunes window appears.

2 Click **iPad** (▢) on the navigation bar.

The iPad control screens appear.

3 Click **Summary**.

4 Click **Sync with this iPad over Wi-Fi** (▢ changes to ☑).

5 Click **Apply**.

6 Disconnect your iPad from your computer.

### Perform a Manual Sync via Wi-Fi

1 Press the **Home** button.

The Home screen appears.

2 Tap **Settings** (⚙).

The Settings screen appears.

**3** Tap **General** (⚙️).

The General screen appears.

**4** Tap **iTunes Wi-Fi Sync**.

The iTunes Wi-Fi Sync screen appears.

**5** Tap **Sync Now**.

The sync runs.

The Sync symbol (↻) appears in the iPad status bar.

The readout shows which part of the sync is currently running.

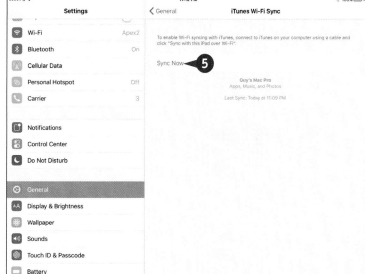

## TIP

**Should I sync my iPad via Wi-Fi or via USB?**

Try both means of syncing and see which suits you best. You can use USB sync even after enabling Wi-Fi syncing, so you do not have to choose one means or the other.

Even though modern Wi-Fi networks and iPads can transfer data at high speeds, you may find that USB sync is still faster and more reliable.

# Explore the Interface and Launch Apps

After you sync the iPad with your computer or set it up with iCloud, you are ready to start using the iPad. When you press the Sleep/Wake button or open the Smart Cover — or the Smart Keyboard on an iPad Pro — the iPad displays the lock screen. You then unlock the iPad to reach the Home screen, which contains icons for running the apps installed on the iPad.

You can quickly launch an app by tapping its icon on the Home screen. From the app, you can return to the Home screen by pressing the Home button. You can then launch another app as needed.

## Explore the Interface and Launch Apps

**1** Press the **Sleep/Wake** button.

The iPad screen lights up and shows the lock screen.

**2** Tap near the **slide to unlock** prompt and drag your finger to the right.

The iPad unlocks, and the Home screen appears.

**A** The iPad has two or more Home screens, depending on how many apps are installed. The gray dots at the bottom of the Home screen show how many Home screens you have. The white dot shows the current Home screen.

**3** Tap **Notes** (▭).

The Notes app opens.

**Note:** If you chose to sync notes with your iPad, the synced notes appear in the Notes app. Otherwise, the list is empty until you create a note.

**4** Tap **New** (✐) to create a new note.

The on-screen keyboard appears automatically.

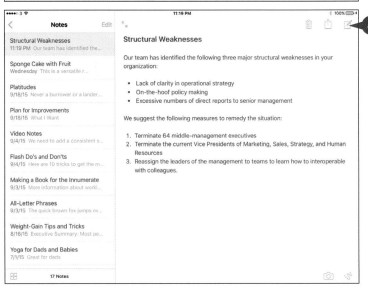

**5** Type a short note.

**B** The note appears in the Notes list.

**C** If the suggestion bar shows the word or phrase you want, tap it to enter it.

**Note:** If the suggestion is in the center, you can enter it by tapping `Spacebar` or another punctuation character.

**D** If you need to hide the keyboard, tap **Hide Keyboard** (⌨).

**E** To delete the note, tap **Delete** (🗑) and then tap **Delete Note** on the pop-up panel.

**6** Press the **Home** button.

The Home screen appears.

**7** Swipe left to display the second Home screen.

You can now launch another app by tapping its icon.

**8** Press the **Sleep/Wake** button or close the Smart Cover.

Your iPad goes to sleep.

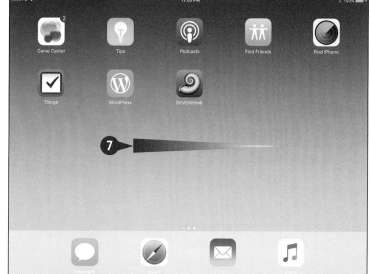

---

**TIP**

**Where do I get more apps to perform other tasks?**

You can find an amazingly wide selection of apps — both free and those you pay for — on the Apple App Store. See Chapter 6 for instructions on finding and downloading the apps you need.

# Using Notification Center

As your communications hub, your iPad handles many types of alerts for you: e-mail messages, text messages, reminders, meetings, and so on.

To help you keep on top of all these alerts, your iPad integrates them into Notification Center. You can quickly access Notification Center from the Home screen or any other screen. After you display Notification Center, you can respond to an alert, view your upcoming appointments, or check on the weather.

## Using Notification Center

① Tap at the top of the screen and swipe your finger down.

Notification Center appears.

Ⓐ The day and date appear.

Ⓑ A weather summary appears.

Ⓒ A summary of your calendar commitments for today appear.

Ⓓ Your calendar for today appears below that.

**Note:** Tap an event in the Calendar area of Notification Center to go to the Calendar app and display that event.

Ⓔ The Today list shows notifications and commitments for today.

Ⓕ The Tomorrow list shows a summary of tomorrow's events.

② To take action on a notification, swipe it left.

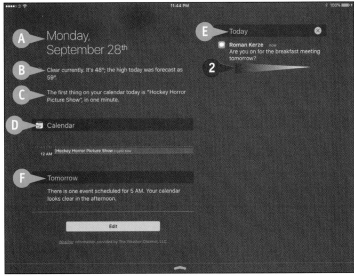

Action buttons for the notification appear.

G You can tap a button to take an action with a notification. For example, tap **Reply** to reply to a message.

3 To customize the notifications shown, tap **Edit**.

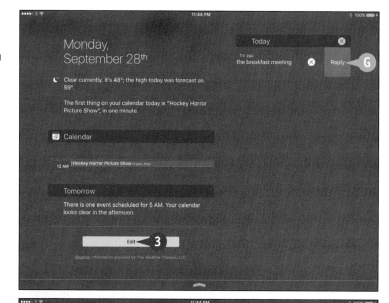

The Edit Widgets dialog opens.

4 To remove a widget, tap **Remove** (⊖) and then tap the textual **Remove** button that appears.

5 To change the order of items, tap a handle (▤) and drag up or down.

6 To add an item from the Do Not Include list to Widgets View, tap **Add** (⊕).

7 Tap **Done**.

The Edit Widgets dialog closes.

8 Tap **Close** (▭) or drag it upward.

Notification Center closes.

**What happens if I receive a notification when my iPad is locked?**
What happens when you receive a notification while the screen is locked depends on the type of notification. For most types of notifications, your iPad displays an alert on the lock screen to alert you to the notification. Unlocking your iPad while the alert is displayed takes you directly to the notification in whatever app it belongs to — for example, to an instant message in the Messages app. If there are multiple alerts, drag across the one you want to open.

# Using Control Center

ontrol Center puts the iPad's most essential controls right where you need them. From Control Center, you can turn Airplane Mode, Wi-Fi, Bluetooth, Do Not Disturb Mode, Mute, and Orientation Lock on or off; control music playback and volume, and direct the audio output to AirPlay devices; change the setting for the AirDrop sharing feature; and quickly access the Clock and Camera apps.

Control Center appears as a pane that you open by swiping upward from the bottom of the screen. After using Control Center, you can drag the pane closed or simply tap the screen above it.

## Using Control Center

### Open Control Center

**1** Tap and swipe up from the very bottom of the screen.

Control Center opens.

**Note:** You can open Control Center from most apps and screens. You may find some exceptions — for example, where iOS interprets an upward swipe as an action within the app.

**A** You can drag the **Brightness** slider to adjust the brightness.

**B** You can drag the **Volume** slider to adjust the volume.

### Control Essential Settings

**1** Tap **Airplane Mode** (✈) to turn Airplane Mode on or off.

**2** Tap **Wi-Fi** (🛜) to turn Wi-Fi on or off.

**3** Tap **Bluetooth** (✱) to turn Bluetooth on or off.

**4** Tap **Do Not Disturb** (☾) to turn Do Not Disturb Mode on or off.

**5** Tap **Mute** (🔔) to turn muting on or off.

**6** Tap **Orientation Lock** (⟳) to turn Orientation Lock on or off.

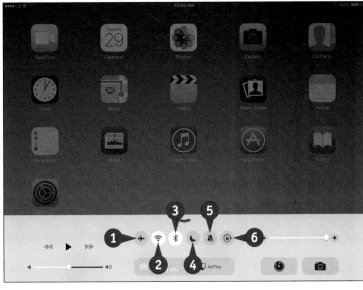

## Choose an AirPlay Device

**1** In Control Center, tap **AirPlay** (▱).

The AirPlay dialog opens.

**2** Tap the AirPlay speaker or Apple TV you want to use.

**3** If you choose an AirPlay TV, set the **Mirroring** switch to On (◯) or Off ( ), as needed.

**4** Tap outside the AirPlay dialog.

The AirPlay dialog closes.

**Note:** To close Control Center, either tap the screen above it or tap near the top line of Control Center and drag the line down to the bottom of the screen.

## Open Clock or Camera

**1** In Control Center, tap **Timer** (🕐) or **Camera** (📷).

The Clock app or the Camera app appears.

**C** You can tap **Music** to display the Music app.

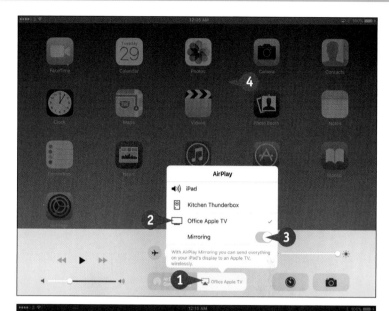

---

**TIP**

**Can I use Control Center from the lock screen?**

Yes, provided this capability is enabled. To turn it on or off, press the Home button, tap **Settings**, tap **Control Center**, and then set the **Access on Lock Screen** switch to On (◯) or Off ( ), as needed. On the Control Center screen, you can also set the **Access Within Apps** switch to On (◯) or Off ( ) to control whether you can access Control Center from within apps.

# CHAPTER 2

# Personalizing Your iPad

In this chapter, you learn how to control notifications, audio preferences, screen brightness, and other key iPad behaviors.

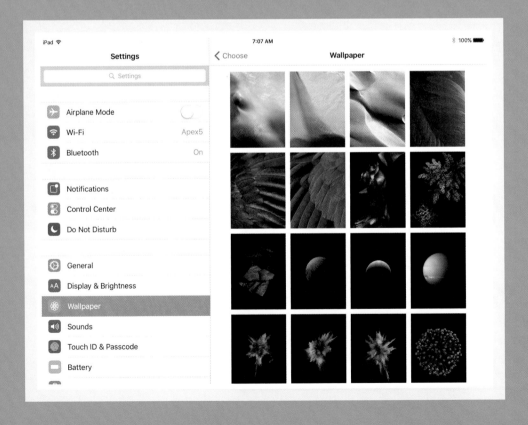

# Find the Settings You Need

To configure your iPad, you work with its settings using the Settings app. This app contains settings for the iPad system software, the apps the iPad includes, and third-party apps you have added.

To reach the settings, you first display the Settings screen, and then display the category of settings you want to configure. In this section, you learn how to open the Settings screen to display the main categories of settings it contains.

## Find the Settings You Need

### Display the Settings Screen

**1** Press **Home**.

The Home screen appears.

**2** Tap **Settings** (⚙).

The Settings screen appears.

**A** You can tap **Search** (🔍) and type a keyword to search for the setting you need.

**3** Tap in the left column and drag up to scroll down the screen to locate the settings category you need.

## Display a Settings Screen

**1** In the left column on the Settings screen, tap the button for the settings you want to display. For example, tap **General** (⚙) to display the General screen.

**B** Tap a button that is followed by > to display another screen of settings.

**C** Tap a button not followed by > to make a selection.

## Display the Settings for an App

**1** On the Settings screen, tap and drag up the left column to scroll down the screen.

**2** Tap the button for the app whose settings you want to display. For example, tap **iBooks** (📖) to display the settings for the iBooks app.

**3** When you finish using the Settings app, press **Home**.

The Home screen appears again.

---

### TIP

**Why do only some apps have a Settings entry?**

The Settings screen contains entries for only those apps that have settings you can configure through iOS, the iPad operating system. Other apps include settings that you configure directly from within the app. This approach is more convenient for apps that have settings you are likely to need to change frequently. A few apps do not have any settings that you can configure.

# Set Up and Configure iCloud

pple's iCloud service enables you to sync items such as your e-mail, contacts, calendars and reminders, Safari bookmarks, photos, and documents and data online. You can also use the Find My iPad feature to locate your iPad when it goes missing.

To use iCloud, you set your iPad to use your Apple ID, and then choose which features to use. If you set up your iPad using iCloud, your account is already active, but you may want to choose different settings for iCloud.

## Set Up and Configure iCloud

**1** Press **Home**.

The Home screen appears.

**2** Tap **Settings** (⚙️).

The Settings screen appears.

**3** Tap **iCloud** (☁️).

The iCloud screen appears.

**4** Type your Apple ID.

**A** If you do not yet have an Apple ID, tap **Create a new Apple ID**, and then follow the prompts.

**5** Type your password.

**6** Tap **Sign In**.

Your iPad signs in to iCloud.

The Find My iPad Enabled dialog opens.

**Note:** iOS automatically enables the Find My iPad feature when you sign into your iCloud account on your iPad. This feature enables you to locate your iPad by signing in to your account on the iCloud website, www.icloud.com. See the section "Locate Your iPad with Find My iPad" in Chapter 12 for details.

**7** Tap **OK**.

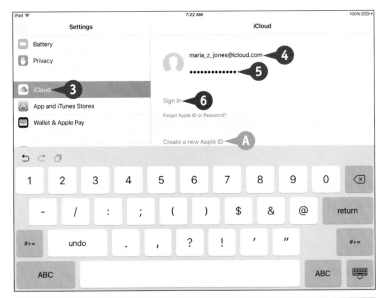

The iCloud controls appear.

B You can tap your Apple ID to display the Apple ID screen, on which you can manage your contact information, devices, password, payment, and more.

C You can tap **Family** or **Set Up Family Sharing** to display the Family screen, on which you configure sharing. See the section "Set Up Family Sharing," later in this chapter, for details.

8 Tap **iCloud Drive** ( ).

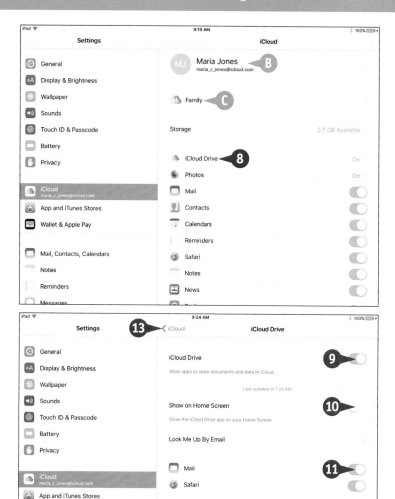

The iCloud Drive screen appears.

9 Set the **iCloud Drive** switch to On ( ) to store files such as your iWork documents in iCloud.

10 Set the **Show on Home Screen** switch to On ( ) to display the iCloud Drive app icon on the Home screen.

11 Set each app's switch to On ( ) or Off ( ), as needed.

12 For a cellular iPad, set the **Use Cellular Data** switch to On ( ) or Off ( ), as needed.

13 Tap **iCloud** ( ).

---

**TIP**

**What does the Look Me Up By Email feature do?**

This feature enables you to control which apps can look you up by the e-mail address you use for your Apple ID. Tap **Look Me Up By Email** on the iCloud Drive screen to display the Look Me Up By Email screen, which displays a list of the apps that have requested permission to look you up. You can then set the switch for an app to Off ( changes to ) if you want to prevent the app from looking you up.

continued ▶

On the Photos screen in iCloud Settings, you can choose to store your entire photo library in iCloud so that you can access your photos and videos from all your devices. You can also decide whether to upload photos automatically, whether to upload bursts of photos, and whether to share photos with other people via iCloud Photo Sharing.

Your other options include iCloud Keychain, which gives you a secure way to store passwords and credit card information across your Apple devices.

## Set Up and Configure iCloud (continued)

The iCloud screen appears.

**14** Choose which features to use by setting the **Mail** (▣), **Contacts** (👤), **Calendars** (📅), **Reminders** ( ), **Safari** (🧭), **Notes** ( ), and **News** (📰) switches to On (⬤) or Off ( ), as needed.

**15** Tap **Photos** (✴).

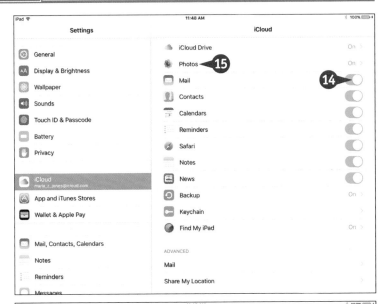

The Photos screen appears.

**16** Set the **iCloud Photo Library** switch to On (⬤) to upload all your photos to iCloud.

**17** Set the **My Photo Stream** switch to On (⬤) to use Photo Stream.

**18** Set the **Upload Burst Photos** switch to On (⬤) to upload bursts you have shot.

**19** Set the **iCloud Photo Sharing** switch to On (⬤) to enable album sharing with other people.

**20** Tap **iCloud** (‹).

The iCloud screen appears again.

**D** You can tap **Backup** (🔄) to display the Backup screen, on which you can configure iCloud backup.

**E** You can tap **Keychain** (🔑) to display the Keychain screen, on which you can enable or disable iCloud Keychain.

**21** Tap **Find My iPad** (🟢).

The Find My iPad screen appears.

**F** You can set the **Find My iPad** switch to Off (⚪ changes to ⚪) to turn off Find My iPad, such as when preparing to erase the iPad so that you can sell it.

**22** Set the **Send Last Location** switch to On (⚪) if you want the iPad to send Apple its location when the battery runs critically low.

**23** Tap **iCloud** (‹).

The iCloud screen appears again.

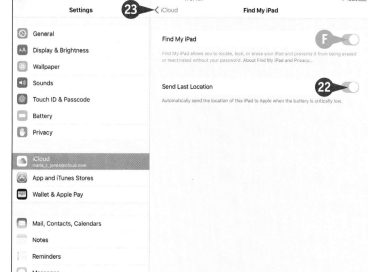

**How much space does iCloud provide?**

iCloud provides 5GB of space for a free account. Content and apps you acquire from Apple do not count against this space. You can buy more space by tapping **Storage** on the iCloud screen, tapping **Manage Storage** to display the Manage Storage screen, tapping **Change Storage Plan**, and following the prompts.

**Should I set the Use Cellular Data switch to On?**

Yes — as long as your data plan has enough capacity, transferring your files across the cellular connection is a great way of keeping them up to date.

# Choose Which Apps Can Give Notifications

**M**any apps can notify you when events occur, such as a message arriving for you in the Messages app. You can choose which apps give notifications for events and which events those notifications concern. You can also specify an app's notification type, choose the order in which notifications appear in Notification Center, and control which notifications the lock screen shows.

You can choose among three notification types for an app. See the tip for details.

## Choose Which Apps Can Give Notifications

**1** Press **Home**.

The Home screen appears.

**2** Tap **Settings** (⚙).

The Settings screen appears.

**3** Tap **Notifications** (🔔).

The Notifications screen appears.

**Ⓐ** If you use Recent sort order, you can set the **Group By App** switch to On (⬤) to group the notifications by their apps.

**4** Tap **Sort Order**.

The Sort Order screen appears.

**5** Tap **Recent** to sort notifications by date. Tap **Manual** to set the sort order manually.

**Ⓑ** If you choose Manual sort order, you can tap a handle (☰) and drag an app to rearrange the list into your preferred order.

**6** Tap **Notifications** (‹).

The Notifications screen appears again.

**7** In the Notification Style list, tap the app for which you want to configure notifications. This example uses Messages (💬).

The screen for the app appears.

**8** Set the **Allow Notifications** switch to On (⬤) to receive notifications from the app.

**9** Set the **Show in Notification Center** switch to On (⬤) or Off (⬤).

**10** Tap **Sounds** and select a sound.

**11** Set the **Badge App Icon** switch to On (⬤) or Off (⬤).

**12** Set the **Show on Lock Screen** switch to On (⬤) or Off (⬤).

**13** In the Alert Style When Unlocked box, tap the alert style to use.

**14** Set the **Show Previews** switch to On (⬤) or Off (⬤).

**15** Tap **Repeat Alerts**.

The Repeat Alerts screen appears.

**16** Tap the repetition frequency you want, such as **Twice**.

**17** Tap **Messages** (⟨).

The screen for the app appears again.

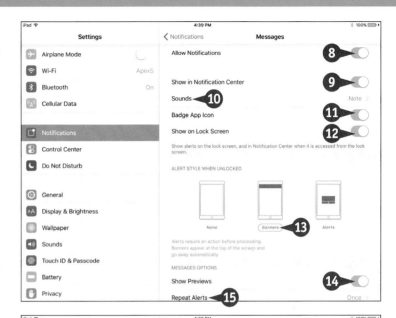

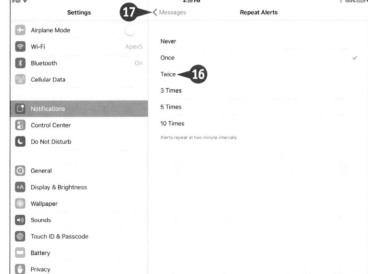

## TIP

**What are the three types of notifications?**
A *badge* is a notification that appears on the app's icon on the Home screen. A *banner* is a pop-up notification that appears briefly at the top of the screen. An *alert* is a dialog that appears in the middle of the screen and stays there until you close it.

# Choose Sounds Settings

To control how your iPad gives you audio feedback, choose settings on the Sounds screen. Here, you can set the volume for the ringer and for alerts, choose your default ringtone for FaceTime and text tone for Messages, and choose whether to receive alerts for calendar items and reminders.

Playing lock sounds helps confirm that you have locked or unlocked your iPad as you intended. Playing keyboard clicks confirms each key press on the on-screen keyboard.

## Choose Sounds Settings

1 Press **Home**.

The Home screen appears.

2 Tap **Settings** (⚙).

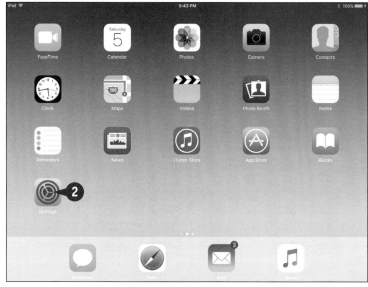

The Settings screen appears.

3 Tap **Sounds** (🔊).

The Sounds screen appears.

4 Tap and drag the **Ringer and Alerts** slider to set the volume.

5 Set the **Change with Buttons** switch to On (⚪) if you want to be able to change the Ringer and Alerts volume by pressing the volume buttons on the side of the iPad.

6 Tap **Ringtone**.

The Ringtone screen appears.

**7** Tap the ringtone you want to hear for FaceTime calls.

Your iPad plays the ringtone so you can decide whether to use it.

**A** You can tap **Store** to buy extra ringtones or alert tones.

**Note:** Tap and drag up to scroll down the Ringtone screen to display the list of alert tones. Tap **Classic**, at the bottom of the Ringtones list, to see the selection of ringtones from early versions of iOS.

**8** Tap **Sounds** (**<**).

The Sounds screen appears again.

**9** Repeat steps **6** to **8** to set other tones, such as text tones.

**10** Set the **Lock Sounds** switch to On (◯) or Off ( ), as needed.

**11** Set the **Keyboard Clicks** switch to On (◯) or Off ( ), as needed.

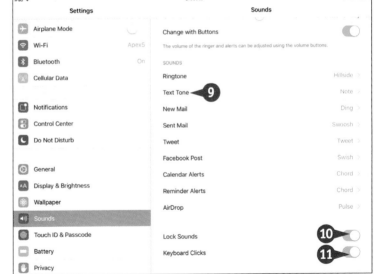

---

**TIP**

**How do I use different ringtones for different callers?**

The ringtone you set in the Ringtone area of the Sounds screen is your default tone for FaceTime calls; the text tone is the default for messaging calls. To set different tones to identify a contact, press **Home** and tap **Contacts** (👤). In the Contacts app, tap the contact, tap **Edit**, and then tap **ringtone**. In the Ringtone dialog, tap the ringtone, and then tap **Done**. You can also change the text tone for the contact. Tap **Done** when you finish editing the contact.

# Choose Display and Brightness Settings

To make the screen easy to see, you can change its brightness. You can also have the iPad's Auto-Brightness feature automatically set the screen's brightness to a level suitable for the ambient brightness that the light sensor on your iPad detects.

To make text on the screen easier to read, you can increase or decrease the text size as needed. You can also turn on the Bold Text setting; this makes more sweeping changes and requires you to restart your iPad.

## Choose Display and Brightness Settings

**1** Press **Home**.

The Home screen appears.

**2** Tap **Settings** (⚙️).

The Settings screen appears.

**3** Tap **Display & Brightness** (AA).

The Display & Brightness screen appears.

**4** Tap the **Brightness** slider and drag it left or right to set brightness.

**5** Set the **Auto-Brightness** switch to On (🔘) or Off ( ), as needed.

**6** Tap **Text Size**.

The Text Size screen appears.

**7** Drag the slider left to decrease the text size or right to increase the text size.

**Note:** Adjusting the text size works only for apps that support the Dynamic Type feature, not all apps that can run on your iPad.

**8** Tap **Display & Brightness** (<).

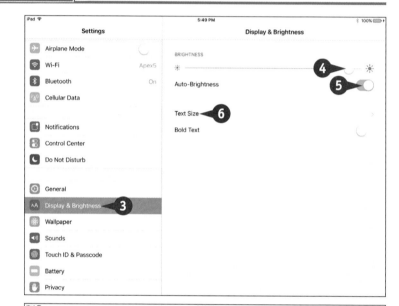

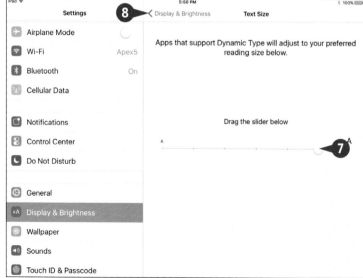

The Display & Brightness screen appears.

**9** If you want to use bold text, set the **Bold Text** switch to On ( ⬤ ).

The Applying This Setting Will Restart Your iPad dialog opens.

**10** Tap **Continue**.

Your iPad restarts.

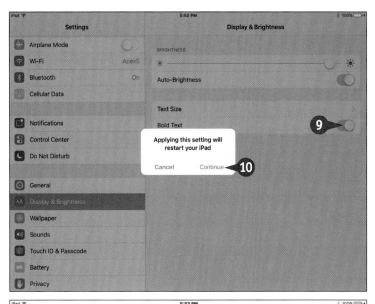

**A** Text appears in a bold font, making it easier to see.

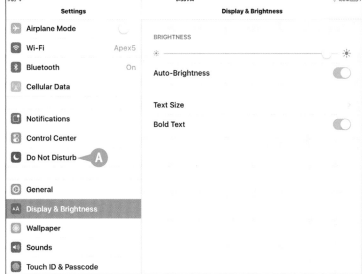

---

## TIPS

**How else can I change the screen brightness?**

Pull up from the bottom of the screen to open Control Center and then drag the **Brightness** slider to the left or right.

**What other settings can I choose to make the screen easier to see?**

The Accessibility screen in the Settings app offers several other settings for making the screen easier to see. These include zooming in and out, inverting the colors, displaying the screen in grayscale, and increasing the contrast. To access these settings, press **Home**, tap **Settings** ( ⚙️ ), tap **General** ( ⚙️ ), and then tap **Accessibility**.

# Set Home Screen and Lock Screen Wallpaper

You can choose which picture to use as the wallpaper that appears in the background. You can use either a static wallpaper or a dynamic, changing wallpaper. You can set different wallpaper for the lock screen — the screen you see when the iPad is locked — and for the Home screen.

When setting the wallpaper, you can choose whether to turn perspective zoom on or off. Perspective zoom gives the three-dimensional effect when you tilt the iPad when looking at the wallpaper.

## Set Home Screen and Lock Screen Wallpaper

**1** Press **Home**.

The Home screen appears.

**2** Tap **Settings** (⚙).

The Settings screen appears.

**3** Tap **Wallpaper** (🌸).

The Wallpaper screen appears.

**4** Tap **Choose a New Wallpaper**.

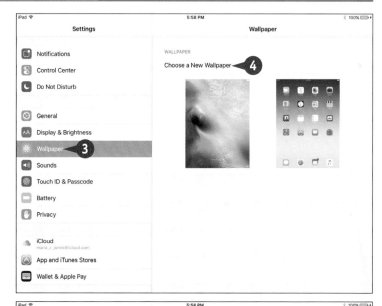

The Choose screen appears.

**5** In the Apple Wallpaper area, tap **Dynamic** or **Stills**. This example uses Stills.

Ⓐ To choose a picture from a different picture category, tap that category. For example, tap **Camera Roll** to display pictures you have taken with the iPad camera or saved from e-mail messages, multimedia messages, or web pages.

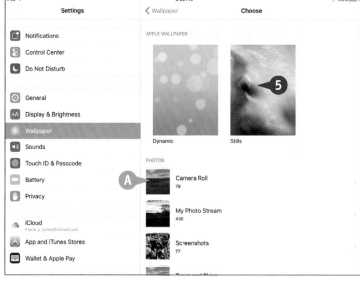

The Wallpaper screen appears.

**6** Tap the wallpaper you want.

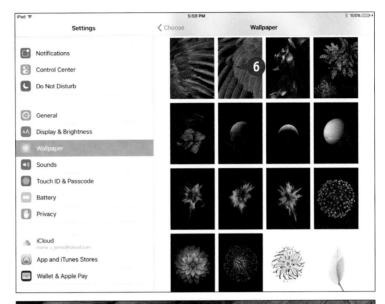

The Wallpaper Preview screen appears.

**7** Tap **Perspective Zoom: On** or **Perspective Zoom: Off** to toggle the perspective zoom on or off.

**8** Tap **Set Lock Screen**, **Set Home Screen**, or **Set Both**.

The Wallpaper screen appears.

**9** Tap **Choose** (<).

The Choose screen appears.

**10** Tap **Wallpaper** (<).

The Wallpaper screen appears.

**Note:** To see the wallpaper, press **Home** to display the Home screen or press the Sleep/Wake button twice to display the lock screen.

## TIP

**How do I use only part of a picture as the wallpaper?**

The iPad wallpapers are the right size for the screen, so you do not need to resize them. But when you choose a photo for the wallpaper, the iPad displays the Move and Scale screen. Pinch in or out to zoom the photo out or in, and tap and drag to move the picture around. When you have chosen the part you want, tap **Set Lock Screen**, **Set Home Screen**, or **Set Both**. Moving and scaling a photo does not edit the original image.

# Choose Privacy and Location Settings

Your iPad contains a huge amount of information about you, the people you communicate with, what you do, and where you go. To keep this information safe, you need to choose suitable privacy and location settings.

Privacy settings enable you to control which apps may access your contacts, calendars, reminders, and photos. You can also choose which apps can use location services, which track your iPad's location using known wireless networks and the Global Positioning System, or GPS, on cellular iPads.

## Choose Privacy and Location Settings

**1** Press **Home**.

The Home screen appears.

**2** Tap **Settings** (⚙️).

The Settings screen appears.

**3** Tap **Privacy** (✋).

The Privacy screen appears.

**4** Tap **Location Services** (➤).

**Note:** To minimize advertisers tracking you, tap **Advertising** on the Privacy screen and set the **Limit Ad Tracking** switch to On (⬤). Then tap **Reset Advertising Identifier** and tap **Reset Identifier** in the confirmation dialog.

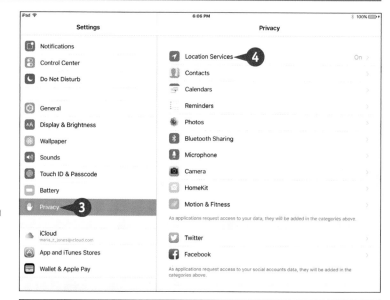

The Location Services screen appears.

**A** If you need to turn location services off completely, set the **Location Services** switch to Off ( ).

**5** To control location sharing, tap **Share My Location**. On the Share My Location screen, set the **Share My Location** switch to On (⬤) or Off ( ), as needed. If you set it to On, tap **From** and choose the sharing device on the Share Location From screen.

**6** Tap an app or feature. This example uses **Camera**.

52

The screen for the app or feature appears.

⑦ In the Allow Location Access list, tap the appropriate button. The options depend on the app, but many apps offer **Never** and **While Using the App**.

⑧ Tap **Location Services** (〈).

The Location Services screen appears.

⑨ Tap **System Services**.

**Note:** For privacy, you may want to set the **Location-Based Alerts** switch on the System Services screen to Off (⬭).

The System Services screen appears.

⑩ Set the switch for each system service to On (⬤) or Off (⬭).

⑪ Set the **Status Bar Icon** switch to On (⬤) to display an arrow in the status bar when the iPad is being tracked.

⑫ Tap **Location Services** (〈).

The Location Services screen appears.

⑬ Tap **Privacy**.

The Privacy screen appears.

⑭ Tap each app or service and choose the apps that can access that app's information.

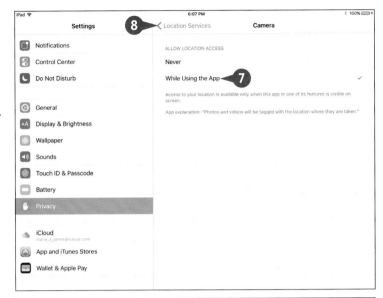

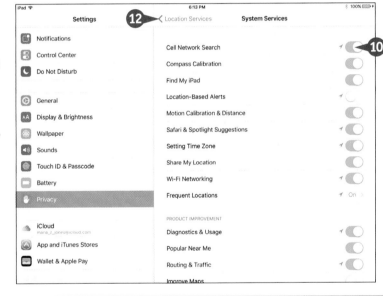

## TIP

**Why do some apps need to use location services?**

Some apps and system services need to use location services to determine where you are. The Maps app uses location services to display your location, and the Compass app needs your position to display accurate compass information. If you allow the Camera app to use location services, it stores location data in your photos. You can sort the photos by location in apps such as Photos or Photoshop Elements on your computer. Other apps use location services to provide context-specific information, such as information about nearby restaurants. For security, review which apps are using location services and turn off any that do not have a compelling reason for doing so.

# Configure Spotlight and Find What You Need

Your iPad can put a huge amount of data in your hand, and you may often need to search to find what you need. To make your search results more accurate and helpful, you can configure the Spotlight Search feature on your iPad.

You can enable or disable suggestions from Siri, the search assistant. You can also turn off searching for items you do not want to see in your search results.

## Configure Spotlight and Find What You Need

### Configure Spotlight Search

1 Press **Home**.

The Home screen appears.

2 Tap **Settings** (⚙).

The Settings screen appears.

3 Tap **General** (⚙).

The General screen appears.

4 Tap **Spotlight Search**.

The Spotlight Search screen appears.

5 Set the **Siri Suggestions** switch to On (⬤) or Off ( ), as needed.

6 In the Search Results list, set each app's switch to On (⬤) or Off ( ), as needed.

7 Tap **General** (<).

The General screen appears again.

## Search for Items Using Spotlight

**1** Press **Home**.

The Home screen appears.

**2** Swipe right.

The Search screen appears.

**3** Tap in the Search field.

The keyboard appears.

**4** Type your search term.

A list of results appears.

**5** Tap the result you want to view.

**A** For a result such as a song, you can tap **Play** (▶) to start playing the song.

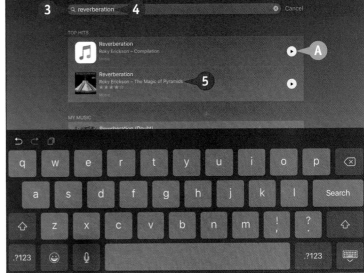

---

**TIP**

**Which items should I make Spotlight search?**

This depends on what you need to be able to search for. For example, if you do not need to search for music, videos, or podcasts, set the switches for the Music, Videos, and Podcasts items on the Spotlight Search screen to Off (  ) to exclude them from Spotlight searches. For normal use, you may want to leave all the switches set to On ( ) and simply ignore the results you do not need.

# Choose Locking and Control Center Settings

To avoid unintentional taps on the screen, your iPad automatically locks itself after a period of inactivity. After locking itself, your iPad turns off its screen and goes to sleep to save battery power.

You can choose how long your iPad waits before locking itself. You may prefer to leave your iPad on longer so that you can continue working, and then lock your iPad manually. You can also choose whether to make Control Center accessible from the lock screen.

## Choose Locking and Control Center Settings

**1** Press **Home**.

The Home screen appears.

**2** Tap **Settings** (⚙).

The Settings screen appears.

**3** Tap **General** (⚙).

The General screen appears.

**4** Tap **Auto-Lock**.

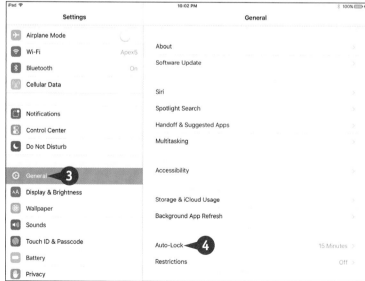

The Auto-Lock screen appears.

**⑤** Tap the interval — for example, **5 Minutes**.

**Note:** Choose the **Never** setting for Auto-Lock if you need to make sure the iPad never goes to sleep. For example, if you are playing music with the lyrics displayed, turning off auto-locking may be helpful.

**⑥** Tap **Control Center** (🔲).

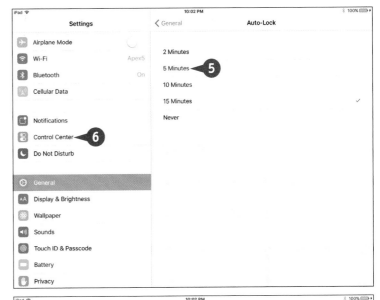

The Control Center screen appears.

**⑦** Set the **Access on Lock Screen** switch to On (🔵) or Off ( ), as needed.

**⑧** Set the **Access Within Apps** switch to On (🔵) or Off ( ), as needed. If you find yourself displaying Control Center unintentionally, try setting this switch to Off ( ).

**Note:** When you turn off access to Control Center from within apps, you can still access it from the Home screen.

## TIP

**How do I put the iPad to sleep manually?**

You can put the iPad to sleep at any point by pressing the Sleep/Wake button for a moment. If your iPad has a Smart Cover or Smart Case, close the cover or case.

Putting the iPad to sleep as soon as you stop using it helps to prolong battery life. If you apply Touch ID or a passcode, as discussed in the section "Secure Your iPad with Touch ID or a Passcode," later in this chapter, putting the iPad to sleep also protects your data sooner.

# Set Up and Use Do Not Disturb Mode

When you do not want your iPad to disturb you, turn on Do Not Disturb Mode. You can configure Do Not Disturb Mode to turn on and off automatically at set times each day; you can also turn Do Not Disturb Mode on and off manually. You can allow particular groups of contacts to bypass Do Not Disturb Mode. You can also allow repeated calls to ring when Do Not Disturb is on.

## Set Up and Use Do Not Disturb Mode

### Configure Do Not Disturb Mode

**1** Press **Home**.

The Home screen appears.

**2** Tap **Settings** (⚙).

The Settings screen appears.

**3** Tap **Do Not Disturb** (🌙).

The Do Not Disturb screen appears.

**4** To schedule regular quiet hours, set the **Scheduled** switch to On (⬤).

**5** Tap **From, To**.

The Quiet Hours dialog opens.

**6** Tap **From**.

**7** Set the From time.

**8** Tap **To**.

**9** Set the To time.

**10** Tap **Allow Calls From**.

The Allow Calls From screen appears.

**11** Tap the group you will allow to call you via FaceTime during quiet hours.

**12** Tap **Do Not Disturb** (‹).

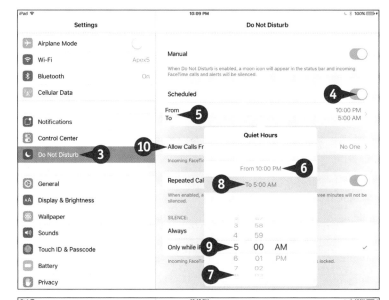

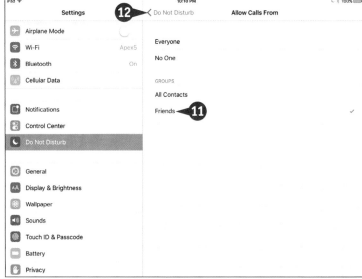

The Do Not Disturb screen appears.

A You can set the **Manual** switch to On ( ) to turn on Do Not Disturb Mode from this screen. It is usually easier to use Control Center to toggle Do Not Disturb Mode on and off.

⑬ Set the **Repeated Calls** switch to On ( ) or Off ( ), as needed.

⑭ In the Silence area, tap **Always** or **Only while iPad is locked**, as needed.

## Turn Do Not Disturb Mode On or Off Manually

① Swipe up from the bottom of the screen.

**Note:** You can open Control Center from the Home screen or from most other screens.

Control Center opens.

② Tap **Do Not Disturb** to turn Do Not Disturb on ( changes to ) or off ( changes to ).

---

**TIP**

**How can I tell whether Do Not Disturb is on?**
When Do Not Disturb is on, a crescent moon symbol appears in the status bar to the left of the battery readout.

# Secure Your iPad with Touch ID or a Passcode

During setup, you secure your iPad using either Touch ID or a passcode. Touch ID uses your fingerprint to unlock the iPad, with a passcode as a backup unlock method. The iPad Air 2, the iPad mini 3, the iPad Pro, and later models have Touch ID; older models, such as the iPad Air and iPad mini 2, do not, and use a passcode without Touch ID.

For added security, you can set the iPad to automatically erase its data after ten failed passcode attempts.

## Secure Your iPad with Touch ID or a Passcode

**1** Press **Home**.

The Home screen appears.

**2** Tap **Settings** (⚙).

The Settings screen appears.

**3** Tap **Touch ID & Passcode**.

**Note:** If your iPad does not support Touch ID, tap **Passcode Lock** to display the Passcode Lock screen.

The Enter Passcode dialog opens.

**4** Type your passcode.

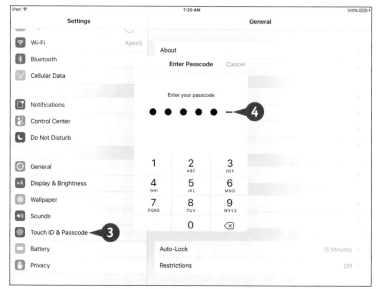

The Touch ID & Passcode screen appears.

**5** Set the **iPad Unlock** switch to On (🔘) to use Touch ID for unlocking.

**6** Set the **Apple Pay** switch to On (🔘) to use Touch ID for Apple Pay.

**7** Set the **App and iTunes Stores** switch to On (🔘) to use Touch ID for store purchases.

**A** You can tap a button in the Fingerprints box to change the button name or delete the fingerprint.

**B** You can tap **Add a Fingerprint** to add another fingerprint to Touch ID.

**C** You can tap **Turn Passcode Off** to turn the passcode off; however, this is seldom wise.

**D** You can tap **Change Passcode** to change your passcode. See the tip for information on changing the passcode type.

**8** Set the **Today** switch to On (⬤) to enable the Today information when the iPad is locked.

**9** Set the **Notifications View** to On (⬤) to enable Notifications View when the iPad is locked.

**10** Set the **Siri** switch to On (⬤) to enable Siri when the iPad is locked.

**11** If you want the iPad to erase all its data after ten failed passcode attempts, set the **Erase Data** switch to On (⬤).

The iPad displays a confirmation dialog.

**12** Tap **Enable**.

**Note:** The Erase Data feature provides effective protection against conventional attackers, but some law-enforcement agencies can defeat it.

**Note:** Even with Touch ID enabled, you must enter your passcode after restarting your iPad or after not using it for 48 hours or longer.

## TIP

**How do I change the type of passcode my iPad uses?**

On the Touch ID & Passcode screen, tap **Change Passcode** to display the Change Passcode dialog. Type your existing passcode to authenticate yourself, and then tap **Passcode Options** to display the Passcode Options pop-up panel. You can then tap **Custom Alphanumeric Code** to create an ultra-secure passcode using letters and numbers; tap **Custom Numeric Code** to create a numeric passcode whose length you choose; or tap **4-Digit Numeric Code** to create a four-digit numeric code, which is easier to type but does not provide serious security.

# Configure Restrictions and Parental Controls

L ike any other computer that can access the Internet, the iPad can reach vast amounts of content not suitable for children or business contexts.

You can restrict the iPad from accessing particular kinds of content. You can use the restrictions to implement parental controls — for example, you can prevent the iPad user from buying content in apps or watching adult-rated movies.

## Configure Restrictions and Parental Controls

**1** Press **Home**.

The Home screen appears.

**2** Tap **Settings** (⚙).

The Settings screen appears.

**3** Tap **General** (⚙).

The General screen appears.

**4** Tap **Restrictions**.

The Restrictions screen appears.

**5** Tap **Enable Restrictions**.

The Set Passcode dialog appears.

**Note:** The passcode you set to protect restrictions is separate from the passcode you use to lock the iPad. Do not use the same code.

**6** Type the passcode.

**Note:** The iPad shows dots instead of your passcode digits in case someone is watching.

The iPad displays the Set Passcode dialog again, this time with the message "Re-enter your Restrictions Passcode."

**7** Type the passcode again.

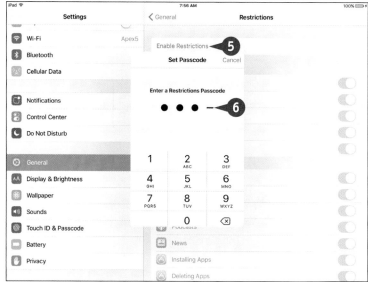

The Restrictions screen appears with the controls in the Allow area now available.

**8** In the Allow area, set each switch to On (●) or Off (   ), as needed.

**9** If you need to change the country used for rating content, tap **Ratings For**. On the Ratings For screen, tap the country, and then tap **Restrictions**.

**10** Choose settings for items in the Allowed Content box. For example, tap **Movies**.

The Movies screen appears.

**11** On the Movies screen, tap the highest rating you will permit.

**12** Tap **Restrictions** (<).

The Restrictions screen appears again.

**13** Set the **In-App Purchases** switch to On (●) or Off (   ), as needed.

**14** Choose other settings in the Privacy box.

**15** Choose settings in the Allow Changes box.

**16** Set the **Multiplayer Games** switch and the **Adding Friends** switch to On (●) or Off (   ), as needed.

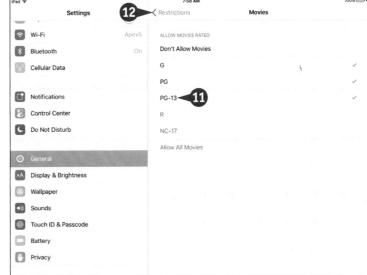

## TIPS

**What are in-app purchases?**

In-app purchases are items that you can buy within apps without needing to use the App Store app. These are a popular and easy way for developers to sell extra features for apps, especially low-cost apps or free apps. They are also an easy way for the iPad user to spend money.

**What do the Privacy settings in Restrictions do?**

The Privacy settings in Restrictions enable you to control which apps can access the location information, contacts, calendars, reminders, photos, and other features on your iPad.

# Set Up Family Sharing

Apple's Family Sharing feature enables you to share purchases from Apple's online services with other family members. You can also share photos and calendars, and you can use the Find My iPhone feature to find your iOS devices and Macs when they go missing.

This section assumes that you are the Family organizer, the person who sets up Family sharing, invites others to participate, and pays for the content they buy on the iTunes Store, the iBooks Store, and the App Store.

## Set Up Family Sharing

**1** Press **Home**.

The Home screen appears.

**2** Tap **Settings** (⚙).

The Settings screen appears.

**3** Tap **iCloud** (☁).

The iCloud screen appears.

**4** Tap **Set Up Family Sharing** (☁).

The Family Sharing dialog opens.

**5** Tap **Get Started**.

The Family Setup dialog opens.

Ⓐ You can tap **add photo** and then either tap **Take Photo** to take a photo with your iPhone's camera or tap **Choose Photo** and select an existing photo for your profile.

**6** Tap **Continue**.

The Sign In dialog opens.

**7** Verify that the Apple ID is correct. Change it if necessary.

**8** Tap **Password** and type your password.

**9** Tap **Next**.

**Note:** If the Share Your Location with Your Family dialog opens, tap **Share Your Location** or **Not Now**, as appropriate.

The Payment Method dialog opens.

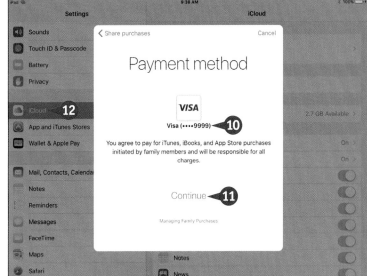

**10** Verify that iOS has identified the means of payment that you want your family to use.

**11** Tap **Continue**.

The Family screen appears.

**12** Tap **iCloud** ( ⬤ ) in the left pane. You can also tap **iCloud** ( ‹ ) at the top of the screen.

The iCloud screen appears.

## TIP

**How do I turn off Family Sharing?**

**1** Press **Home**.

**2** Tap **Settings** ( ⚙ ).

**3** Tap **iCloud** ( ⬤ ).

**4** Tap **Family** ( ⬤ ).

**5** Tap the button with your name and "Organizer" on it.

**6** Tap **Stop Family Sharing** at the bottom of your profile screen.

# Add Family Members to Family Sharing

After enabling Family Sharing and choosing your means of payment, you can add your family members to the group. You can either send an invitation to a family member to join the group or ask her to enter her Apple ID and password on your iPad to join immediately.

If you send an invitation, the family member can join at a time of her choosing by using her own iPhone, iPad, iPod touch, or computer.

## Add Family Members to Family Sharing

### Add a Family Member to Family Sharing

1 Press **Home**.

The Home screen appears.

2 Tap **Settings** (⚙).

The Settings screen appears.

3 Tap **iCloud** (☁).

The iCloud screen appears.

4 Tap **Family** (☁).

The Family screen appears.

5 Tap **Add Family Member**.

The first Add Family Member dialog opens.

**6** Start typing the name.

A list of matches appears.

**7** Tap the appropriate match.

**8** Tap **Next**.

**Note:** If the Verify Security Code dialog opens, type the security code — the three- or four-digit Card Verification Value code, or CVV code — for the credit card or debit card, and then tap **Next**.

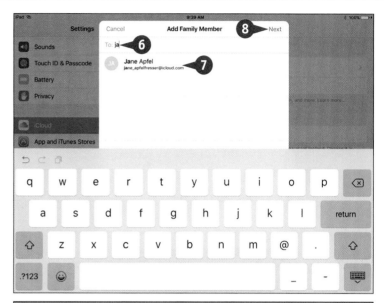

The second Add Family Member dialog opens.

**A** If the family member is not present, tap **Send an Invitation**. iOS sends the invitation.

**9** If the family member is present, tap **Ask *Name* to Enter Password**.

The Enter Password screen appears.

**10** Ask the family member to enter her Apple ID and password.

**11** Tap **Done**.

iOS adds the family member to Family Sharing.

## TIPS

**How many people can I add to Family Sharing?**

Family Sharing works for up to six people, so you can add five other people to your account.

**How do I control who can approve purchase requests from Family Sharing members?**

On the Family screen in the Settings app, tap the name of the adult involved. The profile screen for the adult appears. Set the **Parent/Guardian** switch to On ( ) to enable the adult to approve Ask to Buy requests.

# Choose Date, Time, and Region Settings

To keep yourself on time and your data accurate, you need to make sure your iPad is using the correct date and time. You can choose between having your iPad set the date and time automatically and setting them yourself. To choose date and time settings, you use the Date & Time screen in the Settings app. To make dates, times, and other data appear in the formats you prefer, you may need to change the Language & Region settings on your iPad.

## Choose Date, Time, and Region Settings

### Choose Date and Time Settings

**1** Press **Home**.

The Home screen appears.

**2** Tap **Settings** (⚙).

The Settings screen appears.

**3** Tap **General** (⚙).

The General screen appears.

**4** Tap **Date & Time**.

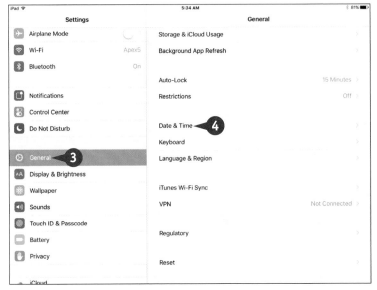

The Date & Time screen appears.

**5** Set the **24-Hour Time** switch to On (⬤) if you want to use 24-hour times.

**6** To set the date and time manually, set the **Set Automatically** switch to Off (⬤ changes ◯).

**7** Tap the button showing the date and time.

The controls for setting the date and time appear.

**8** Set the date and time.

**9** Tap **General** (‹).

The General screen appears.

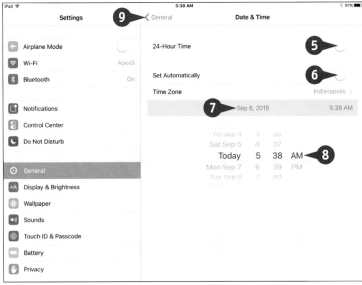

## Choose Language & Region Settings

**①** From the General screen, tap **Language & Region**.

The Language & Region screen appears.

**②** Tap **Region**.

The Region dialog opens.

**③** Tap the region you want, which places a check mark next to it.

**④** Tap **Done**.

The Region dialog closes.

**Note:** From the Language & Region screen, you can also change the language used for the iPad user interface.

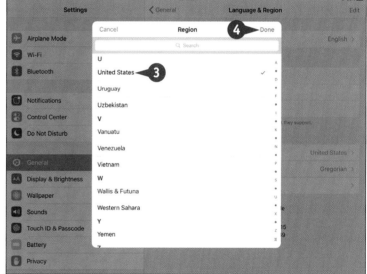

---

**How does the iPad set the date and time automatically?**
The iPad sets the date and time automatically by using time servers, which are computers on the Internet that provide date and time information to computers that request it. The iPad automatically determines its geographical location so that it can request the right time zone from the time server.

# Set Up Your Social Networking Accounts

Your iPad can connect to various social networks, including Facebook, Twitter, Flickr, and Vimeo. iOS makes it easy to post updates, photos, and videos to your accounts on these social networks by selecting the appropriate item and using the Share sheet.

Before you can use a social network, you must enter the details of your account, as described in this section. To use the social network fully, you can also install the social network's app.

## Set Up Your Social Networking Accounts

### Open the Settings App and Set Up Your Twitter Account

**1** Press **Home**.

The Home screen appears.

**2** Tap **Settings** (⚙).

The Settings screen appears.

**3** On the Settings screen, tap **Twitter** (🐦).

The Twitter screen appears.

**A** If the Install button appears, tap **Install** to install the app. Then return to the Settings app and continue with these steps.

**4** Type your username.

**Note:** To create a new Twitter account, tap **Create New Account** and follow the resulting screens.

**5** Type your password.

**6** Tap **Sign In**.

Twitter verifies your username and password, and then sets up your account on the iPad.

**B** You can tap **Update Contacts** if you want Twitter to pick up e-mail addresses and phone numbers from the contacts on your iPad and add them to your Twitter contacts.

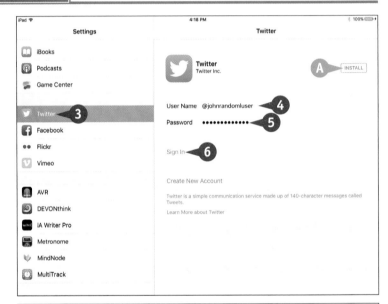

## Set Up Your Facebook Account

1. On the Settings screen, tap **Facebook** (f).

   The Facebook screen appears.

C. If the Install button appears, tap it to install the app. Then return to the Settings app and continue with these steps.

2. Type your username.

**Note:** To create a new Facebook account, tap **Create New Account**.

3. Type your password.

4. Tap **Sign In**.

5. On the information screen, tap **Sign In**. Facebook verifies your username and password, and the Facebook screen appears with your account enabled.

6. Set the **Calendars** switch to On (⬤) or Off ( ), as needed.

7. Set the **Contacts** switch to On (⬤) or Off ( ), as needed.

D. You can tap **Update All Contacts** if you want Facebook to pick up e-mail addresses and phone numbers from the contacts on your iPad and add them to your Facebook contacts.

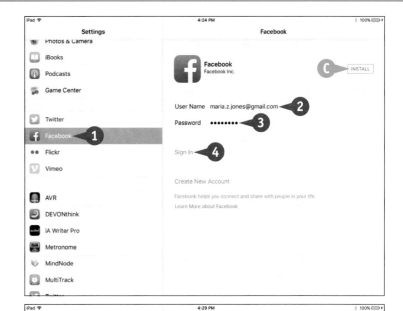

---

## TIP

**How do I set up a Flickr account or a Vimeo account?**
To set up a Flickr account or a Vimeo account, tap **Flickr** (••) or **Vimeo** (v) on the Settings screen. If the Install button appears, the app is not yet installed, so you need to tap **Install** to install it. You can then return to the Settings app, type your username and password, and tap **Sign In**.

# CHAPTER 3

# Working with Voice and Accessibility

Your iPad includes the Siri personal assistant, helpful accessibility features, and integration with your Mac.

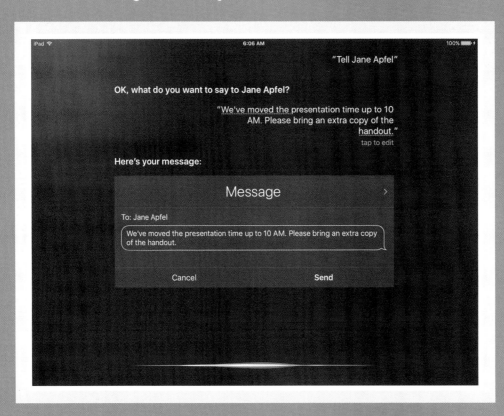

# Give Commands with Siri

The powerful Siri feature on your iPad enables you to take essential actions by using your voice to tell your iPad what you want. Siri requires an Internet connection, because the speech recognition runs on servers in Apple's data center.

You can use Siri either with the iPad's built-in microphone or with a microphone on a headset. Unless you are in a quiet environment, you are free to speak loudly and clearly, or you can speak as close to the built-in microphone as possible, a headset microphone provides better results than the built-in microphone.

## Open Siri

From the Home screen or any app, press the Home button or the headset clicker button for several seconds.

The Siri screen appears, showing the "What can I help you with?" prompt. Siri also plays a tone to indicate that it is ready to take your commands.

When your iPad is connected to a power source, you can also activate Siri by saying "Hey Siri" if the Voice Activation feature is turned on.

## Send an E-Mail Message

Say "E-mail" and the contact's name, followed by the message. Siri creates an e-mail message to the contact and enters the text. Review the message, and then tap Send to send it.

You can also say "E-mail" and the contact's name and have Siri prompt you for the various parts of the message. This approach gives you more time to collect your thoughts.

If your Contacts list has multiple e-mail addresses for the contact, Siri prompts you to choose the address to use.

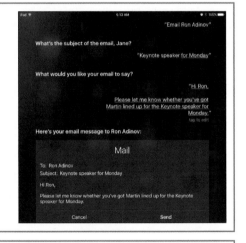

## Set an Alarm

Say "Set an alarm for 5AM" and check the alarm that Siri displays.

You can turn the alarm off by tapping its switch (⬜ changes to ⬛).

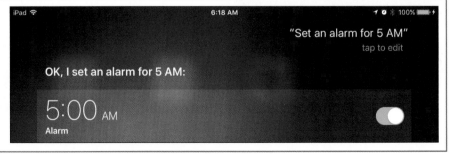

## Send a Text Message

Say "Tell" or "Text" and the contact's name. When Siri responds, say the message you want to send. For example, say "Tell Kelly Wilson" and then "I am stuck in traffic, but I'll be there in an hour." Siri creates a text message to the contact, enters the text, and sends the message when you say "Send" or tap **Send**.

You can also say "Tell" and the contact's name followed immediately by the message. For example, "Tell Bill Sykes the package will arrive at 10AM."

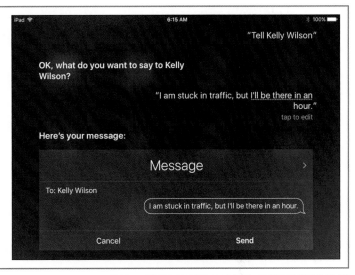

## Set a Reminder for Yourself

Say "Remind me" and the details of what you want Siri to remind you of. For example, say "Remind me to take the wireless transmitter to Acme Industries tomorrow morning." Siri listens to what you say and creates a reminder. Check what Siri has written, and then tap **Confirm** if it is correct.

## Set Up a Meeting

Say "Meet with" and the contact's name, followed by brief details of the appointment. For example, say "Meet with Don Williamson for lunch at noon on Thursday." Siri listens and warns you of any scheduling conflict. Siri then displays the appointment for you to check.

If you tap Confirm, Siri sends a meeting invitation to the contact if it finds an e-mail address. Siri adds the meeting to your calendar.

# Dictate Text Using Siri

Oone of Siri's strongest features is its capability to transcribe your speech quickly and accurately into correctly spelled and punctuated text. Using your iPad, you can dictate into any app whose keyboard displays the microphone icon (🎤), so you can dictate e-mail messages, notes, documents, and more. To dictate, simply tap the microphone icon (🎤), speak after Siri beeps, and then tap **Done**.

To get the most out of dictation, it is helpful to know the standard terms for dictating punctuation, capitalization, symbols, layout, and formatting.

## Insert Punctuation

To insert punctuation, use standard terms: "comma," "period" (or "full stop"), "semicolon," "colon," "exclamation point" (or "exclamation mark"), "question mark," "hyphen," "dash" (for a short dash, –), or "em dash" (for a long dash, —).

You can also say "asterisk" (*), "ampersand" (&), "open parenthesis" and "close parenthesis," "open bracket" and "close bracket," and "underscore" (_).

For example, say "buy eggs comma bread comma and cheese semicolon and maybe some milk period nothing else exclamation point" to enter the text shown here.

## Insert Standard Symbols

To insert symbols, use these terms: "at sign" (@), "percent sign" (%), "greater-than sign" (>) and "less-than sign" (<), "forward slash" (/) and "backslash" (\), "registered sign" (®), and "copyright sign" (©).

For example, say "fifty-eight percent forward slash two greater than ninety-seven percent forward slash three" to enter the computation shown here.

## Insert Currency Symbols

To insert currency symbols, say the currency name and "sign." For example, say "dollar sign" to insert $, "cent sign" to insert ¢, "euro sign" to insert €, "pound sterling sign" to insert £, and "yen sign" to insert ¥.

For example, say "the cost is dollar sign six or euro sign five per person" to enter the text shown here.

## Control Layout

You can control layout by creating new lines and new paragraphs as needed. A new paragraph enters two line breaks, creating a blank line between paragraphs.

To create a new line, say "new line." To create a new paragraph, say "new paragraph."

For example, say "dear Anna comma new paragraph thank you for the parrot period new paragraph it's the most unusual gift I have ever had period" to enter the text shown here.

## Control Capitalization

You can apply capitalization to the first letter of a word or to a whole word. You can also switch capitalization off temporarily to force lowercase:

- Say "cap" to capitalize the first letter of the next word.
- Say "caps on" to capitalize all the words until you say "caps off."
- Say "no caps" to prevent automatic capitalization of the next word — for example, "no caps Monday" produces "monday" instead of "Monday."
- Say "no caps on" to force lowercase of all words until you say "no caps off."

For example, say "give the cap head cap dining cap table a no caps french polish period" to enter the text shown here.

## Insert Quotes and Emoticons

To insert double quotes, say "open quotes" and "close quotes." To insert single quotes, say "open single quotes" and "close single quotes."

To enter standard emoticons, say "smiley face," "frown face," and "wink face."

For example, say "she said comma open quotes I want to go to Paris next summer exclamation point close quotes" to enter the text shown here.

# Gather and Share Information with Siri

Y ou can use Siri to research a wide variety of information online — everything from sports and movies to restaurants worth visiting or worth avoiding. You can also use Siri to perform hands-free calculations.

When you need to share information quickly and easily, you can turn to Siri. By giving the right commands, you can quickly change your Facebook status or post on your wall. Similarly, you can send tweets using your Twitter account.

## Find Information About Sports

Launch Siri and ask a question about sports. For example:

- "Siri, when's the next Patriots game?"
- "Did the Lakers win their last game?"
- "When's the end of the NBA season?"
- "Can you show me the roster for the Maple Leafs?"

## Find Information About Movies

Launch Siri and ask a question about movies. For example:

- "How good is the movie *The Transporter Refueled*?"
- "Siri, where is the movie *War Room* playing in Indianapolis?"
- "What's the name of Michael Douglas' latest movie?"
- "Who's the star of *The Man from U.N.C.L.E.*?"

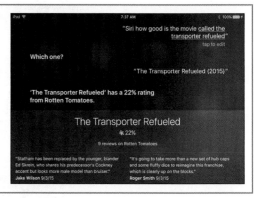

## Find a Restaurant

Launch Siri, and then tell Siri what type of restaurant you want. For example:

- "Where's the best Mexican food in Spokane?"
- "Where can I get sushi in Albuquerque?"
- "Is there a brewpub in Minneapolis?"

## Address a Query to the Wolfram Alpha Computational Knowledge Engine

Launch Siri, and then say "Wolfram" and your question. For example:

- "Wolfram, what is the cube of 27?"

- "Wolfram, minus 20 Centigrade in Kelvin."

- "Wolfram, tangent of 60 degrees."

- "Wolfram, give me the chemical formula of formaldehyde."

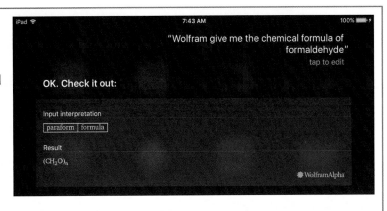

## Update Your Facebook Status or Post a Comment on Your Wall

Launch Siri and give the appropriate command:

- "Update my Facebook status," and then give details when Siri prompts you.

- "Post on my Facebook Wall," and then dictate the post when Siri prompts you.

If the post turns out to your liking, tap **Post**.

## Send a Tweet

Launch Siri, and then say "Tweet" and the text of the tweet. If necessary, tap the tap to edit prompt and edit the text of the tweet manually.

When you are satisfied with the tweet, tap **Send**.

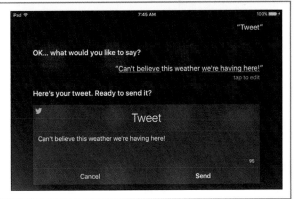

# Configure Siri to Work Your Way

To get the most out of Siri, spend a few minutes configuring it. You can set the language Siri uses, choose between using a female voice and a male voice, and control when Siri should give you voice feedback. You can also enable or disable Voice Activation or temporarily turn Siri off.

Most important, you can tell Siri which contact record contains your information, so that Siri knows your name, address, phone numbers, e-mail address, and other essential information.

## Configure Siri to Work Your Way

**1** Press **Home**.

The Home screen appears.

**2** Tap **Settings** (⚙).

The Settings screen appears.

**3** Tap **General** (⚙).

The General screen appears.

**4** Tap **Siri**.

The Siri screen appears.

**5** Set the **Siri** switch to On (⬤).

**6** Set the **Allow "Hey Siri"** switch to On (⬤) if you want to be able to activate Siri by saying "Hey, Siri!"

**7** Tap **Language**.

The Language screen appears.

**8** Tap the language you want to use, which places a check mark next to it.

**9** Tap **Siri** (❮).

The Siri screen appears again.

**10** Tap **Siri Voice**.

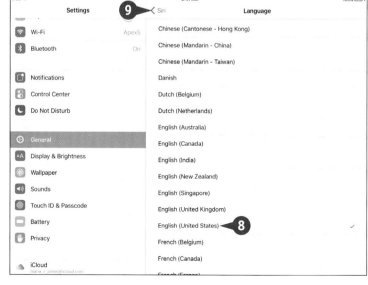

The Siri Voice screen appears again.

**11** In the Accent box, tap the accent you want, such as **American**.

**12** In the Gender box, tap **Male** or **Female**.

**13** Tap **Siri** (**<**).

The Siri screen appears again.

**14** Tap **Voice Feedback**.

The Voice Feedback screen appears.

**15** Tap **Always On**, **Control with Ring Switch**, or **Hands-Free Only** to specify when you want to receive voice feedback from Siri.

**16** Tap **Siri** (**<**).

The Siri screen appears again.

**17** Tap **My Info**.

The Contacts dialog appears.

**Note:** To change which contacts appear in the Contacts dialog, tap **Groups**, select the groups to display, and then tap **Done**.

**18** Tap the contact record that contains your information.

The name appears on the My Info button.

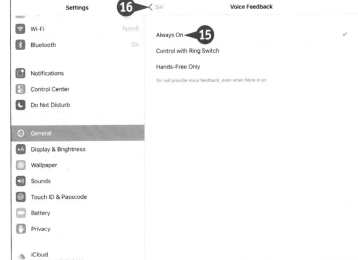

## TIP

**Does Apple store the details of what I ask Siri?**

Yes, but not in a way that will come back to haunt you. When you use Siri, your iPad passes your input to servers in the Apple data center in North Carolina, USA, for processing. The servers analyze your request and tell Siri how to respond to it. The Apple data center stores the details of your request and may analyze them to determine what people use Siri for and work out ways of making Siri more effective. Apple does not associate your Siri data with other data Apple holds about you — for example, the identity and credit card data you used to pay for iTunes Match.

# Using VoiceOver to Identify Items On-Screen

If you have trouble identifying the iPad controls on-screen, you can use the VoiceOver feature to read them to you. VoiceOver changes the standard iPad finger gestures so that you tap to select the item whose name you want it to speak, double-tap to activate an item, and flick three fingers to scroll. VoiceOver can make your iPad easier to use. Your iPad also includes other accessibility features, which you can learn about in the next section.

## Using VoiceOver to Identify Items On-Screen

**1** Press **Home**.

The Home screen appears.

**2** Tap **Settings** (⚙).

The Settings screen appears.

**3** Tap **General** (⚙).

The General screen appears.

**4** Tap **Accessibility**.

The Accessibility screen appears.

**5** Tap **VoiceOver**.

**Note:** You cannot use VoiceOver and Zoom at the same time. If Zoom is on when you try to switch VoiceOver on, your iPad prompts you to choose which to use.

The VoiceOver screen appears.

**6** Set the **VoiceOver** switch to On (⚪).

**7** Tap **VoiceOver Practice**.

**A** A selection border appears around the button, and VoiceOver speaks its name.

**8** Double-tap **VoiceOver Practice**.

**9** Practice tapping, double-tapping, triple-tapping, and swiping.

**10** Tap **Done** to select the button, and then double-tap **Done**.

**11** On the VoiceOver screen, tap **Speaking Rate** to select it, and then swipe up or down to adjust the rate. Swiping is the VoiceOver gesture for adjusting the slider.

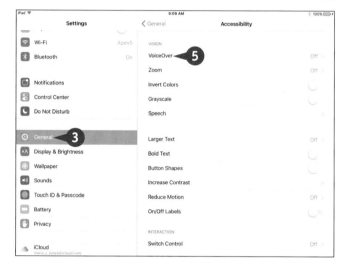

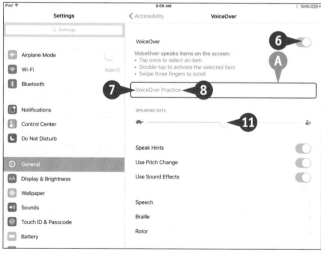

**12** Swipe up with three fingers.

The screen scrolls down.

**13** Set the **Speak Hints** switch to On (⬤) to have VoiceOver give you hints.

**14** Set the **Use Pitch Change** switch to On (⬤) if you want VoiceOver to use different pitches.

**15** Set the **Use Sound Effects** switch to On (⬤) to use sound effects.

**16** Tap **Typing Feedback** to select it, and then double-tap.

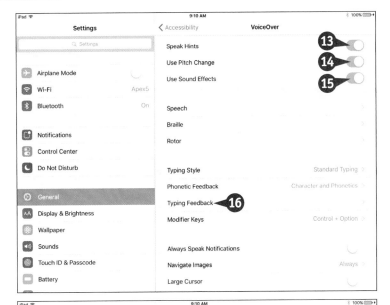

The Typing Feedback screen appears.

**17** In the Software Keyboards area, tap and then double-tap the feedback type you want: **Nothing**, **Characters**, **Words**, or **Characters and Words**.

**18** In the Hardware Keyboards area, tap and then double-tap the feedback type you want: **Nothing**, **Characters**, **Words**, or **Characters and Words**.

**19** Tap and then double-tap **VoiceOver** (❮).

The VoiceOver screen appears again.

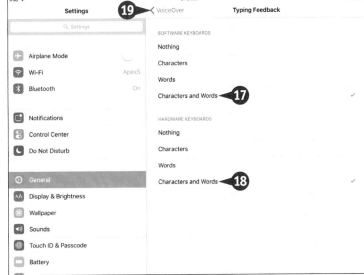

## TIP

**Is there an easy way to turn VoiceOver on and off?**

Yes. You can set your iPad to toggle VoiceOver on or off when you use the accessibility shortcut, which is pressing the Home button three times in rapid sequence. At the bottom of the Accessibility screen, tap **Accessibility Shortcut** to display the Accessibility Shortcut screen, and then tap **VoiceOver** to place a check mark next to it.

# Configure Other Accessibility Features

To help you see the screen better, iOS provides a full-featured zoom capability. After turning on zooming, you can display the Zoom Controller to give yourself easy control of zoom, choose the zoom region, and set the maximum zoom level.

The Follow Focus feature makes the zoomed area follow the focus on-screen. The Smart Typing feature makes iOS switch to Window Zoom when the keyboard appears, so that text is zoomed but the keyboard is regular size.

## Configure Other Accessibility Features

**1** Press **Home**.

The Home screen appears.

**2** Tap **Settings** (⚙).

The Settings screen appears.

**3** Tap **General** (⚙).

The General screen appears.

**4** Tap **Accessibility**.

The Accessibility screen appears.

**5** Tap **Zoom**.

The Zoom screen appears.

**6** Set the **Zoom** switch to On (○).

**A** The Zoom window appears if the Zoom Region is set to Window Zoom.

**7** Set the **Follow Focus** switch to On (○) or Off ( ).

**8** Set the **Smart Typing** switch to On (○) or Off ( ).

**9** Set the **Show Controller** switch to On (○).

**B** The Zoom Controller appears.

**10** Drag the **Maximum Zoom Level** slider to set the maximum zoom level.

**11** Tap **Idle Visibility**.

The Idle Visibility screen appears.

**12** Drag the slider to set the visibility percentage for the Zoom Controller when it is idle.

**Note:** Move the slider on the Idle Visibility screen to the left to make the controller fade more after you have not used it for a while.

**13** Tap **Zoom** (<).

The Zoom screen appears again.

**14** Tap **Zoom Region**.

The Zoom Region screen appears.

**15** Tap **Full Screen Zoom** or **Window Zoom**, as needed.

**Note:** Window Zoom displays a movable window frame that you can position over the area you want to zoom, leaving the rest of the screen unchanged.

**16** Tap **Zoom** (<).

The Zoom screen appears again.

**17** Tap **Zoom Filter**.

The Zoom Filter screen appears.

**18** Tap the zoom filter you need: **None**, **Inverted**, **Grayscale**, **Grayscale Inverted**, or **Low Light**.

**19** Tap **Zoom** (<).

The Zoom screen appears again.

**20** Tap **Accessibility** (<).

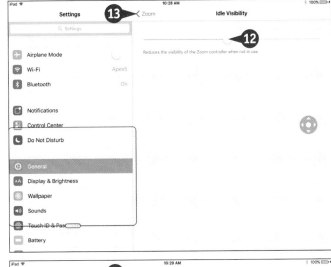

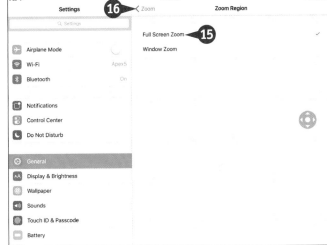

**TIP**

**Is there an easy way to turn the Zoom feature on and off?**
Yes. You can set your iPad to toggle Zoom on or off when you invoke the accessibility shortcut by pressing the Home button three times in rapid sequence. From the Accessibility screen, tap **Accessibility Shortcut** to display the Accessibility Shortcut screen. Tap **Zoom** to place a check mark next to it. You can also use the Home button triple-press to toggle the VoiceOver feature, the Invert Colors feature, the Grayscale feature, the Switch Control feature, or the AssistiveTouch feature.

continued ▶

To make your iPad's screen easier to read, you can invert the colors or switch the screen to grayscale. You can also increase the text size, make the text bold, and make iOS display the shapes around buttons so you can see exactly where they are.

iOS also includes a range of features that can help with hearing problems. You can connect a hearing aid, make the LED flash to warn you about alerts, and play mono audio instead of stereo audio.

## Configure Other Accessibility Features (continued)

The Accessibility screen appears.

**C** You can set the **Invert Colors** switch to On (⬤) to invert the colors.

**D** You can set the **Grayscale** switch to On (⬤) to make the screen appear in grayscale.

**Note:** Setting the **Grayscale** switch to On (⬤) does not reduce the amount of power needed for the display.

**21** To use larger type on-screen, tap **Larger Text**, choose settings on the Larger Type screen, and then tap **Accessibility** (〈).

**22** Tap **Speech**.

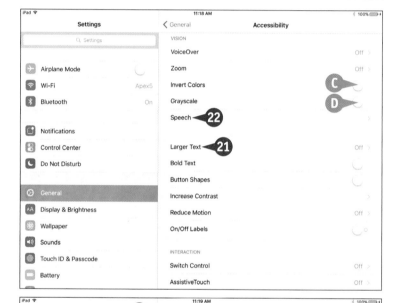

The Speech screen appears.

**23** Set the **Speak Selection** switch to On (⬤) to enable your iPad to speak selected text. If you turn this feature on, the Voices button, Speaking Rate slider, and Highlight Content switch appear, and you can set them.

**24** Set the **Speak Screen** switch to On (⬤) to enable your iPad to speak the content of the screen.

**25** Set the **Speak Auto-text** switch to On (⬤) to make your iPad speak automatic corrections.

**26** Tap **Accessibility** (〈).

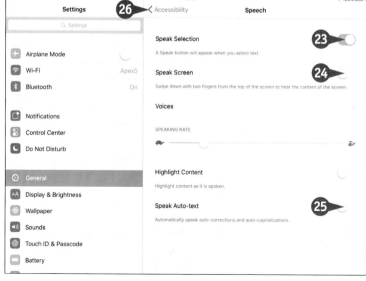

The Accessibility screen appears again.

**27** To display text in boldface, set the **Bold Text** switch to On ( ). This setting requires your iPad to restart.

**28** To display a shape around each on-screen button, set the **Button Shapes** switch to On ( ).

**E** Buttons such as General display the button shapes.

**29** To increase the contrast, tap **Increase Contrast** and choose settings on the Increase Contrast screen.

**30** Set the **On/Off Labels** switch to On ( ) if you want to display labels on the switches — I for On, 0 for Off.

**31** Set the **Mono Audio** switch to On ( ) if you want to use mono audio.

**32** Drag the audio balance slider to the left or the right as needed.

**33** Choose other options as needed in the Media, Learning, and Interaction sections.

**What does the Reduce Motion feature do?**
The Reduce Motion feature reduces the amount of movement that occurs when you tilt the iPad when displaying a screen such as the Home screen, where the icons appear to float above the background. To turn Reduce Motion on, tap **Reduce Motion** on the Accessibility to display the Reduce Motion screen, and then set the **Reduce Motion** switch to On ( ).

# Using a Hardware Keyboard

Your iPad includes several on-screen keyboards that appear automatically when you tap a text field on the screen. You can switch among the keyboards as necessary to type the characters you need, and you can undock the keyboard or split it so that you can type easily with two thumbs while holding the iPad.

If you need to type extensively, you may prefer to connect a hardware keyboard to your iPad. This section details your options for a hardware keyboard, explains how to connect it, and shows you how to use it.

## Choose a Hardware Keyboard

For the iPad Pro, you can get Apple's Smart Keyboard, which connects via the custom Smart Connector on the iPad Pro. For other iPads, the main means of connecting a keyboard to the iPad is by using Bluetooth, which is usually effective and convenient for most purposes. The alternative means of connection is by connecting a Lightning-to-USB connector to the iPad's Lightning port and then

connecting a standard USB keyboard, but this works for only some keyboard models; if not, the iPad displays a Cannot Use Device dialog to warn you about the problem.

Many types of Bluetooth keyboards work well with iPads, but it is a good idea to verify the compatibility of any particular model before buying it. Keyboards designed specifically for the iPad, or for iOS devices in general, often include dedicated keys for functions such as displaying the Home screen, controlling the volume, and launching apps.

One option is to get a keyboard case designed specifically for the iPad model you have. This approach works well if you do not already have an iPad case, it is convenient for you to keep the iPad in the keyboard case, and you do not plan to switch iPad models in the near future. Some keyboard cases fully enclose the iPad, whereas others act as a protective cover for the screen but leave the iPad's back exposed.

For more flexibility, you can get a Bluetooth keyboard designed for use with iOS but not customized for any particular model. You can then use the keyboard with any iOS device.

For the greatest flexibility, you can use any Bluetooth keyboard that is compatible with iOS. For example, if you already have a Bluetooth keyboard, you may want to see if it works with your iPad.

## Connect the Keyboard to the iPad

Once you have gotten your keyboard, connect it to your iPad. This section assumes you are using Bluetooth.

Unlock the iPad, press **Home** to display the Home screen, and then tap **Settings** (⚙) to display the Settings screen. Tap **Bluetooth** (◈) to display the Bluetooth screen, and set the **Bluetooth** switch to On (◯).

Turn the keyboard on, and then put the keyboard into pairing mode. How you do this depends on the keyboard, so you may need to read its documentation, but it often involves pressing either a dedicated pairing button or pressing and holding the power button until lights begin flashing in a particular pattern.

Tap the keyboard's button in the Devices list on the Bluetooth screen. The Bluetooth Pairing Request dialog opens, showing a pairing code. Type this code on the keyboard and press **Return** or **Enter** to authenticate the connection.

## Configure the Keyboard

After connecting the keyboard, you can simply type on it after tapping a text field on the screen. But you can also change the keyboard layout if necessary.

To change the keyboard layout, press **Home** to display the Home screen, and then tap **Settings** (⚙) to display the Settings screen. Tap **General** (⚙) to display the General screen, and then tap **Keyboard** to display the Keyboards screen. Tap **Hardware Keyboard** at the top of the screen to display the Hardware Keyboard screen, and then tap the language you are using, such as **English**. On the screen that appears, such as the English screen, tap the layout you want, such as **Dvorak** or **U.S. International – PC.**

# Using Your iPad with Your Mac

Ⅰf you have a Mac, you can enjoy the impressive integration that Apple has built into iOS and OS X. Apple calls this integration Continuity. Continuity involves several features including Handoff, which enables you to pick up your work or play seamlessly on one device exactly where you have left it on another device. For example, you can start writing an e-mail message on your Mac and then complete it on your iPad.

To use Continuity, your iPad must be running iOS 8 or a later version, and your Mac must be running OS X 10.10, which is called Yosemite, or a later version. Your Mac must have Bluetooth 4.0 hardware. In practice, this means a Mac mini or MacBook Air from 2011 or later, a MacBook Pro or iMac from 2012 or later, a MacBook from 2014 or later, or a Mac Pro from 2013 or later.

## Enable Handoff and Suggested Apps on Your iPad

To enable your iPad to communicate with your Mac, you need to enable the Handoff feature. Press the Home button to display the Home screen, tap **Settings** (⚙) to open the Settings app, and then tap **General** (⚙) to display the General screen. Tap **Handoff & Suggested Apps** to display the Handoff & Suggested Apps screen, and then set the **Handoff** switch to On (◯).

On this screen, you can also set the **Installed Apps** switch to On (◯) to display suggested apps on your iPad's lock screen and in the app switcher.

## Enable Handoff on Your Mac

You also need to enable Handoff on your Mac. To do so, click **Apple** (🍎) on the menu bar and then click **System Preferences** to open the System Preferences window. Click **General** to display the General pane. Click **Allow Handoff between this Mac and your iCloud devices** (☐ changes to ☑). You can then click **System Preferences** on the menu bar and click **Quit System Preferences** to quit System Preferences.

## Work on the Same Task on Your Mac and Your iOS Devices

With Handoff enabled, you can easily start a task on one device, pick it up on another device, and finish it on a third. For example, you can start writing an e-mail message on your Mac at home, continue it on your iPhone as you commute, and then finish it on your iPad while waiting for a meeting to start.

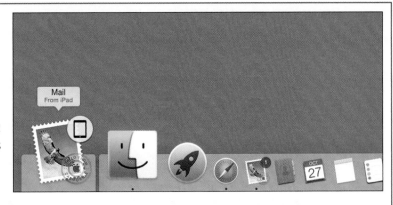

## Send and Receive Text Messages from Your Mac

Your Mac can already send and receive messages via Apple's iMessage service, but when your cellular iPad's Internet connection is available, your Mac can send and receive Short Message Service (SMS) and Multimedia Messaging Service (MMS) messages directly. This capability enables you to manage your messaging smoothly and tightly from your Mac.

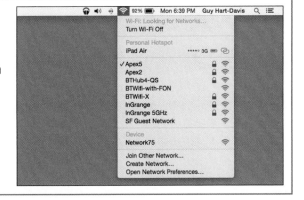

## Get Your Mac Online with Personal Hotspot

With Continuity, you can use your cellular iPad as a hotspot for your Mac without having to set up the Portable Hotspot feature. Click **Wi-Fi** on the menu bar on your Mac and then click your iPad's entry on the pop-up menu to connect. The iPad's menu entry on the Wi-Fi pop-up menu shows the signal strength and battery life, enabling you to make sure you don't run your iPad down unusably low.

# CHAPTER 4

# Setting Up Communications

In this chapter, you learn how to add your e-mail accounts to the Mail app, choose how and when your iPad gets your mail, and control how the messages appear. You also learn how to make your contacts appear the way you prefer, choose alert options for calendar events, and set your default account for notes.

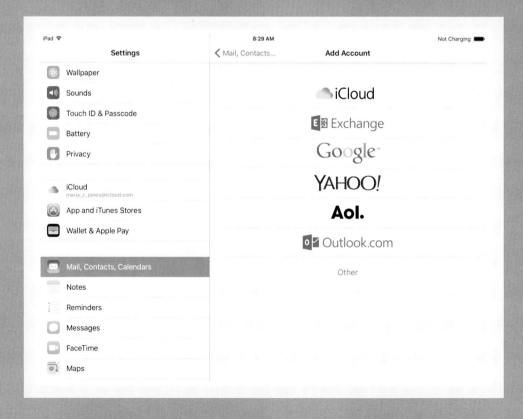

# Set Up Your Mail Accounts

You can set up your iCloud Mail account simply by setting up your iCloud account on your iPad. Beyond that, you can set up other e-mail accounts manually by working directly on the iPad, as explained in this section. To set up an e-mail account, you need to know the e-mail address and password, as well as the e-mail provider. You may also need to know the addresses of the mail servers the account uses. For Microsoft Exchange, you must know the domain name as well; see the next section, "Set Up an Exchange Server Account."

## Set Up Your Mail Accounts

**1** Press **Home**.

The Home screen appears.

**2** Tap **Settings** (⚙).

The Settings screen appears.

**Note:** If you have not yet set up an e-mail account on the iPad, you can also open the Add Account screen by tapping Mail on the Home screen.

**3** Tap **Mail, Contacts, Calendars** (✉).

The Mail, Contacts, Calendars screen appears.

**4** Tap **Add Account**.

**Note:** This example uses a Google account. Different account types require you to enter different information. For example, for some account types, you must type a description for the e-mail account and your name the way you want it to appear in outgoing messages.

The Add Account screen appears.

**5** Tap the kind of account you want to set up.

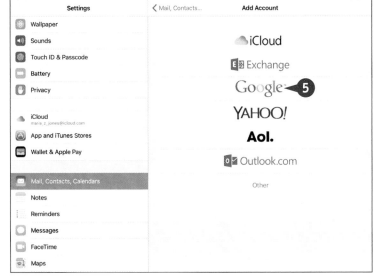

The screen for setting up that type of account appears.

**6** Type the e-mail address.

**7** Type the password.

**8** Tap **Sign in**.

**Note:** For some e-mail account types, you tap a different button than Sign In, such as **Next**.

**Note:** For a Google account, the iOS Would Like To screen appears, making sure you know that iOS will view and manage your mail, manage your calendars, and manage your contacts. Click **Accept**.

The configuration screen for the account appears. The options vary depending on the account type.

**9** Make sure the **Mail** switch is set to On (⚪).

**10** Set the **Contacts** switch to On (⚪) or Off ( ).

**11** Set the **Calendars** switch to On (⚪) or Off ( ).

**12** Set the **Notes** switch to On (⚪) or Off ( ).

**Note:** If the Reminders switch appears, set it to On (⚪) or Off ( ), as needed.

**13** Tap **Save**.

The account appears on the Mail, Contacts, Calendars screen.

**TIP**

**How do I change the name for an e-mail account?**

To change the name displayed for the account, press **Home**, tap **Settings** (⚙), and then tap **Mail, Contacts, Calendars** (▢). Tap the account and then tap **Account**. Tap **Description** and type the name that you want to have appear for the account, such as **Work E-Mail** or **Main Google Account**. Tap **Done** and then tap **Mail, Contacts, Calendars** (<).

# Set Up an Exchange Server Account

You can set up your iPad to connect to Microsoft Exchange Server or Office 365 for e-mail, contacts, calendaring, reminders, and notes.

Before setting up your Exchange account, ask an administrator for the details you need. They include your e-mail address, your password, the server name, and the domain name, if required. You may be able to set up the account using only the e-mail address and password, but often you need the server name and domain as well.

## Set Up an Exchange Server Account

**1** Press **Home**.

The Home screen appears.

**2** Tap **Settings** (⚙️).

The Settings screen appears.

**3** Tap **Mail, Contacts, Calendars** (✉️).

The Mail, Contacts, Calendars screen appears.

**4** Tap **Add Account**.

The Add Account screen appears.

**5** Tap **Exchange**.

The first Exchange dialog opens.

**6** Tap **Email** and type your e-mail address.

**7** Tap **Password** and type your password.

**8** Tap **Description** and type a descriptive name for the account.

**Note:** The description is to help you identify the account easily.

**9** Tap **Next**.

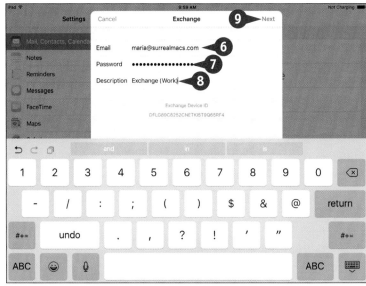

The second Exchange dialog opens.

**Note:** If the configuration dialog for the Exchange account opens at this point, go to step **14**.

**10** Tap **Server** and type the server's address.

**11** Tap **Domain** and type the domain, if needed.

**12** Tap **Username** and type your username.

**13** Tap **Next**.

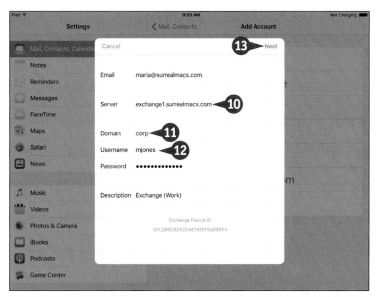

The configuration dialog for the Exchange account opens.

**14** Set the **Mail** switch to On (◯) or Off ( ), as needed.

**15** Set the **Contacts** switch to On (◯) or Off ( ), as needed.

**16** Set the **Calendars** switch to On (◯) or Off ( ), as needed.

**17** Set the **Reminders** switch to On (◯) or Off ( ), as needed.

**18** Set the **Notes** switch to On (◯) or Off ( ), as needed.

**19** Tap **Save**.

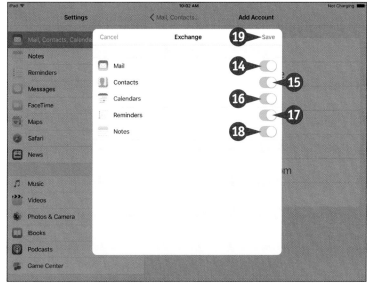

## TIPS

**How do I know whether to enter a domain name when setting up my Exchange account?**
You need to ask an administrator, because some Exchange installations require you to enter a domain, whereas others do not.

**How do I set up an Office 365 e-mail account?**
Use the method explained in this section, but use outlook.office365.com as the server's address. Your username is typically your full e-mail address; if in doubt, ask an administrator.

# Set Your Default Account and Create Signatures

If you set up multiple e-mail accounts on your iPad, you need to set your default account. This is the account from which the Mail app sends messages, unless you choose to use another account for a particular message.

You can save time by using e-mail signatures. A signature is text that the Mail app automatically adds to each message you compose — for example, your name and contact information. The default iPad signature is "Sent from my iPad."

## Set Your Default Account and Create Signatures

**1** Press **Home**.

The Home screen appears.

**2** Tap **Settings** (⚙).

The Settings screen appears.

**3** Tap **Mail, Contacts, Calendars** (✉).

The Mail, Contacts, Calendars screen appears.

**4** In the Mail section, tap **Default Account**.

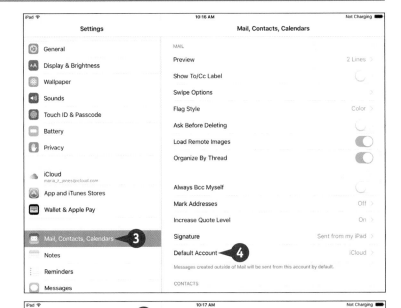

The Default Account screen appears.

**5** Tap the account you want to make the default.

**6** Tap **Mail, Contacts, Calendars** (‹).

The Mail, Contacts, Calendars screen appears again.

**7** Tap **Signature**.

The Signature screen appears.

**8** Tap **All Accounts** if you want to use the same signature for each e-mail account. Tap **Per Account** to use different signatures.

**Note:** If you do not want to use a signature, simply delete the default signature.

If you tap **Per Account** in step **8**, a separate area appears for each account.

**9** Type the text of the signature or signatures.

**Note:** To make your signatures easy to read, keep them to four lines or fewer and use plain text without formatting.

**10** Tap **Mail, Contacts, Calendars** (⟨).

The Mail, Contacts, Calendars screen appears.

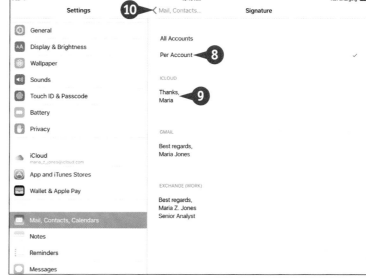

**TIP**

**How do I send a message from an e-mail account other than the default account?**

After starting to compose a message, tap **Cc/Bcc, From** to display the Cc, Bcc, and From lines. Tap **From** to display the pop-up menu of e-mail addresses, and then tap the address you want to use.

When you reply to a message, Mail sends the reply from the account to which the message was sent, even if this is not your default account. To send the reply from a different account, tap **Cc/Bcc, From**, tap **From**, and then tap the address.

# Choose How Your iPad Gets Your E-Mail

Your iPad can get your e-mail messages by using two different technologies, Push and Fetch. With Push, the e-mail server "pushes" your new messages to your iPad as soon as the server receives them. With Fetch, your iPad checks in periodically with the server and downloads any new messages.

Push is normally more convenient than Fetch, but if your e-mail provider does not support Push, use Fetch and set a suitable interval for checking for messages. You can also check manually for e-mail at any point.

## Choose How Your iPad Gets Your E-Mail

1 Press **Home**.

The Home screen appears.

2 Tap **Settings** (⚙).

**Note:** Push uses more battery power, especially if you receive many messages or large attachments.

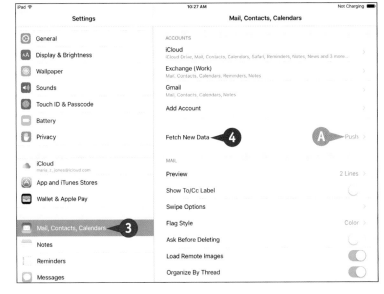

The Settings screen appears.

3 Tap **Mail, Contacts, Calendars** (✉).

The Mail, Contacts, Calendars screen appears.

Ⓐ The Fetch New Data button shows Push if Push is enabled or Off if Push is disabled.

4 Tap **Fetch New Data**.

100

The Fetch New Data screen appears.

**5** To use Push for any of your e-mail accounts, set the **Push** switch to On (⬤).

**Note:** The Fetch New Data screen shows only the options that are available for the accounts.

**6** To control how frequently Fetch runs, tap **Every 15 Minutes**, **Every 30 Minutes**, **Hourly**, or **Manually**.

**7** If you need to use different settings for an account, tap that account.

The account's screen appears.

**8** Tap **Push**, **Fetch**, or **Manual**, as needed.

**Note:** Push is not available for some types of accounts.

**Ⓑ** If the account displays the Pushed Mailboxes list, as iCloud and Exchange do, tap to select each mailbox you want to push.

**9** Tap **Fetch New Data** (‹).

The Fetch New Data screen appears.

**10** Tap **Mail, Contacts, Calendars** (‹).

The Mail, Contacts, Calendars screen appears again.

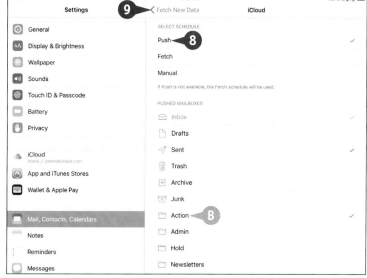

**TIP**

**How do I check manually for new e-mail messages?**
In a mailbox, tap the list of messages, drag down, and then release it. A progress icon indicates that Mail is checking for new messages.

# Control How Your iPad Displays Your E-Mail

You can configure the Mail app to suit the way you work. You can choose how many lines to include in the message preview, decide whether to display the To/CC label, and control whether Mail prompts you before deleting a message.

To make messages easy to read, you can change the minimum font size. You can also choose whether to load remote images in messages and whether to increase the indentation on messages you reply to or forward to others.

## Control How Your iPad Displays Your E-Mail

① Press **Home**.

The Home screen appears.

② Tap **Settings** (⚙).

The Settings screen appears.

③ Tap **Mail, Contacts, Calendars** (✉).

The Mail, Contacts, Calendars screen appears.

④ Set the **Show To/Cc Label** switch to On (◯) or Off (◯ ).

⑤ Set the **Load Remote Images** switch to On (◯) or Off (◯ ).

⑥ Tap **Preview**.

The Preview screen appears.

⑦ Tap the number of lines you want to see in previews.

⑧ Tap **Mail, Contacts, Calendars** (‹).

The Mail, Contacts, Calendars screen appears again.

⑨ Tap **Flag Style**.

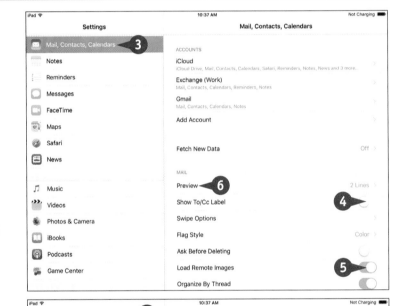

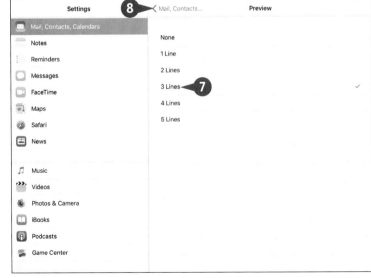

The Flag Style screen appears.

**10** Tap **Color** or **Shape** to set the flag style.

**11** Tap **Mail, Contacts, Calendars** (<).

The Mail, Contacts, Calendars screen appears again.

**12** Tap **Increase Quote Level**.

The Increase Quote Level screen appears.

**13** Set the **Increase Quote Level** switch to On (⬤) or Off ( ).

**14** Tap **Mail, Contacts, Calendars** (<).

The Mail, Contacts, Calendars screen appears again.

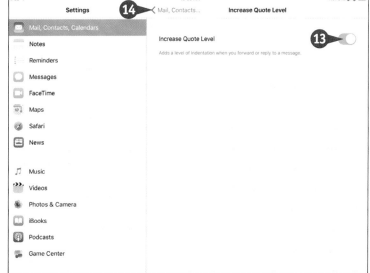

## TIPS

**Why turn off Load Remote Images?**
Loading a remote image enables the sender to find out that you have opened the message. When Mail requests the remote image, the server that provides the image can log the date and time and your Internet connection's IP address, which reveals your approximate location.

**What is Always Bcc Myself useful for?**
Most e-mail services automatically put a copy of each message you send or forward into a folder with a name such as Sent. If your e-mail service does not use a Sent folder, set the **Always Bcc Myself** switch to On (⬤) to send a bcc copy of each message to yourself. You can then file these messages for reference.

# Organize Your E-Mail Messages by Threads

The Mail app gives you two ways to view e-mail messages. You can view the messages as a simple list, or you can view them with related messages organized into threads, which are sometimes called *conversations*.

Having Mail display your messages as threads can help you navigate your Inbox quickly and find related messages easily. You may find threading useful if you tend to have long e-mail conversations, because threading reduces the number of messages you see at once.

## Organize Your E-Mail Messages by Threads

### Set Mail to Organize Your Messages by Thread

**1** Press **Home**.

The Home screen appears.

**2** Tap **Settings** (⚙).

The Settings screen appears.

**3** Tap **Mail, Contacts, Calendars** (✉).

The Mail, Contacts, Calendars screen appears.

**4** Set the **Organize By Thread** switch to On (◯).

## Read Messages Organized into Threads

**1** Press **Home**.

The Home screen appears.

**2** Tap **Mail** (✉).

The Mailboxes screen appears.

**3** Tap the mailbox.

The Inbox for the account appears.

**Ⓐ** Two chevrons on the right (»») indicate a threaded message.

**4** Tap the threaded message.

The Thread screen appears.

**Ⓑ** The Thread pane shows the list of threaded messages.

**5** Tap the message you want to display.

**Ⓒ** The message appears.

**6** Tap the button (‹) in the upper-left corner of the Thread pane, such as the **Inbox** button, when you want to return from the thread to the mailbox.

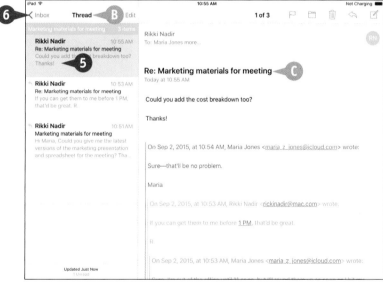

**What does the Ask Before Deleting switch do?**

This switch lets you control whether your iPad displays the Trash Message dialog to confirm deletion of a message by tapping **Delete** (🗑). Set **Ask Before Deleting** to On (⬤) if you find you tap **Delete** (🗑) by accident sometimes — for example, when using your iPad on public transit.

# Using the VIP Inbox

The Mail app includes an inbox named VIP for collecting your most important messages so that you do not miss any. Mail automatically monitors your incoming messages and adds those from your designated VIPs to the VIP inbox.

To start using your VIP inbox, you must add people to the VIP list. You can add people either from your Contacts list or from e-mail messages you receive. After designating your VIPs, you can tap the VIP inbox to display its contents.

## Using the VIP Inbox

**1** Press **Home**.

The Home screen appears.

**2** Tap **Mail** (◻).

The Mailboxes screen appears.

**3** Open the VIP list as follows:

**A** If Information (ⓘ) appears on the VIP button in the Mailboxes list, tap **Information** (ⓘ). Your VIP list already contains VIPs, so tapping the VIP button opens the mailbox rather than the VIP list.

**B** If Information (ⓘ) does not appear, tap **VIP**.

The VIP List pane appears.

**4** Tap **Add VIP**.

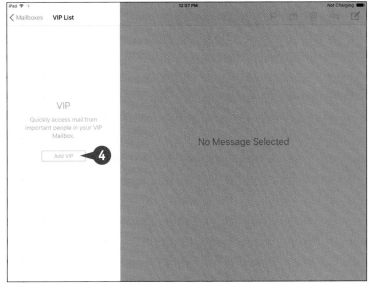

The Contacts list opens in the left pane. If All Contacts appears, you are viewing all your contacts. If Contacts appears, you are viewing only some groups.

**C** You can change the groups displayed by tapping **Groups**, making your choices on the Groups screen, and then tapping **Done**.

**5** Tap the contact you want to make a VIP.

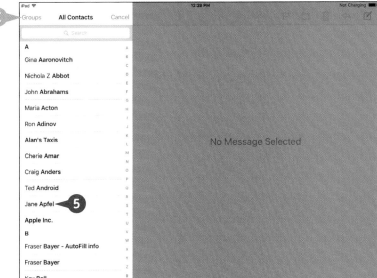

---

TIP

**Is there another way to add someone to my VIP list?**
Yes. Open a message you have received, and then tap the sender's name. In the Sender dialog, tap **Add to VIP** to add the sender to your VIP list.

continued ▶

# Using the VIP Inbox (continued)

You can configure notifications for your VIP group, enabling you to distinguish incoming messages from VIPs from other incoming e-mail messages. For example, you can assign the VIP group a distinctive sound for Mail notifications.

You may also want to show mail previews on the lock screen so that you can determine whether an incoming VIP e-mail requires you to unlock your iPad immediately.

## Using the VIP Inbox (continued)

Ⓓ The VIP List pane appears again, with the contact now added.

Ⓔ You can tap **Add VIP** and repeat step **5** as needed to add all your VIPs to the VIP list.

**6** Tap **VIP Alerts**.

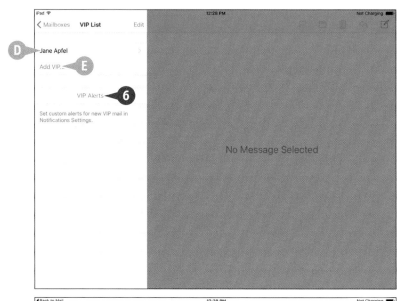

The Notifications screen in the Settings app appears.

**7** Tap **Mail** (📧).

The Mail screen appears.

**8** Make sure the **Allow Notifications** switch is set to On (●).

**9** Tap **VIP**.

The VIP pane appears.

**10** Set the **Show in Notification Center** switch to On (●) to display VIP messages in Notification Center.

**11** Tap **Sounds**, tap the sound on the Sounds screen, and then tap **VIP** to return to the VIP screen.

**12** Set the **Badge App Icon** switch to On (●) to display a badge on the Mail icon.

**13** Set the **Show on Lock Screen** switch to On (●) to display VIP messages on the lock screen.

**14** In the Alert Style When Unlocked area, tap **None**, **Banners**, or **Alerts**, as you prefer.

**15** Set the **Show Previews** switch to On (●) to include message previews.

**16** Tap **Back to Mail**.

The VIP List screen in the Mail app appears.

---

**TIP**

**How do I remove a VIP?**

Press Home, tap **Mail** (✉), and then tap **Information** (ⓘ) on the VIP button to display the VIP List pane. Tap **Edit** to open the list for editing, tap **Delete** (⊖) to the left of the VIP's name, and then tap the textual **Delete** button that appears to the right of the VIP's name.

# Choose How Your iPad Displays Your Contacts

You can set your iPad to sort and display the contacts in your preferred order for easy browsing. You can sort contacts either by first name or by last name; you can display contacts either by first name or last name; and you can choose whether and how to shorten last names — for example, by using the first initial and last name.

You can also control whether iOS displays suggested contacts it has found in e-mail messages. See the tip for details.

## Choose How Your iPad Displays Your Contacts

**1** Press **Home**.

The Home screen appears.

**2** Tap **Settings** (⚙️).

The Settings screen appears.

**3** Tap **Mail, Contacts, Calendars** (📧).

The Mail, Contacts, Calendars screen appears.

**4** In the Contacts area, tap **Sort Order**.

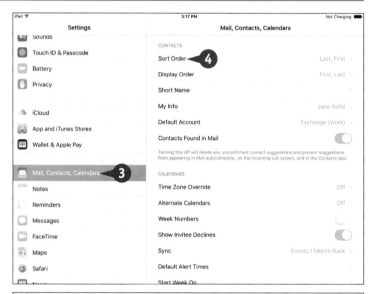

The Sort Order screen appears.

**5** Tap **First, Last** to sort by first name and then last name, or tap **Last, First** to sort by last name and then first name.

**6** Tap **Mail, Contacts, Calendars** (〈).

**7** On the Mail, Contacts, Calendars screen, tap **Display Order**.

**8** On the Display Order screen, tap **First, Last** to display the first name and then the last name, or tap **Last, First** to display the last name and then the first name.

**9** Tap **Mail, Contacts, Calendars** (〈).

**10** On the Mail, Contacts, Calendars screen, tap **Short Name**.

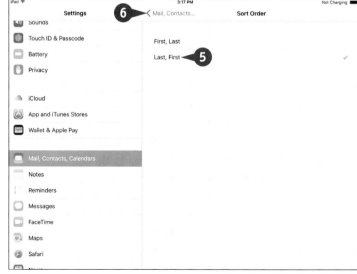

The Short Name screen appears.

11 Set the **Short Name** switch to On ( ) if you want to use name shortening.

12 Tap your preferred means of shortening names: **First Name & Last Initial**, **First Initial & Last Name**, **First Name Only**, or **Last Name Only**.

13 Set the **Prefer Nicknames** switch to On ( ) if you want Contacts to display nicknames instead of proper names.

14 Tap **Mail, Contacts, Calendars** (‹).

15 On the Mail, Contacts, Calendars screen, tap **Default Account**.

The Default Account screen appears.

16 Tap the account to use for new contacts by default.

17 Tap **Mail, Contacts, Calendars** (‹).

The Mail, Contacts, Calendars screen appears again.

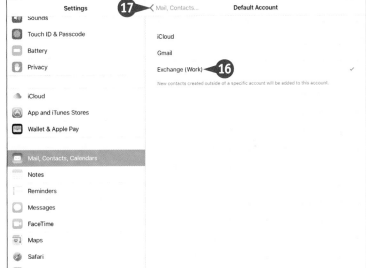

**TIP**

**What does the Contacts Found in Mail switch control?**
Set the **Contacts Found in Mail** switch to On ( ) if you want iOS to display suggestions for contacts. These suggestions show contact information that iOS has identified in e-mail messages but that you have not confirmed as being contacts. The suggestions appear in Mail's auto-completion as you type recipient names, on the incoming call screen when you receive FaceTime calls, and in the Contacts app.

# Choose Alert Options for Calendar Events

Your iPad enables you to sync your calendars via iCloud and other online services. To help keep on schedule, you can set default alert times for calendar events. You can set a different alert time for each type of event — for example, 15 minutes' notice for a regular event and a week's notice for a birthday. You can also turn on the Time to Leave feature to make the Calendar app allow travel time based on your location and current traffic.

## Choose Alert Options for Calendar Events

**1** Press **Home**.

The Home screen appears.

**2** Tap **Settings** (⚙).

The Settings screen appears.

**3** Tap **Mail, Contacts, Calendars** (✉).

The Mail, Contacts, Calendars screen appears.

**4** Tap **Sync**.

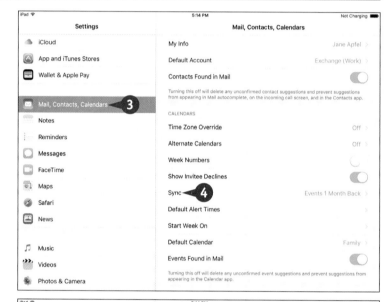

The Sync screen appears.

**5** Tap the period of events you want to sync. For example, tap **Events 1 Month Back**.

**6** Tap **Mail, Contacts, Calendars** (〈).

The Mail, Contacts, Calendars screen appears again.

**7** Tap **Default Alert Times**.

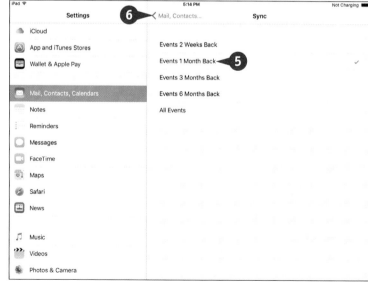

The Default Alert Times screen appears.

**8** Set the **Time To Leave** switch to On (⬤) to have your iPad use your location to determine a suitable departure time for events.

**9** Tap the event type for which you want to set the default alert time. For example, tap **Events**.

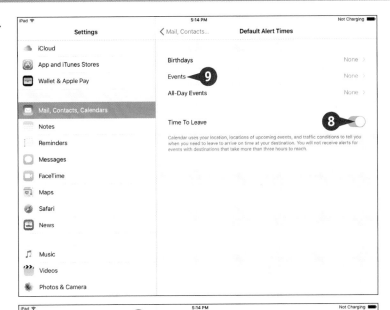

The corresponding screen appears — the Events screen, the Birthdays screen, or the All-Day Events screen.

**10** Tap the amount of time for the warning. For example, for an event, tap **15 minutes before**.

**11** Tap **Default Alert Times** (〈).

The Default Alert Times screen appears.

**12** Tap **Mail, Contacts, Calendars** (〈).

The Mail, Contacts, Calendars screen appears again.

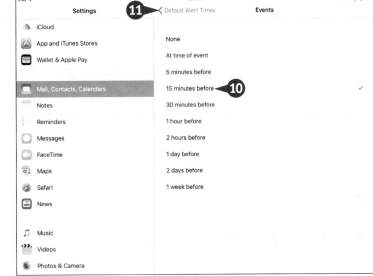

**TIP**

**What does the Events Found in Mail switch control?**

Set the **Events Found in Mail** switch to On (⬤) if you want the Calendar app to display suggested event details. These are possible events that iOS has identified in e-mail messages but that you have not confirmed as events. This feature can be helpful; but if you find the suggested events are imaginary or irrelevant, set the **Events Found in Mail** switch to Off (  ).

# Choose Your Default Calendar and Time Zone

When you use multiple calendars on your iPad, you should set your default calendar. This is the calendar that receives events you create outside any specific calendar. For example, if you have a Work calendar and a Home calendar, you can set the Home calendar as the default calendar.

If you travel to different time zones, you may need to specify which time zone to show event dates and times in. Otherwise, Calendar uses the time zone for your current location.

## Choose Your Default Calendar and Time Zone

**1** Press **Home**.

The Home screen appears.

**2** Tap **Settings** (⚙).

The Settings screen appears.

**3** Tap **Mail, Contacts, Calendars** (✉).

The Mail, Contacts, Calendars screen appears.

**4** In the Calendars section, tap **Time Zone Override**.

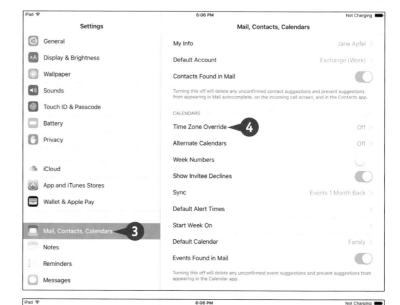

The Time Zone Override screen appears.

**5** Set the **Time Zone Override** switch to On (◯).

**6** Tap **Time Zone**.

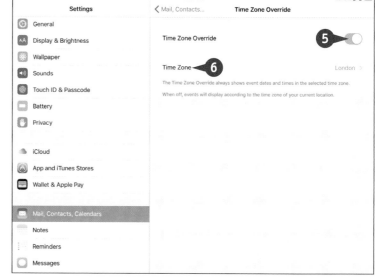

The Time Zone screen appears.

**7** Type the first letters of a city in the time zone.

**8** Tap the search result you want.

The Time Zone Override screen appears.

**9** Tap **Mail, Contacts, Calendars** (‹).

The Mail, Contacts, Calendars screen appears again.

**10** Tap **Default Calendar**.

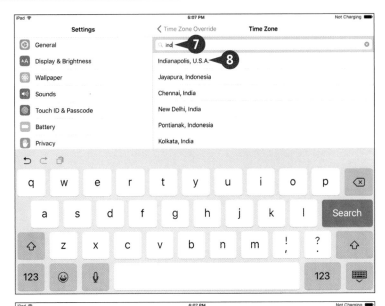

The Default Calendar screen appears.

**11** Tap the calendar you want to make the default.

**12** Tap **Mail, Contacts, Calendars** (‹).

The Mail, Contacts, Calendars screen appears again.

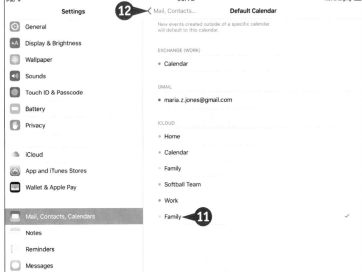

---

**TIP**

**How do I choose which calendars to display in the Calendar app?**

You choose the calendars in the Calendar app, not in the Settings app. Press **Home** to display the Home screen, tap **Calendar** (📅), and then tap **Calendars**. In the Show Calendars dialog, tap to place a check mark on each calendar you want to display. Tap to remove a check mark from each calendar you want to hide, and then tap **Done**.

# Choose Settings for Notes

As described earlier in this chapter, you can set up multiple e-mail accounts on your iPad. Each e-mail account can synchronize notes if the e-mail service supports them.

You can choose whether to store notes directly on your iPad as well as — or instead of — in online accounts. You can set the default account for notes you create using Siri. You can also choose the default style for the first line of new notes.

## Choose Settings for Notes

**1** Press **Home**.

The Home screen appears.

**2** Tap **Settings** (⚙).

The Settings screen appears.

**3** Tap **Notes** (▭).

The Notes screen appears.

**4** Set the **"On My iPad" Account** switch to On (⬤) if you want to be able to store notes on your iPad instead of in online accounts.

**5** Tap **Default Account for Siri**.

The Default Account for Siri screen appears.

**6** Tap the account in which you want to store new notes you create using Siri.

**7** Tap **Notes** (<).

116

The Notes screen appears again.

**8** Tap **New Notes Start With**.

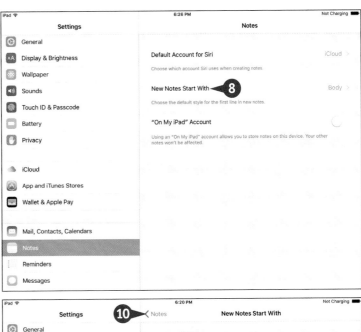

The New Notes Start With screen appears.

**9** Tap the style — Title, Heading, or Body — with which you want each new note to start.

**10** Tap **Notes** (<).

The Notes screen appears again.

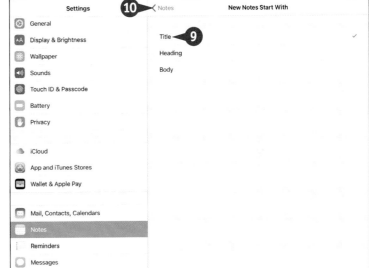

**Should I enable the "On My iPad" Account feature?**
Usually, it is best to store your notes online, such as in your iCloud account, so that you can access them from all your iOS devices and your computers. But if you need to work with notes in places in which your iPad does not have Internet access, enable the "On My iPad" Account so that you can store notes locally.

# CHAPTER 5

# Networking and Communicating

Your iPad connects to the Internet through wireless networks and Wi-Fi hotspots; if it has cellular capability, it can connect through the cellular network as well. The iPad also has Bluetooth connectivity for connecting headsets and other devices. Once connected to the Internet, you can send instant messages, share your news on Twitter, post updates to Facebook, and make video calls with FaceTime.

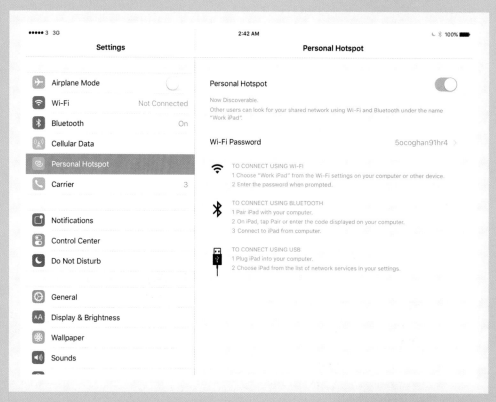

# Using Airplane Mode

Normally, you will want to keep your iPad connected to the Internet so that you can send and receive messages and browse the web. But when you do not need or may not use the cellular network or Wi-Fi, you can turn on the Airplane Mode feature to cut off all connections.

Turning on Airplane Mode turns off Wi-Fi and Bluetooth connections as well. But you can also turn Wi-Fi and Bluetooth on and off separately when you need to.

## Using Airplane Mode

**1** Press **Home**.

The Home screen appears.

**2** Tap **Settings** (⚙️).

The Settings screen appears.

**3** To turn Airplane Mode on, set the **Airplane Mode** switch to On (⚪).

**Note:** When your iPad has a wireless network connection, it uses that connection instead of the cellular connection. This helps keep down your cellular network usage and often provides a faster connection.

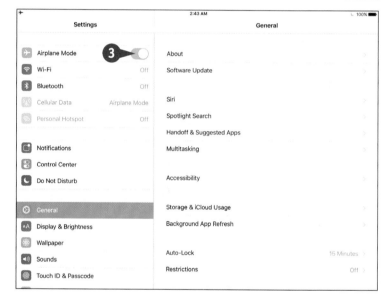

**A** The iPad turns off all cellular, Wi-Fi, and Bluetooth connections. An airplane icon (✈️) appears in the status bar.

**4** To turn on Wi-Fi, tap **Wi-Fi** (📶).

The Wi-Fi screen appears.

**5** Set the **Wi-Fi** switch to On (⚪).

Ⓑ The list of available networks appears in the Choose a Network section.

Ⓒ If your iPad detects a known network, it connects automatically, and the network moves out of the Choose a Network list up to below the Wi-Fi switch. If not, you can connect to a network manually as described in the section "Connect to Wi-Fi Networks," later in this chapter.

⑥ Tap **Bluetooth** (🔵).

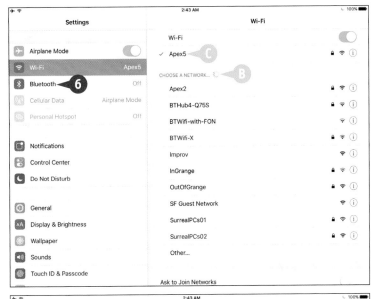

The Bluetooth screen appears.

⑦ Set the **Bluetooth** switch to On (🔵) if you need to use Bluetooth devices while Airplane Mode is on.

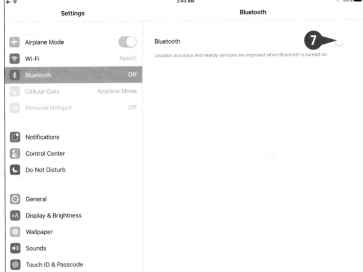

**If I turn on Wi-Fi and Bluetooth on a non-cellular iPad, what effect does Airplane Mode have?**
Even if you turn on both Wi-Fi and Bluetooth, Airplane Mode keeps your iPad's Location Services feature disabled. If your iPad has cellular connectivity, turning on Airplane Mode also keeps the Global Positioning System — GPS — feature disabled.

# Connect Bluetooth Devices to Your iPad

To extend the functionality of your iPad, you can connect devices to it that communicate using the wireless Bluetooth technology.

For example, you can connect a Bluetooth keyboard so that you can quickly type e-mail messages, notes, or documents. Or you can connect a Bluetooth headset so that you can listen to music and make and take FaceTime calls. If you connect a Bluetooth headset or headphones, you need to tell the iPad which audio device to use.

## Connect Bluetooth Devices to Your iPad

### Set Up a Bluetooth Device

**1** Press **Home**.

The Home screen appears.

**2** Tap **Settings** (⚙).

The Settings screen appears.

**3** Tap **Bluetooth** (❋).

The Bluetooth screen appears.

**4** Set the **Bluetooth** switch to On (◯).

**5** Turn on the Bluetooth device and make it discoverable.

**Note:** Read the Bluetooth device's instructions to find out how to make the device discoverable via Bluetooth.

Ⓐ The My Devices list shows devices you have already paired with your iPad.

Ⓑ The Other Devices list shows unpaired devices.

**6** Tap the device's button.

Your iPad attempts to pair with the device.

**7** If the Bluetooth Pairing Request dialog opens, type the code to confirm the pairing request.

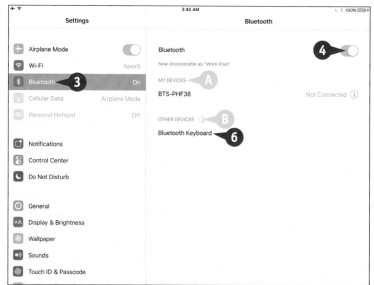

The iPad pairs with the device and then connects to it.

The device appears in the My Devices list.

The Connected readout indicates that the device is connected.

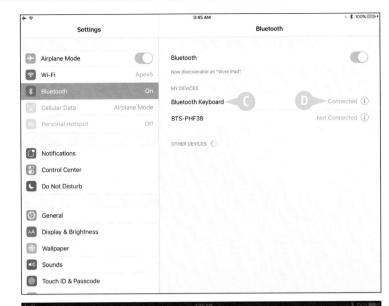

## Choose the Device for Playing Audio

**1** Tap and swipe up from the bottom of the screen.

Control Center opens.

**2** Tap **AirPlay** (🖵).

The AirPlay dialog appears.

**3** Tap the AirPlay device you want to use.

**4** Tap the screen above Control Center.

Control Center closes.

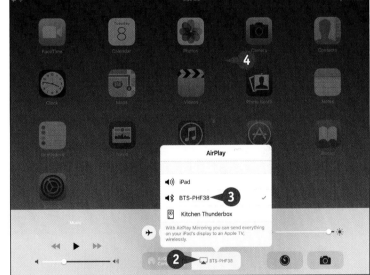

**How do I stop using a Bluetooth device?**
When you no longer need to use a particular Bluetooth device, tell your iPad to forget it. Press **Home**, tap **Settings** (⚙), and then tap **Bluetooth** (⬙). On the Bluetooth screen, tap **Information** (ⓘ) for the device. On the device's screen, tap **Forget This Device**, and then tap **Forget Device** in the confirmation dialog.

# Control Cellular Data and Background Refresh

I f you have a cellular iPad, you can monitor and control its use of cellular data using the Cellular screen in the Settings app. You can also turn on and off the Data Roaming feature, which enables some iPads to access the Internet using other carriers' networks, usually at extra cost.

You can also use the Background App Refresh feature to control which apps refresh their content via Wi-Fi or cellular connections when running in the background rather than as the foreground app.

## Control Cellular Data and Background Refresh

**1** Press **Home**.

The Home screen appears.

**2** Tap **Settings** (⚙).

The Settings screen appears.

**3** Tap **Cellular Data** (📶).

The Cellular Data screen appears.

**4** If you need to turn cellular data off altogether, set the **Cellular Data** switch to Off ( ). Normally, you will want to leave this switch set to On (⬤).

**5** If the **Enable 4G** switch is available, set it to On (⬤) to enable 4G connectivity.

**6** Set the **Data Roaming** switch to On (⬤) if you need to use data roaming.

Ⓐ The Current Period readout shows how much cellular data your iPad has used on your regular carrier.

Ⓑ The Current Period Roaming readout shows data roaming usage.

**7** In the Use Cellular Data For area of the Cellular screen, set each app's switch to On (⬤) or Off ( ), as needed.

**8** At the bottom of the Cellular Data screen, set the **Wi-Fi Assist** switch to On ( ) if you want your iPad to automatically use cellular data when it detects that Wi-Fi connectivity is poor.

**C** You can tap **Reset Statistics** to reset your usage statistics.

**9** Tap **General** ( ).

The General screen appears.

**10** Tap **Background App Refresh**.

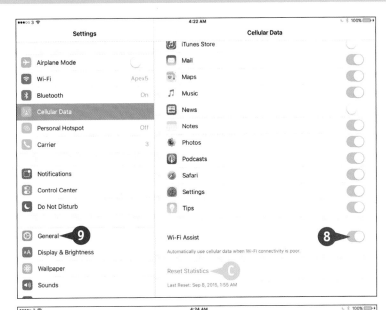

The Background App Refresh screen appears.

**11** Set the **Background App Refresh** switch to On ( ) or Off ( ), as needed.

**12** Set each individual app switch to On ( ) or Off ( ), as needed.

**13** Tap **General** ( < ).

The General screen appears again.

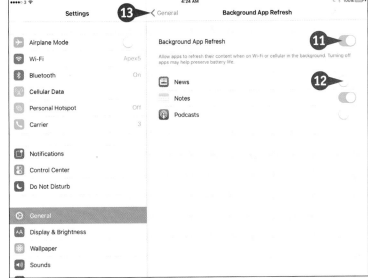

**Which apps and features should I allow to use cellular data?**

Allow those apps and features you find most helpful to use cellular data, but watch out for apps and features that use data heavily. For example, syncing Reading List involves transferring only small amounts of data, so it is unlikely to eat through your data allowance. By contrast, iCloud documents, iTunes, and FaceTime can require large amounts of data in a short time. Review your cellular data usage periodically and restrict any apps that consume too much data.

# Connect Your iPad to a Different Carrier

The SIM card in your cellular iPad makes it connect automatically to a particular carrier's network. Depending on whether your iPad is locked to your carrier — and if so, whether that carrier permits connections to different carriers — you may be able to connect manually to a different carrier's network when you go out of range of your carrier's network. You may need to set up an account with the other carrier, pay extra charges to your standard carrier, or change SIM cards.

## Connect Your iPad to a Different Carrier

1 Press **Home**.

The Home screen appears.

2 Tap **Settings** (⚙).

The Settings screen appears.

3 Tap **Carrier** (📞).

The Network Selection screen appears.

4 Set the **Automatic** switch to Off ( ).

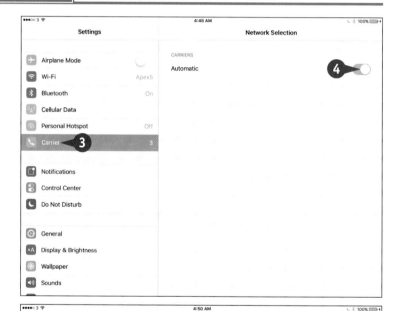

The list of available carriers appears.

5 Tap the carrier you want to use.

**Note:** When you want to switch back to your regular carrier, set the **Automatic** switch on the Network Selection screen to On (🔘).

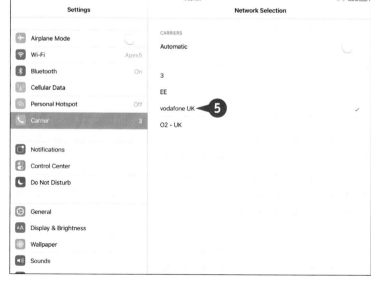

# Specify Your iPad's Cellular Access Point

ormally, your cellular iPad connects automatically to a suitable cellular access point for its network carrier. But under some circumstances you may need to specify which access point to use. This is a specialized and relatively unusual move you perform from the APN Settings screen in the Settings app. APN, short for Access Point Name, is the name of a particular gateway between a cellular network and the Internet.

## Specify Your iPad's Cellular Access Point

**1** Press **Home**.

The Home screen appears.

**2** Tap **Settings** (⚙).

The Settings screen appears.

**3** Tap **Cellular Data** (📶).

The Cellular Data screen appears.

**4** Tap **APN Settings**.

The APN Settings screen appears.

**5** Type the name of the APN.

**6** Type the username if you need to provide one.

**7** Type the password if applicable.

**A** You can tap **Reset Settings** to reset the cellular settings on your iPad to their defaults.

**8** Tap **Cellular Data** (‹).

The Cellular Data screen appears again.

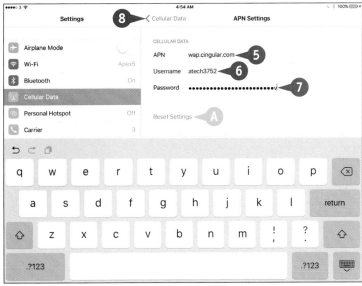

*A*irDrop is a technology for sharing files swiftly and easily with iOS devices and Macs near your iPad via Wi-Fi or Bluetooth. For example, you can use AirDrop to share a photo or a contact record. You can use AirDrop in any app that displays a Share button (⬆).

You can turn AirDrop on and off, as needed. When AirDrop is on, you can choose between accepting items only from your contacts or from everyone.

## Share Items via AirDrop

### Turn AirDrop On or Off

**1** Swipe up from the bottom of the screen.

Control Center opens.

**Ⓐ** The readout shows the AirDrop status: *AirDrop*, indicating the feature is off; *AirDrop: Contacts Only*; or *AirDrop, Everyone*.

**2** Tap **AirDrop** (📡).

The AirDrop dialog opens.

**3** Tap **Off**, **Contacts Only**, or **Everyone**, as needed.

The AirDrop dialog closes.

The AirDrop readout shows the AirDrop setting you chose.

**4** Tap the screen above Control Center.

Control Center closes.

## Share an Item via AirDrop

**1** Open the app that contains the item. For example, tap **Photos** on the Home screen.

**2** Navigate to the item you want to share. For example, tap a photo to open it.

**3** Tap **Share** (⬆).

The Share sheet appears.

**B** In some apps, you can select other items to share at the same time. For example, in Photos, you can select other photos.

**4** In the AirDrop area, tap the device to which you want to send the item.

**Note:** AirDrop between Macs and iOS devices works only for Macs from 2012 and later and iOS devices that have the Lightning connector rather than the earlier, larger Dock connector.

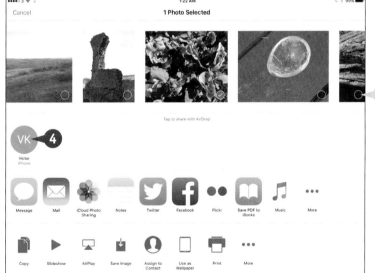

---

**TIP**

**How do I receive an item via AirDrop?**

When someone tries to send you an item via AirDrop, your iPad displays a pop-up message. Tap **Accept** or **Decline**, as appropriate. If you tap **Accept**, your iPad receives the item, stores it in the appropriate app, and opens it in that app. So when you receive a photo, the Photos app opens and displays it.

# Share Your Cellular iPad's Internet Access

Your cellular iPad can not only access the Internet from anywhere it has a suitable connection to the cell network, but it can also share that Internet access with your computer or other devices. This feature is called *Personal Hotspot*. For you to use Personal Hotspot, your iPad's carrier must permit you to use it. Some carriers simply charge the Personal Hotspot data as part of the iPad allowance, but others charge an extra fee per month for using the feature.

## Share Your Cellular iPad's Internet Access

### Set Up Personal Hotspot

**1** Press **Home**.

The Home screen appears.

**2** Tap **Settings** (⚙).

The Settings screen appears.

**3** Tap **Personal Hotspot** (◉).

The Personal Hotspot screen appears.

**Note:** If you want to use the existing Wi-Fi password, go to step **8**.

**4** Tap **Wi-Fi Password**.

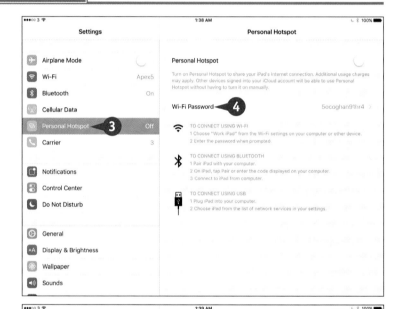

The Wi-Fi Password screen appears.

**5** Tap ⓧ to clear the default password.

**6** Type the password you want to use.

**7** Tap **Done**.

**Note:** You can connect up to five computers or other devices, such as an iPod touch, to the Internet by using Personal Hotspot on your iPad. Because the devices share the connection, the more devices transferring data, the slower each device's data rate will be.

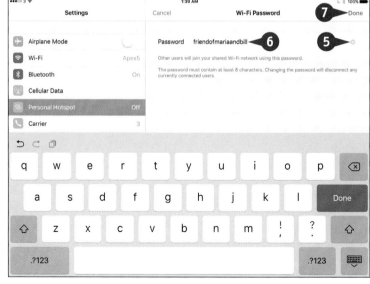

The Personal Hotspot screen appears again.

**8** Set the **Personal Hotspot** switch to On (![on]).

**A** The Now Discoverable readout appears.

**B** The wireless network's name appears for reference.

**9** Connect your computer or device to Personal Hotspot. See the tip for details.

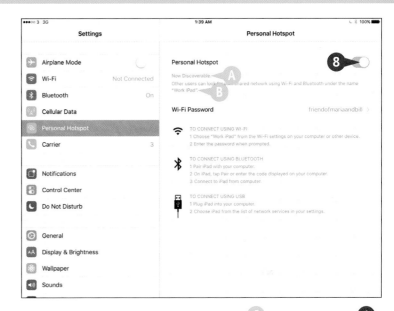

## Stop Using Personal Hotspot

**C** When Personal Hotspot is active, the Personal Hotspot blue bar appears across the top of the screen, showing the number of connections.

**1** Tap the **Personal Hotspot** bar.

**Note:** If you find it hard to tap the Personal Hotspot bar, press **Home**, tap **Settings** (![icon]), and then tap **Personal Hotspot** (![icon]).

The Personal Hotspot screen appears.

**2** Set the **Personal Hotspot** switch to Off ( ).

---

**TIP**

**How do I connect my Mac or PC to Personal Hotspot?**

The simplest way is to join the Personal Hotspot Wi-Fi network as you would any other wireless network. Alternatively, connect your Mac or PC to your iPad via the USB cable. On a Mac, Control +click **System Preferences** in the Dock and click **Network**. In the Network Preferences pane, click **iPad USB** and then click **Apply**. In Windows, if the Set Network Location dialog opens, click **Home Network** and then click **Close**.

# Connect to Wi-Fi Networks

Acellular iPad can connect to the Internet either via the cell phone network or via a Wi-Fi network. To conserve your data allowance, use a Wi-Fi network instead of the cell phone network whenever you can. A Wi-Fi–only iPad always uses Wi-Fi for connecting to the Internet.

The first time you connect to a Wi-Fi network, you must provide the network's password. After that, the iPad stores the password, so you can connect to the network without typing the password again.

## Connect to Wi-Fi Networks

### Connect to a Network Listed on the Wi-Fi Screen

**1** Press **Home**.

The Home screen appears.

**2** Tap **Settings** (⚙).

The Settings screen appears.

**3** Tap **Wi-Fi** (📶).

The Wi-Fi screen appears.

**4** Set the **Wi-Fi** switch to On (⚪).

The Choose a Network list appears.

Ⓐ A lock icon (🔒) indicates the network uses security, such as a password.

**5** Tap the network you want to connect to.

**Note:** If the network does not have a password, your iPad connects to it without prompting you for a password.

The Enter Password dialog appears.

**6** Type the password.

**Note:** The Join button turns blue when you have entered enough characters for a Wi-Fi password. Until then, the Join button is unavailable.

**7** Tap **Join**, and your iPad connects to the wireless network.

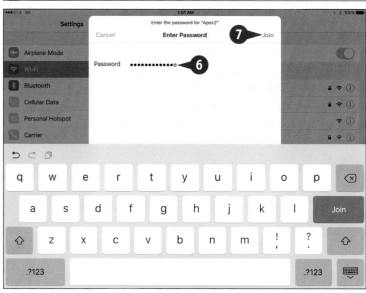

**B** The Wi-Fi network your iPad has connected to appears at the top of the screen with a check mark to its left.

**C** The Wi-Fi signal icon (📶) in the status bar and on the Wi-Fi screen shows the strength of the Wi-Fi signal. The more bars that appear, the stronger the signal is.

## Connect to a Network Not Listed on the Wi-Fi Screen

**Note:** A wireless network configured not to broadcast its network name does not appear on the Wi-Fi screen.

**1** On the Wi-Fi screen, tap **Other**.

The Other Network dialog opens.

**2** Type the network name.

**3** Tap **Security**.

**4** Tap the security type — for example, **WPA2**.

**5** Tap **Other Network**.

**6** Type the password in the Password field.

**7** Tap **Join**.

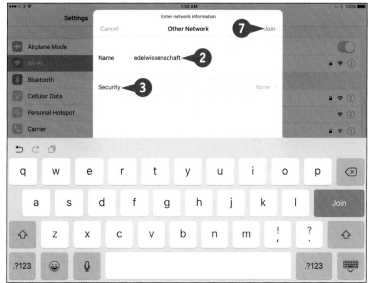

**What does the Ask to Join Networks switch control?**
Your iPad automatically connects to networks it has connected to before. Set the **Ask to Join Networks** switch to On (⬤) if you want your iPad to prompt you when wireless networks are available that your iPad has never used.

**How do I stop using a particular wireless network?**
Tap **Information** (ⓘ) to the right of the network's name on the Wi-Fi screen. On the network's screen, tap **Forget This Network**. In the dialog that opens, tap **Forget**.

# Log In to Wi-Fi Hotspots

When you are in town or on the road, you can log in to Wi-Fi hotspots to enjoy fast Internet access.

You can find Wi-Fi hotspots at many locations, including coffee shops and restaurants, hotels, and airports. Some municipal areas, and even some parks and highway rest stops, also provide public Wi-Fi. Some Wi-Fi hotspots charge for access, whereas others are free to use.

## Log In to Wi-Fi Hotspots

**1** Press **Home**.

The Home screen appears.

**2** Tap **Settings** (⚙).

The Settings screen appears.

**3** Tap **Wi-Fi** (🛜).

The Wi-Fi screen appears.

**4** If Wi-Fi is off, set the **Wi-Fi** switch to On (⚪).

The list of wireless networks appears.

**5** Tap the Wi-Fi hotspot you want to join.

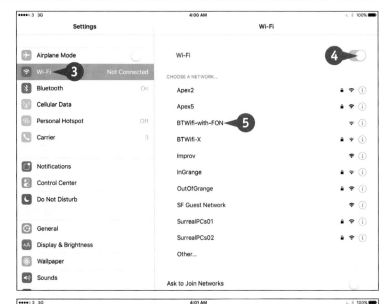

The iPad joins the hotspot.

**A** The Wi-Fi network your iPad has connected to appears at the top of the screen with a check mark to its left.

**6** Press **Home**.

134

The Home screen appears.

**7** Tap **Safari** ( ).

Safari opens.

The login screen for the Wi-Fi hotspot appears.

**8** Type your login details.

**9** Tap **Login** or an equivalent button.

After connecting to the hotspot, you can use the Internet. For example, you can browse the web using Safari or send and receive e-mail using the Mail app.

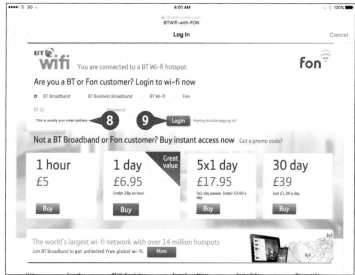

**What precautions should I take when using Wi-Fi hotspots?**

The main danger is that you may connect to a malevolent network. To stay safe, connect only to hotspots provided by reputable establishments — for example, national hotel chains or restaurant chains — instead of hotspots run by unknown operators.

When you finish using a Wi-Fi hotspot you will not use again, tell the iPad to forget the network by tapping next to the network's name, tapping **Forget This Network**, and then tapping **Forget** in the confirmation dialog. Forgetting the network ensures the iPad does not connect to another network that has the same name, security type, and password — but is in fact a malevolent hotspot set up to trap traffic from the genuine hotspot.

# Connect to a Network via VPN

I f you use your iPad for work, you may need to connect it to your work network via virtual private networking, or VPN, across the Internet. You can also use VPN to change your iPad's apparent geographical location — for example, to use a U.S.-restricted media service when you are located in another country.

VPN uses encryption to create a secure connection across the Internet. By using VPN, you can connect securely from anywhere you have an Internet connection.

## Connect to a Network via VPN

### Set Up the VPN Connection on the iPad

**1** Press **Home**.

The Home screen appears.

**2** Tap **Settings** (⚙).

The Settings screen appears.

**3** Tap **General** (⚙).

The General screen appears.

**4** Tap **VPN**.

The VPN screen appears.

**5** Tap **Add VPN Configuration**.

**Note:** If your iPad already has a VPN you want to use, tap it, and then go to step **1** of the next set of steps, "Connect to the VPN."

The Add Configuration dialog opens.

**6** Tap **Type**; select the VPN type, such as **L2TP**, in the Type dialog that opens; and then tap **Back** (‹).

**7** Fill in the details of the VPN.

**8** Set the **Send All Traffic** switch to On (⬤) if you want all your Internet traffic to go via the VPN.

**9** Tap **Done**.

## Connect to the VPN

**1** On the VPN screen, set the **Status** switch to On (⬤).

The iPad connects to the VPN.

**Ⓐ** The Status readout shows *Connected*.

**Ⓑ** The VPN indicator appears in the status bar.

**2** Work across the network connection as if you were connected directly to the network.

**Ⓒ** You can tap **Information** (ⓘ) to display information about the connection, including the assigned IP address and the connection time.

**3** When you are ready to disconnect from the VPN, set the **Status** switch on the VPN screen to Off ( ).

**Ⓓ** You can turn the VPN on and off by using the VPN switch in the left column.

**Is there an easier way to set up a VPN connection?**
Yes. An administrator can provide the VPN details in a file called a configuration profile, either via e-mail or via a web page. When you install the configuration profile, your iPad adds the VPN automatically. You can then connect to the VPN.

**How can I connect to a VPN type that iOS does not support?**
Look for an app designed to connect to this type of VPN. Ask the VPN's administrator for details of the VPN and suggestions on which app to use.

# Send Instant Messages

When you need to communicate quickly with another person, but do not need to speak to him, you can send an instant message using the Messages app.

The Messages app runs on the iPad, the iPhone, and the iPod touch; and on the Mac running OS X El Capitan (version 10.11), OS X Yosemite (version 10.10), OS X Mavericks (version 10.9), or OS X Mountain Lion (version 10.8). You can use Messages to send instant messages to other users of Messages on these devices. You can send either straightforward text messages or messages that include photos or videos.

## Send Instant Messages

**1** Press **Home**.

**2** Tap **Messages** (⬭).

The Messages screen appears.

**3** Tap **New Message** (✎).

The New Message screen appears.

**4** Start typing the contact's name, address, or phone number.

Ⓐ Alternatively, you can tap **Add Contact** (⊕) and then tap the contact in the Contacts dialog.

A list of matches appears.

**5** Tap the appropriate contact.

Messages starts a new message to the contact.

**6** Tap in the text field, and then type your message.

**7** To add a photo, tap **Add Photo** (📷).

The Add Photo dialog opens.

Ⓑ If the photo you want appears in the scrolling bar at the top of the dialog, you can tap the photo to insert it quickly.

**8** Tap **Photo Library**.

Ⓒ You can tap **Take Photo or Video** to take a photo or video with the camera (see Chapter 11), and then send it with the message.

The Photos dialog opens.

**Note:** You can tap **Hide Keyboard** (⌨) to hide the keyboard so that you can see the photos better.

**9** Tap the album or other collection that contains the photo.

The album or collection opens.

**10** Tap the photo.

The photo opens in the Choose Photo dialog.

**11** Tap **Use**.

**D** The photo appears in the message.

**Note:** You can attach another photo or video by repeating steps **7** to **11**.

**12** Tap **Send**.

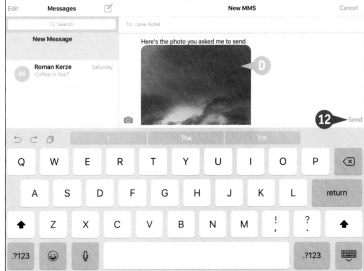

**Is there another way to send a photo or video?**
Yes. You can start from the Camera app or the Photos app. This way of sending a photo or video is handy when you are taking photos or videos or when you are browsing your photos or videos. Tap the photo or video you want to share, and then tap **Share** (⬆). On the Share sheet, tap **Message** (💬). Your iPad starts a message containing the photo or video in Messages. You can then address and send the message.

# Mute a Conversation or Share Your Location

Y ou may need to mute a Messages conversation temporarily while you focus on other things. You can mute a conversation by displaying the Details screen for the conversation and setting the Do Not Disturb switch to On.

From the Details screen for a conversation, you can also share your current location by sending an embedded link for the Maps app, enabling the recipient to see exactly where you are. You can also share your location for a specific length of time with all your contacts.

## Mute a Conversation or Share Your Location

### Open Messages and Display the Details Screen for the Conversation

1. Press **Home**.

   The Home screen appears.

2. Tap **Messages** (○).

   The Messages screen appears.

3. Tap the conversation you want to view.

   The conversation appears.

4. Tap **Details**.

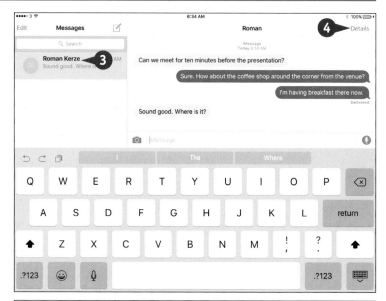

### Turn On Do Not Disturb for the Conversation

1. On the Details screen, set the **Do Not Disturb** switch to On (○).

**Note:** After you turn on Do Not Disturb for a conversation, your iPad does not display notifications for that conversation.

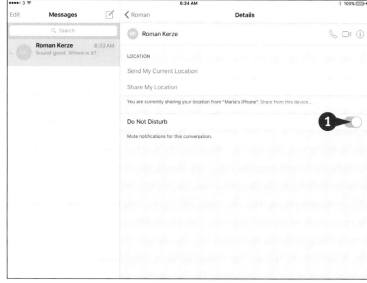

## Share Your Location

**1** On the Details screen, tap **Share My Location**.

A dialog opens.

**2** Tap **Share for One Hour**, **Share Until End of Day**, or **Share Indefinitely**, as needed.

Your friends can now track your location through Messages for the period of time you chose.

**3** To send your current location, tap **Send My Current Location**.

Message displays a thumbnail of a map showing your current location.

**A** You can tap the thumbnail to view the map full-screen. You can tap **Directions To Here** to get directions to this location. Tap **Done** when you are ready to return to the conversation.

Messages sends the location to your contact.

**TIP**

**How do I stop sharing my location?**
In the conversation, tap **Details** to display the Details screen, and then tap **Stop Sharing My Location**. This button also displays the amount of time left until sharing will stop automatically.

# Manage Your Instant Messages

I f you send and receive many messages, the Messages interface may get so full that it becomes hard to navigate. To keep your messages under control, you can forward messages to others and delete messages you do not need to keep. You can either delete messages from a conversation, leaving the conversation's other messages, or delete the entire conversation.

## Manage Your Instant Messages

### Forward or Delete One or More Messages from a Conversation

**1** Press **Home**.

The Home screen appears.

**2** Tap **Messages** ( ).

The Messages screen appears.

**3** In the Messages column, tap the appropriate conversation.

The messages in the conversation appear.

**4** Tap and hold the first of the messages you want to forward or delete.

**5** Tap **More**.

A selection button ( ) appears to the left of each message.

**A** Messages selects the message you tapped ( ).

**B** You can tap another selection button ( changes to ) to select that message.

**6** Tap **Forward** ( ).

Messages starts a new message containing the forwarded messages.

**C** Instead of forwarding the messages, you can tap **Delete** ( ) to delete them from the conversation.

**D** You can tap **Delete All** to delete all the messages.

**7** Address the message and tap **Send** to send it.

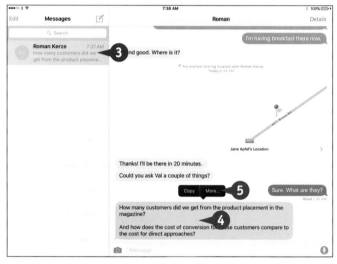

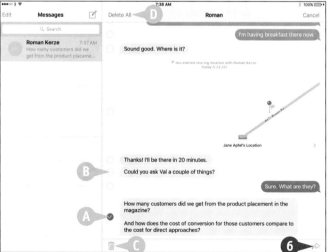

142

## Delete a Conversation

**1** Press **Home**.

The Home screen appears.

**2** Tap **Messages** (◯).

The Messages screen appears.

**3** Tap **Edit**.

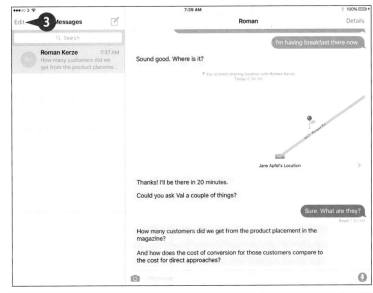

The Messages column switches to Edit Mode.

**4** Tap the selection button (◯) for the conversation you want to delete (◯ changes to ✓).

The Delete button appears.

**5** Tap **Delete**.

Messages deletes the conversation and turns off Edit Mode.

**Note:** You can also delete a conversation by tapping it in the conversation list, swiping to the left, and then tapping **Delete**.

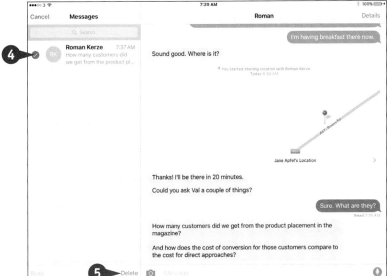

### Can I resend a message?

Yes. You can resend a message in either of these ways:

- If a red icon with an exclamation point appears next to the message, the message has not been sent. Tap the icon and then tap **Try Again** to attempt to send the message again.

- If the message has been sent, tap and hold the message text, and then tap **Copy** to copy it. Tap and hold in the message text field, and then tap **Paste** to paste in the text. Tap **Send** to send the message.

# Share Your Updates Using Twitter

Many iOS apps are fully integrated with Twitter, the online microblogging service. To send a short textual tweet, you can use the Twitter app. To send a photo, you can start from the Photos app and create a tweet in moments.

When tweeting, you can choose to add your location to the tweet. Adding the location can help your followers understand and appreciate your posts, but it also raises privacy concerns — for example, concerns about stalking.

## Share Your Updates Using Twitter

### Send a Text Tweet

1 Press **Home**.

The Home screen appears.

2 Tap **Twitter** (🐦).

**Note:** If Twitter does not appear, tap **Settings** (⚙), tap **Twitter**, and then tap **Install**.

The Twitter app opens.

3 Tap **New Tweet** (✎).

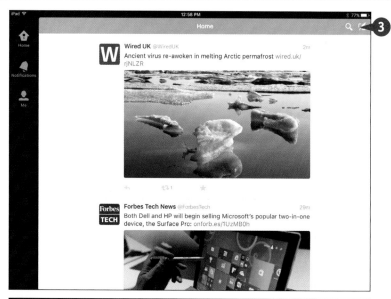

The New Tweet screen appears.

4 Type the text of the tweet.

**Note:** You can also tap the microphone icon (🎤) to activate Siri, and then dictate the text of the tweet.

5 Tap **Location** (📍) if you want to add your location to the tweet.

6 Tap **Tweet**.

Twitter posts the tweet to your Twitter account.

## Send a Photo Tweet

**1** Press **Home**.

The Home screen appears.

**2** Tap **Photos** (🌸).

The Photos app opens.

**3** Navigate to the photo you want to tweet. For example, tap **Albums** and then tap the album that contains the photo.

**4** Tap the photo to display it.

**5** Tap **Share** (📤).

The Share sheet appears.

**6** Tap **Twitter** (🐦).

The Twitter dialog opens, showing the tweet with the photo attached.

**7** Type the tweet.

**8** If you want to add the location to the tweet, tap **Location**. In the Location dialog, tap the location, and then tap **Twitter** to return to the Twitter dialog.

**9** Tap **Post**.

Your iPad posts the tweet to your Twitter account.

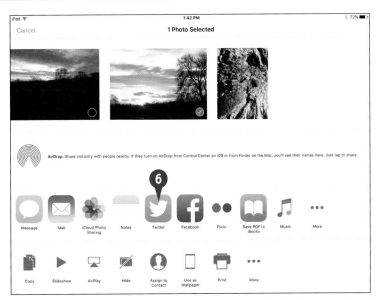

---

**TIP**

**How do I read other people's tweets?**

To read other people's tweets, use the Twitter app. Press **Home** to display the Home screen, tap **Twitter** (🐦), and then tap **Home** (🏠) to catch up on tweets from the Twitter accounts you are following.

# Post Updates on Facebook

If you have an account on Facebook, the world's biggest social network, you can post updates directly from your iPad with a minimum of fuss.

When you are using the Facebook app, you can easily start a post from within it by tapping the Status button. But you can also start from apps that contain content suitable for Facebook posts. For example, you can post a photo from the Photos app to Facebook.

## Post Updates on Facebook

### Post an Update from the Facebook App

**1** Press **Home**.

The Home screen appears.

**2** Tap **Facebook** (![icon]).

The Facebook app opens.

**Note:** If Facebook does not appear, tap **Settings** (![icon]), tap **Facebook** (![icon]), and then tap **Install**.

**3** On your Facebook app home page, tap **Status** (![icon]).

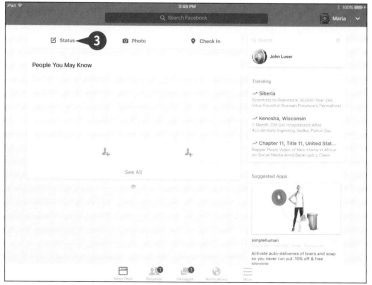

The Update Status dialog opens.

**4** Type the update.

**5** To choose whom to share the update with, tap **To**, tap the appropriate people or groups in the Share With dialog, and then tap **Done**.

**6** To add the location to the update, tap **Location** (![icon]).

**7** To add a photo or video, tap **Photo** (![icon]). You can then take a new photo or video or select an existing one.

**8** To add your current activity, tap **Activity** (![icon]) and tap the appropriate activity.

**9** Tap **Post**.

## Post a Photo Update

**1** Press **Home**.

The Home screen appears.

**2** Tap **Photos** (🌸).

The Photos app opens.

**3** Navigate to the photo you want to post. For example, tap **Albums** and then tap the album that contains the photo.

**4** Tap the photo to display it.

**5** Tap **Share** (📤).

The Share sheet appears.

**6** Tap **Facebook** (f).

The Facebook dialog appears, with the photo ready for posting.

**7** Type the text for the update.

**8** To choose the album, tap **Album**, and then tap the album in the Choose Album dialog.

**9** Tap **Location**, tap the location in the Location dialog, and then tap **Facebook** to return to the Facebook dialog.

**10** To specify the audience, tap **Audience**, and then tap the appropriate group in the Audience dialog.

**11** Tap **Post**.

iOS posts the update to your Facebook account.

### TIP

**From what other apps can I post updates to Facebook?**

You can post updates to Facebook from any app to which the developer has added Facebook integration. For example, you can post a location from the Maps app or a lecture from iTunes U to Facebook.

To see whether you can post updates to Facebook from an app, tap **Share** (📤) from the app. If Facebook (f) appears on the Share sheet, you can post an update to Facebook.

# Chat Face-to-Face Using FaceTime

By using the FaceTime feature on your iPad, you can enjoy video chats with any of your contacts who have an iPhone 4 or later, an iPad 2 or later, an iPad mini or later, a fourth-generation or later iPod touch, or the FaceTime for Mac application.

To make a FaceTime call, you and your contact must both have Apple IDs or iPhones. Your iPad must also be connected to either a Wi-Fi network or the cellular network.

## Chat Face-to-Face Using FaceTime

**1** Press **Home**.

The Home screen appears.

**Note:** On a cellular iPad, use a Wi-Fi network instead of the cellular network if possible. Not only does a wireless network usually give better performance, but you also do not use up your cellular data allowance.

**2** Tap **FaceTime** ().

The FaceTime app opens.

**3** Tap **Video**.

**Note:** Tap **Audio** if you want to make an audio-only FaceTime call.

**4** Tap **Enter name, email, or number** and start typing the contact's name, e-mail address, or number.

**Note:** After making FaceTime calls, you can call a FaceTime contact quickly from the Recents list.

**5** Tap the appropriate match.

The contact's record opens.

**6** Tap **Video Call** ().

148

The iPad starts a FaceTime call, showing your video preview.

**7** When your contact answers, smile and speak.

**Note:** Tap to display the on-screen controls. They disappear automatically if you do not use them for a few seconds.

When the connection is established, your iPad displays the caller full-screen, with your video inset.

**8** If you need to mute your microphone, tap **Mute** (). Tap **Mute** () when you want to turn muting off again.

**9** If you need to show your contact something using the rear-facing camera, tap **Switch Cameras** (). Your inset video then shows the picture that is being sent to your contact. Tap **Switch Cameras** () when you are ready to switch back.

**10** When you are ready to end the call, tap **End** ().

**Note:** When your iPad receives a FaceTime request, and the screen shows who is calling, aim the camera at your face, and then tap **Answer** to answer.

## TIP

**Are there other ways of starting a FaceTime call?**

Yes. Here are three other ways of starting a FaceTime call:

- In the Contacts app, tap the contact to display the contact record, and then tap **FaceTime** ().
- In a Messages conversation, tap **Details**, and then tap **FaceTime** ().
- Ask Siri to call a contact via FaceTime. For example, press and hold **Home** to summon Siri, and then say "FaceTime John Smith."

# CHAPTER 6

# Working with Apps

You can customize the Home screen to optimize the layout of the icons you need most and to organize them into folders. You can switch quickly among open apps; use the iPad's multitasking features; and manage your apps by installing apps, updating apps to the latest versions, and removing apps you do not use. You can also apply formatting and use Cut, Copy, and Paste.

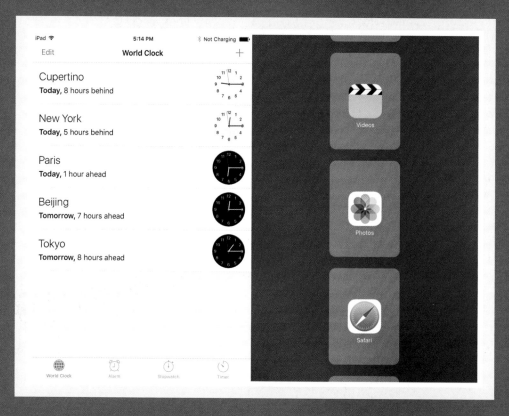

# Customize the Home Screen

You can customize the Home screen to put the apps you use most frequently within easy reach. When the existing Home screens fill up with icons, the iPad adds more Home screens automatically, as needed.

You can also create more Home screens — up to 11 screens total — and move the app icons among them. You can customize the Home screen on your iPad, as described here. If you synchronize your iPad with a computer, you can use iTunes instead. This is an easier way to make extensive changes.

## Customize the Home Screen

### Unlock the Icons for Customization

**1** Press **Home**.

The Home screen appears.

**2** Tap and drag left or right to display the Home screen you want to customize.

**A** You can also tap the dot for the Home screen you want to display.

**3** Tap and hold the icon you want to move.

**Note:** You can tap and hold any icon until the apps start jiggling. Usually, it is easiest to tap and hold the icon you want to move, and then drag the icon.

The icons start to jiggle, indicating that you can move them.

### Move an Icon Within a Home Screen

**1** After unlocking the icons, drag the icon to where you want it.

The other icons move out of the way.

**2** When the icon is in the right place, drop it by lifting your finger from the screen.

The icon stays in its new position.

## Move an Icon to a Different Home Screen

**1** After unlocking the icons, drag the icon to the left edge of the screen to display the previous Home screen or to the right edge to display the next Home screen.

The previous Home screen or next Home screen appears.

**2** Drag the icon to where you want it.

The other icons move out of the way.

**3** Drop the icon.

The icon stays in its new position.

## Stop Customizing the Home Screen

**1** Press **Home**.

The icons stop jiggling.

**Note:** You can customize the icons at the bottom of the Home screen. You can add icons, up to a total of six, by dragging and dropping them from the main part of the Home screen. You can also remove the default icons by dragging them to the main part of the Home screen.

## TIP

**How can I put the default apps back on the first Home screen?**

Press **Home**, tap **Settings** (⚙), and then tap **General** (⚙). Tap and drag up to scroll down the screen, and then tap **Reset**. On the Reset screen, tap **Reset Home Screen Layout**, and then tap **Reset** in the dialog that opens. Press **Home** to return to the Home screen.

When you reset the Home screen, iOS arranges the icons for third-party apps in alphabetical order, starting after the last of the default apps.

# Organize Apps with Folders

You can organize the Home screen by arranging the icons into folders. The default Home screen layout on your iPad does not include any folders, but you can create as many as you need.

You create a folder by dragging one icon onto another icon. Doing this creates a folder containing both items. You can then rename the folder and add other items to it. To run an app stored in a folder, you open the folder to reveal its contents, and then tap the app.

## Organize Apps with Folders

### Create a Folder

**1** Display the Home screen that contains the item you want to put into a folder.

**2** Tap and hold the item until the icons start to jiggle.

**Note:** When creating a folder, you may find it easiest to first put at least the first two items you will add to the folder on the same screen.

**3** Drag one of the app icons you want to place in the folder and hold it over the icon of another app destined for the folder.

The iPad creates a folder, puts both icons in it, and assigns a default name based on the genre.

**4** Tap **Delete** (⊗) in the folder name field.

The keyboard appears.

**5** Type the name for the folder.

**6** Tap outside the folder.

**Note:** You can also tap **Done** on the keyboard.

The iPad applies the name to the folder.

**7** Press **Home**.

The icons stop jiggling.

## Open an Item in a Folder

**1** Display the Home screen that contains the folder.

**2** Tap the folder's icon.

The folder's contents appear, and the items outside the folder fade.

**Ⓐ** If necessary, tap a dot to display a different screen in the folder.

**3** Tap the item you want to open.

The item opens.

## Add an Item to a Folder

**1** Display the Home screen that contains the item.

**2** Tap and hold the item until the icons start to jiggle.

**3** Drag the icon on top of the folder, hold it there for a moment, and drop it there.

**Note:** If the folder is on a different Home screen from the icon, drag the icon to the left edge to display the previous Home screen or to the right edge to display the next Home screen.

The item goes into the folder.

**4** Press **Home** to stop the icons from jiggling.

### TIP

**How do I take an item out of a folder?**

**1** Tap the folder to display its contents.

**2** Tap and hold the item until the icons start to jiggle.

**3** Drag the item out of the folder. The folder closes and the Home screen appears.

**4** Drag the item to where you want it, and then drop it.

# Switch Quickly from One App to Another

You can run many apps on your iPad at the same time, switching from one app to another as needed. The most straightforward way to switch among apps is to press **Home** to display the Home screen and then tap the icon for the app you want to start using.

For faster switching among apps that are already running, use the App Switcher. The App Switcher also enables you to close running apps.

## Switch Quickly from One App to Another

**1** Press **Home**.

The Home screen appears.

**2** Tap the app you want to launch.

The app's screen appears.

**3** Start using the app as usual.

**4** Press **Home** twice in quick succession.

**Note:** If you have set the **Gestures** switch on the Multitasking screen in the Settings app to On ( ), you can also display the App Switcher by swiping four fingers up from the bottom of the screen. You can also swipe left or right with four fingers to switch among the running apps.

The App Switcher appears, showing a carousel of apps. Each app shows a thumbnail of the app's current screen, with the app's icon above it.

**A** The app you were using appears on the right.

**B** The previous app appears next, with more of its thumbnail visible at the front of the carousel.

**C** Other apps appear further to the left in the order you last used them.

**5** If necessary, swipe right until you can see the app you want.

**6** Tap the app in the App Switcher.

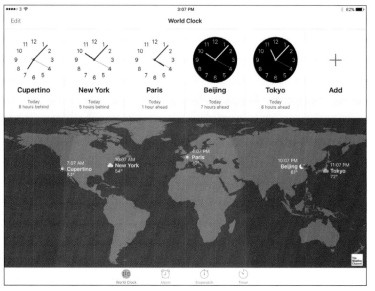

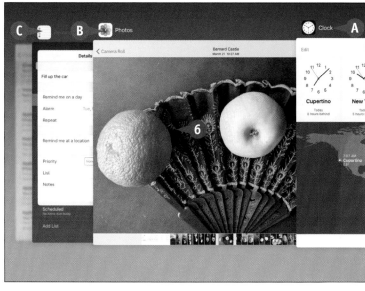

The app appears, and you can work in it as usual. For example, in the Photos app, tap a thumbnail in the thumbnail bar to display a photo.

**7** When you are ready to switch back, press **Home** twice in quick succession.

The App Switcher appears.

**8** Scroll right if necessary, and then tap the app to which you want to return.

The app appears, ready to resume from where you stopped using it.

**TIP**

**How do I stop an app that is not responding?**

If an app stops responding, you can quickly close it from the app-switching screen. Press **Home** twice to open the app-switching screen. Scroll right if necessary until you can see the problem app, and then swipe it upward so it disappears off the screen. You can then either tap the app you want to use or press **Home** to return to the Home screen.

You can use this move to close any app that you no longer want to use, whether or not it has stopped responding.

# Multitask with Split-Screen Views

Your iPad normally runs each app full-screen, so you see a single app at a time. But on recent iPad models you can also split the screen between two apps in any of three ways.

The Slide Over feature displays a second app in the rightmost third of the screen. The Split View feature divides the screen evenly between the two apps. The Picture-in-Picture feature displays a video in a pop-up window over another app or the Home screen.

## Multitask with Split-Screen Views

### Enable and Configure Multitasking

1. Press **Home**.

   The Home screen appears.

2. Tap **Settings** (⚙).

   The Settings screen appears.

3. Tap **General** (⚙)

   The General screen appears.

4. Tap **Multitasking**.

The Multitasking screen appears.

5. Set the **Allow Multiple Apps** switch to On (⬤) to enable multitasking.

6. Set the **Persistent Video Overlay** switch to On (⬤) if you want to be able to overlay a playing video on other screens.

7. Set the **Gestures** switch to On (⬤) if you want to be able to give multitasking gestures with four or five fingers. See the tip for details on the gestures.

8. Tap **General** (‹).

   The General screen appears.

158

## Use Two Apps with Slide Over and Split View

1 With an app open that you want to use, swipe in from the right side of the screen.

**Note:** You can use the multitasking views in either landscape orientation or portrait orientation.

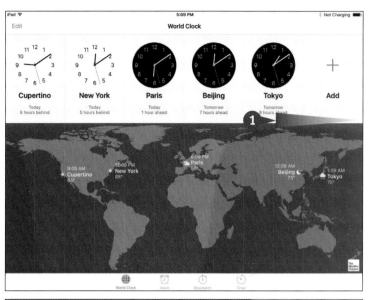

An app appears in the right third of the screen.

**Note:** If, instead of an app appearing, the list of apps appears, go to step **3**.

2 Tap the gray bar at the top of the app's pane and pull down.

TIP

**What multitasking gestures can I use?**

To display the Home screen, place four or five fingers apart on the screen and pinch them together.

To display the App Switcher, swipe up from the bottom of the screen with four or five fingers.

To switch among running apps, swipe left or right with four or five fingers.

continued ▶

Y ou can multitask with many of the apps that come with your iPad and with many third-party apps. But some apps cannot run in either Slide Over or Split View. For example, the Settings app can run only full-screen, so you cannot multitask with it. Other apps can run in Slide Over but not in Split View.

## Multitask with Split-Screen Views (continued)

The right-hand pane displays apps you can use in the split-screen views.

**Note:** Unlike in the App Switcher, which shows only apps that are currently running, the apps in the right-hand pane in Slide Over view may or may not be running.

**3** Tap the app you want to display.

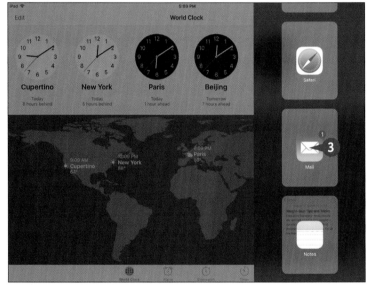

The app appears in the right-hand pane.

You can start using the app as usual.

**4** Tap the handle between the apps and drag left.

iOS switches to Split View, dividing the screen evenly between the apps.

You can work in either app.

**Note:** Drag the handle between the apps all the way to the left to switch the right-hand app to full-screen. Drag the handle all the way to the right to switch the left-hand app to full-screen.

**5** To switch apps in the right-hand pane, tap the gray bar at the top of the pane and pull down.

The list of apps appears.

**6** Tap the app you want to use.

The app appears in the right-hand pane.

---

**TIP**

**Do the split-screen and pop-up features work with all iPad models?**

The Split View feature requires an iPad Air 2 or later model, such as an iPad mini 4 or an iPad Pro.

The Slide Over feature and the Picture-in-Picture feature both require an iPad mini 2, an iPad Air, or a later model.

continued ▶

The Picture-in-Picture feature enables you to switch a video you are playing from full-screen to a small floating window. You can reposition the floating window in any of the four quadrants of the screen so that you can continue to watch the video while working in another app — or in two other apps using Slide Over or Split View.

The Picture-in-Picture feature works only on some iPad models, such as the iPad mini 2, iPad mini 4, iPad Air 2, and the iPad Pro.

**Multitask with Split-Screen Views** (continued)

### Use the Picture-in-Picture Feature

**1** Press **Home**.

The Home screen appears.

**2** Tap **Videos** (⯮).

The Videos app opens.

**3** Tap the video you want to view.

The video starts playing.

**4** Press **Home**.

The video shrinks down to a floating window and continues playing unless you pause it.

The Home screen appears, with the video window floating above it.

**5** Tap the app you want to launch. This example uses **Notes** (⬜).

The category screen appears, showing its lists of apps.

**Note:** Tap and drag sideways to see more apps in a list, or tap and drag up to see other lists.

**5** Tap the app you want to view.

The app's dialog opens.

**Note:** To understand what an app does and how well it does it, look at the app's rating, read the description, and read the user reviews.

**A** You can tap **Share** (⬆) to share the app's details with others via e-mail, messaging, AirDrop, or other means.

**6** Tap the price button or the **Get** button.

The price button or Get button changes to an Install App button.

**7** Tap **Install App**.

**8** If the iPad prompts you to sign in, type your password and tap **OK**.

**Note:** If you have not created an App Store account already, the iPad prompts you to create one now.

The iPad downloads and installs the app.

**9** Tap **Open** to launch the app.

## TIP

**Why does the App Store not appear on the Home screen or when I search?**

If the App Store does not appear on the Home screen, and if searching for it does not show a result, the iPad has restrictions applied that prevent you from installing apps. You can remove these restrictions if you know the restrictions passcode. Press **Home**, tap **Settings** (⚙), and then tap **General** (⚙). Scroll down, and then tap **Restrictions**. Type the passcode in the Enter Passcode dialog, and then set the **Installing Apps** switch to On ( ⚪ changes to ⚫ ).

# Update and Remove Apps

To keep the apps running smoothly on your iPad, you should install app updates when they become available. Most updates for paid apps are free, but you must usually pay to upgrade to a new version of the app. You can download and install updates using the App Store app on your iPad.

When you no longer need an app, you can remove it from the iPad and recover the space it was occupying.

## Update and Remove Apps

### Update an App

**1** Press **Home**.

The Home screen appears.

**A** The badge on the App Store icon shows the number of available updates.

**2** Tap **App Store** ().

The App Store app opens.

The Updates screen appears.

**3** Tap **Updates** (⬆ changes to ⬇).

**B** You can tap **Update** to update a single app.

**4** Tap **Update All**.

**Note:** If the Apple ID Password dialog opens, type your password and then tap **OK**.

Your iPad downloads and installs the updates.

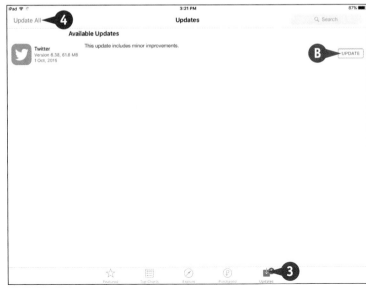

## Remove an App from the iPad

**1** Press **Home**.

The Home screen appears.

**2** Display the Home screen that contains the app you want to delete.

**3** Tap and hold the item until the icons start to jiggle.

**4** Tap **Delete** (⊗) on the icon.

The Delete dialog appears.

**5** Tap **Delete**.

The iPad deletes the app, and the app's icon disappears.

## TIP

**Can I reinstall an app after removing it?**

Yes, you can easily reinstall an app. Press **Home**, tap **App Store** (Ⓐ), and then tap **Purchased** (ⓟ changes to ⓟ) to display the Purchased screen. Tap the **Not on This iPad** tab at the top and then locate the app; you can tap **Search Purchased Apps** and search by keyword if necessary. Then tap **Install** (⬇) to install the app.

# Manage Automatic Downloads and Your Apple ID

The App Store and iTunes Store can automatically download apps, music, and other content for you. You can turn off automatic downloads if you prefer to keep manual control, and on a cellular iPad, you can control whether downloads can use the cellular network.

From the iTunes & App Store screen in the Settings app, you can also view the details of your current Apple ID and switch from one Apple ID to another.

## Manage Automatic Downloads and Your Apple ID

### Choose Which Items to Download Automatically

1 Press **Home**.

The Home screen appears.

2 Tap **Settings** (⚙).

The Settings screen appears.

3 Tap **App and iTunes Stores** (Ⓐ).

The App and iTunes Stores screen appears.

4 Set the **Music** switch to On (◯) or Off ( ), as needed.

5 Set the **Apps** switch to On (◯) or Off ( ), as needed.

6 Set the **Books** switch to On (◯) or Off ( ), as needed.

7 Set the **Updates** switch to On (◯) or Off ( ), as needed.

8 If you have a cellular iPad, set the **Use Cellular Data** switch to On (◯) or Off ( ), as needed.

9 Set the **Installed Apps** switch to On (◯) or Off ( ) to control whether your iPad can suggest apps for you to try.

## Switch Apple ID or View Its Details

**1** On the iTunes & App Store screen in the Settings app, tap **Apple ID**.

The Apple ID dialog opens.

**2** To switch the Apple ID, tap **Sign Out**.

**3** Tap **Apple ID** and type the e-mail address for the Apple ID you want to use.

**4** Tap **Password** and type the password.

**5** Tap **Sign In**.

Your iPad signs in using the Apple ID.

**6** To view the details of your current Apple ID, tap **View Apple ID**.

The Account dialog appears.

**7** Examine the Apple ID as needed:

**A** Tap **Apple ID** to display the My Apple ID web page in Safari.

**B** Tap **Family Sharing** to view information in the Family Sharing dialog.

**C** Tap **Payment Information** to display an Account dialog that contains your credit- or debit-card details.

**D** Tap **Country/Region** to change your country or region.

**8** Tap **Done** when you finish reviewing your Apple ID.

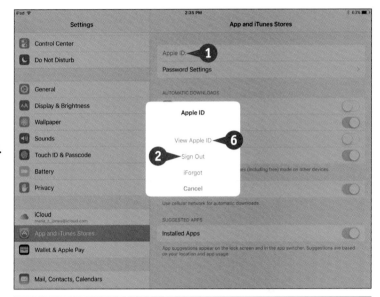

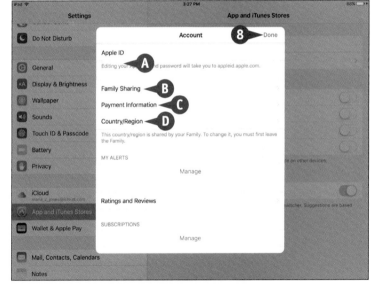

---

## TIP

### Is it a good idea to download items automatically?

Whether you download items automatically is up to you, but having the items appear on your iPad without your intervention is often helpful. If your iPad has cellular capability and you set the **Use Cellular Data** switch to On (⬤), monitor your data usage carefully. Most e-book files are small, but music and video files can go through your cellular allowance quickly. Be especially careful about downloading apps automatically, because some of them are huge.

# Enter Text Quickly in Apps

Even though your iPad does not come with a physical keyboard, it offers powerful time-saving features that enable you to enter text quickly in the apps you use. You can split and reposition the on-screen keyboard to make it easier to use, or keep it in its standard docked position. You can enter words more quickly by accepting predictive text suggestions. And you can configure keyboard settings and create your own shortcuts to enter boilerplate text quickly.

## Enter Text Quickly in Apps

### Undock and Split the Keyboard and Use Predictions

① In an app that supports text input, tap a text field.

The keyboard appears in its docked position at the bottom of the screen.

② Tap and hold **Hide Keyboard** (⌨).

The keyboard pop-up menu opens.

③ Tap **Undock**.

The keyboard moves up the screen.

④ Start typing a word.

Suggested words or phrases appear.

⑤ Tap the word or phrase you want to insert.

⑥ Tap and hold **Hide Keyboard** (⌨).

⑦ Tap **Split**.

The keyboard splits.

**Note:** With the keyboard split, you can type using "ghost" keys on the opposite side of the keyboard. For example, tap to the right of the T key to type Y, and tap to the left of the Y key to type T.

**Note:** Tap and drag **Hide Keyboard** (⌨) to move the undocked or split keyboard up or down.

⑧ Tap and hold **Hide Keyboard** (⌨).

⑨ Tap **Merge** or **Dock and Merge**, as needed.

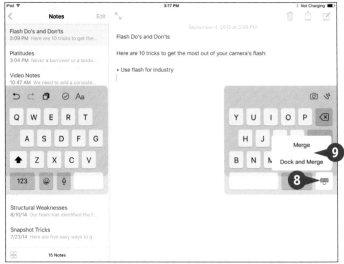

## Configure Keyboard Settings and Create Shortcuts

**1** Press **Home**.

**2** Tap **Settings** (⚙).

**3** Tap **General** (⚙).

The General screen appears.

**4** Tap **Keyboard**.

The Keyboard screen appears.

**5** Set the **Auto-Capitalization** switch, **Auto-Correction** switch, **Check Spelling** switch, **Enable Caps Lock** switch, **Predictive** switch, **Split Keyboard** switch, and **"." Shortcut** switch to On ( ⬤ ) or Off ( ), as needed.

**Note:** The "." Shortcut switch enables you to type a period by pressing Spacebar twice in quick succession.

**6** Tap **Text Replacement**.

The Text Replacement screen appears.

**7** Tap **Add** (+).

**8** Type the word or phrase.

**9** Type the shortcut to use for entering the word or phrase.

**10** Tap **Save**.

**Note:** To prevent the spell checker from querying a word, create a shortcut with the word as the phrase text but with no shortcut. The spell checker then accepts the word as correct.

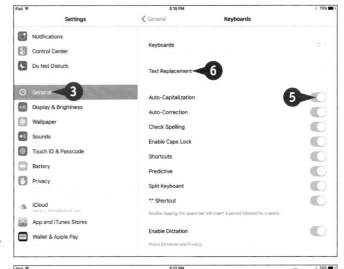

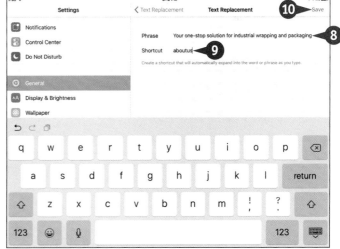

---

### TIP

**How can I use a hardware keyboard with my iPad?**

You can connect a Bluetooth keyboard to your iPad. You can use either a standard Bluetooth keyboard, such as the Apple Wireless Keyboard, or a Bluetooth keyboard designed specifically for the iPad, such as a keyboard built into a case or a stand that props up the iPad to a suitable angle for typing. You can also connect many USB keyboards by using an Apple Lightning-to-USB Camera Adapter, which you can buy from the Apple Store. For the iPad Pro, you can get Apple's Smart Keyboard, which attaches to the Smart Connector pins on the iPad.

# Cut, Copy, and Paste Text

Y our iPad enables you to copy existing text and paste it elsewhere. For example, you can copy text from a note and paste it into an e-mail message you are composing.

If the text is in a document you can edit, you can cut — remove — the text from the document instead of copying it. If the text is in a document you cannot edit, you can copy the text but not cut it.

## Cut, Copy, and Paste Text

### Select and Copy Text

**①** Tap and hold a word in the text you want to copy.

**Note:** If the text is editable, either double-tap a word to select it, or tap the word to position the insertion point and then tap **Select** on the command bar to display the selection handles.

**Ⓐ** A selection highlight with handles appears around the word.

**Ⓑ** The command bar appears above the selection.

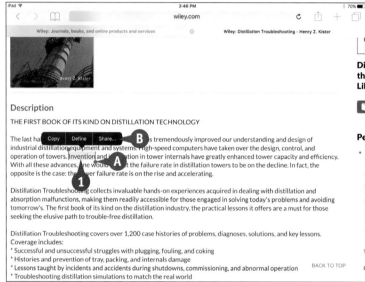

**②** Drag the handles of the selection highlight around the text that you want.

**③** Tap **Copy**.

**Note:** If the text is editable, you can tap **Cut** on the command bar to cut the text from the document, placing it on the Clipboard.

Your iPad places the text on the Clipboard, a hidden storage area.

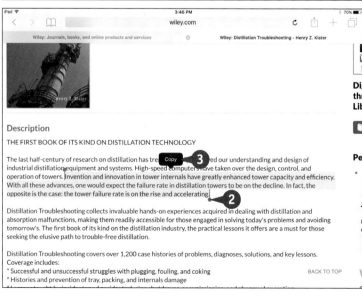

## Paste the Content You Have Copied or Cut

**1** Open the app in which you want to paste the text.

**Note:** This example shows text being pasted into a new message in the Mail app.

**2** Tap where you want to paste the text.

**C** In some apps, you can also tap **Paste** (⌷) on the bar above the keyboard to paste.

**3** Tap **Paste**.

**D** The pasted text appears in the document.

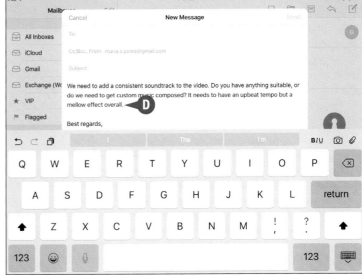

## TIPS

**How many items can I store on the Clipboard?**
You can store only one item on the Clipboard at a time. Each item you cut or copy replaces the existing item on the Clipboard. But until you replace the existing item on the Clipboard, you can paste it as many times as needed.

**Can I transfer the contents of the Clipboard to my computer?**
You cannot transfer the Clipboard's contents directly to your computer, but you can easily transfer them indirectly. For example, you can paste them into an e-mail message and send it to yourself.

# Bold, Italicize, Underline, and Replace Text

Some apps enable you to add formatting such as boldface, underline, and italics to text to make parts of it stand out. For example, you can apply formatting in e-mail messages you create using the Mail app and in various apps for creating word-processing documents.

To apply formatting, you first select the text, and then choose options from the pop-up command bar. Some apps also offer other text commands, such as replacing a word or phrase from a menu of suggestions.

## Bold, Italicize, Underline, and Replace Text

### Apply Bold, Italics, and Underline

1 Tap and hold the text to which you want to apply bold, italics, or underline.

A command bar appears.

2 Tap **Select**.

**Note:** Some apps have their own formatting tools, many of which are more extensive than the standard formatting tools shown here.

**Note:** Some e-mail services and notes services do not support formatting.

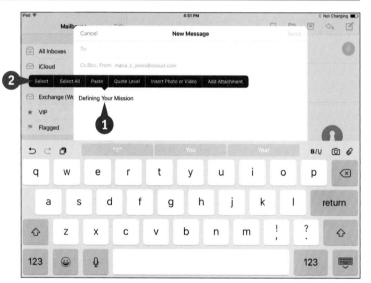

Part of the text is highlighted and handles appear.

3 Drag the handles to select the text that you want to bold, italicize, or underline.

4 Tap the **B***I*U button in the command bar.

A In some apps, you can also tap **B***I*U on the bar above the keyboard to display a formatting bar.

The command bar displays formatting options.

5 Tap **Bold**, **Italics**, or **Underline**, as needed.

The text takes on the formatting you chose.

6 Tap outside the selected text to deselect it.

## Replace Text with Suggested Words

**1** Double-tap the word you want to replace.

**Note:** You can tap and hold in the word, and then tap **Select** on the command bar to select the word.

> Selection handles appear around the word.
>
> The command bar appears.

**2** Tap **Replace**.

> The command bar displays suggested replacement words.

**3** Tap the word with which you want to replace the selected word.

> Your iPad replaces the word.

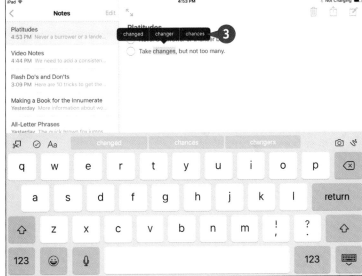

---

### TIP

**What does the Quote Level button on the command bar in Mail do?**

Tap the **Quote Level** button when you need to increase or decrease the quote level of your selected text. When you tap Quote Level, the command bar displays an Increase button and a Decrease button. Tap **Increase** to increase the quote level, indenting the text more, or **Decrease** to decrease the quote level, reducing the existing indent.

# CHAPTER 7

# Browsing the Web and Sending E-Mail

**Your iPad is fully equipped to browse the web and send e-mail via a Wi-Fi connection or cellular network.**

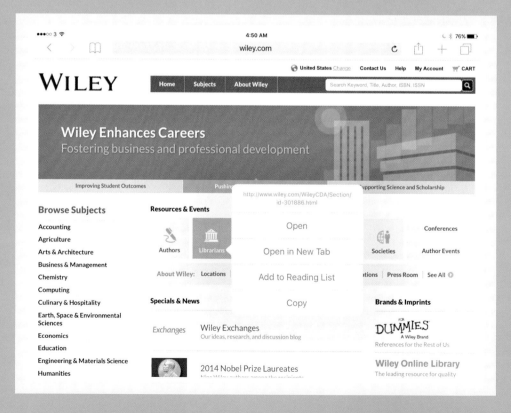

# Browse the Web with Safari

Your iPad comes equipped with the Safari app for browsing the web. You can quickly go to a web page by typing its address in the Address box or by following a link. The Address box includes a search function, so you can type in either a web page address or a search term.

You can either browse a single web page at a time or open multiple pages in separate tabs and switch back and forth among them.

## Browse the Web with Safari

### Open Safari and Navigate to Web Pages

1 Press **Home**.

2 Tap **Safari** ( ).

Safari opens and loads the last web page that was shown. If you closed all pages the last time you used Safari, the app displays the Top Sites screen.

3 Tap the Address box.

The keyboard appears.

4 Tap **Delete** ( ) if you need to delete the contents of the Address box.

5 Type the address of the page you want to open.

6 Tap **Go**.

Safari displays the page.

7 Tap a link on the page.

Safari displays that page.

Ⓐ After going to a new page, tap **Back** ( ) to display the previous page. You can then tap **Forward** ( ) to go forward again to the page you just went back from. Tap and hold **Back** ( ) or **Forward** ( ) to display a list of pages you can go back or forward to.

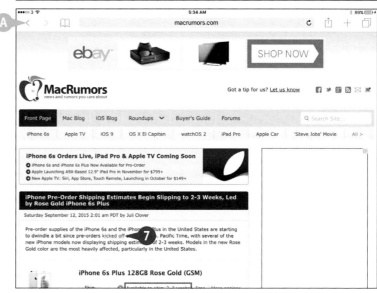

## Open Multiple Pages and Navigate Among Them

**1** Tap **New Tab** (+) at the right end of the tab bar.

Safari displays a new tab.

**2** Tap in the Address box.

The keyboard appears.

**3** Type the address for the page you want to display.

**B** If a suitable search result appears in the suggestions list, tap it to display that page.

**Note:** You can also go to a page by using a bookmark, as described in the next section, "Access Websites Quickly with Bookmarks."

**4** Tap **Go**.

**C** The page appears.

**5** To switch to another page, tap its tab.

**D** You can tap **Close** (⊗) to close the active page.

**Note:** To change the order of the tabs, tap a tab and drag it to the left or right. Release the tab when it appears where you want it.

**TIP**

**How can I type a web page address more easily?**
You have to type most of the address manually, but you can use Safari's shortcut for entering the domain suffix, such as .com or .net. Tap and hold the period key, and then tap the suffix on the pop-up panel that appears. Alternatively, you can open a link from another app — for example, by tapping a link in a message in Mail. If you have the web page address as text rather than as a link, copy it and paste it into the Address box, and then tap **Go**.

# Access Websites Quickly with Bookmarks

To avoid having to type web addresses, you will probably want to use bookmarks to access websites you value.

By syncing your existing bookmarks in iCloud to your iPad, you can instantly access your preferred web pages. You can also use the iCloud Tabs feature to view tabs that are open in Safari on your other devices or create bookmarks on your iPad, as discussed in the next section, "Create Bookmarks to Access Pages Quickly."

## Access Websites Quickly with Bookmarks

### Open the Bookmarks Screen

1 Press **Home**.

The Home screen appears.

2 Tap **Safari** (  ).

Safari opens.

3 Tap **Bookmarks** (  ).

The Bookmarks panel appears.

4 If the Bookmarks list does not appear, tap **Bookmarks** (  ) at the top of the Bookmarks panel.

The Bookmarks list appears.

### Explore Your History

1 In the Bookmarks panel, tap **History**.

A scrollable list of the web pages you have recently visited appears.

Ⓐ Safari divides the list by times, such as This Evening, This Morning, and specific days.

**Note:** You can delete an item from your history by swiping its button left in the History panel and then tapping **Delete**, which appears to the right of the button.

## Explore a Bookmarks Category and Open a Bookmarked Page

**1** In the Bookmarks panel, tap the bookmarks folder or category you want to see. For example, tap **Bookmarks Menu**.

**Note:** You can delete a bookmarks folder or a bookmark by swiping its button left in the Bookmarks panel and then tapping **Delete**, which appears to the right of the button.

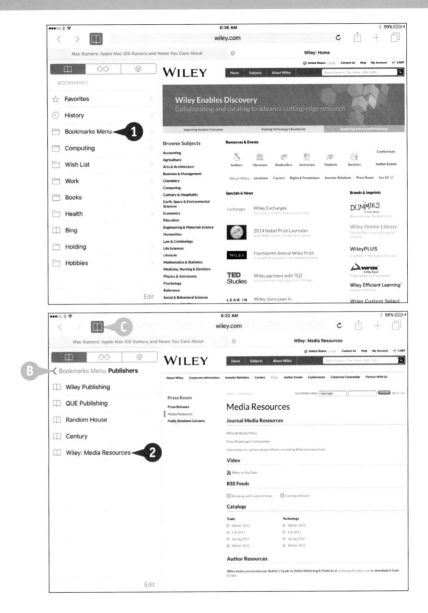

The contents of the folder or category appear. For example, the contents of the Bookmarks Menu folder appear.

**Note:** If the folder you opened contains subfolders, tap the subfolder you want to open.

**2** Tap the page you want to view.

**B** Alternatively, tap **Back** (**<**) in the upper-left corner one or more times to go back.

**C** You can tap **Bookmarks** (⬚) to close the Bookmarks panel or simply leave it open.

TIP

### How can I quickly access a website?

Creating a bookmark within Safari — as discussed in the next section, "Create Bookmarks to Access Pages Quickly" — is good for sites you access now and then, but if you access a site frequently, create an icon for it on your Home screen. Open the site in Safari. Tap **Share** (⬆), tap **Add to Home Screen** (➕), edit the name in the Add to Home dialog, and then tap **Add**. You can then go straight to the page by tapping its icon on the Home screen.

# Create Bookmarks to Access Pages Quickly

When you find a page you want to access again, create a bookmark for it. If you have set your iPad to sync Safari information with iCloud, that bookmark becomes available to the other devices you sync with iCloud.

If you create many bookmarks, it is usually helpful to store them in multiple folders. You can create folders easily on your iPad and choose which folder to store each bookmark in.

## Create Bookmarks to Access Pages Quickly

### Create a Bookmark

**1** Press **Home**.

The Home screen appears.

**2** Tap **Safari** (🧭).

Safari opens and displays the last web page you were viewing.

**3** Navigate to the web page you want to bookmark.

**4** Tap **Share** (⬆️).

The Share sheet appears.

**5** Tap **Add Bookmark** (📖).

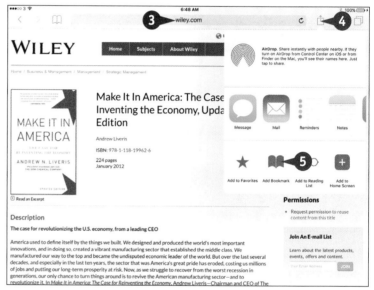

The Add Bookmark dialog opens.

**6** Edit the suggested name, or type a new name.

**7** Tap **Location** and then tap the folder in which you want to create the bookmark.

**Note:** The Location button shows the last bookmarks folder you used. In this example, the last folder was Favorites.

**8** Tap **Save**.

Safari creates the bookmark.

## Create a Bookmark Folder

**1** In **Safari**, tap Bookmarks (▢).

The Bookmarks panel opens.

**2** Tap **Bookmarks** (▢).

The Bookmarks list appears.

**3** Tap **Edit** at the bottom of the list.

The Bookmarks panel changes to editing mode.

A Delete icon (⊖) appears to the left of each bookmark.

A movement handle (☰) appears to the right of each bookmark.

**4** Tap **New Folder**.

The Edit Folder dialog opens.

**5** Type a descriptive name for the folder.

**6** Tap **Location** and then tap the folder in which to store the new folder.

**7** Tap **Back** (<).

**8** Tap **Done** in the Bookmarks panel.

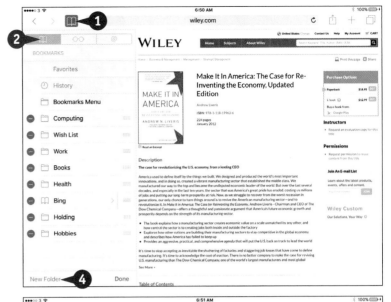

---

**TIP**

**How do I change a bookmark I have created?**

Tap **Bookmarks** (▢) to display the Bookmarks panel, and then navigate to the bookmark you want to change. Tap **Edit** to display a button for opening a bookmark to change it, a handle (☰) for dragging it up or down the list, and a Delete button (⊖) for deleting it.

# Keep a Reading List of Web Pages

When you want to save a web page in its current state so you can read it later, use the Reading List feature in Safari. Reading List enables you to quickly save the current web page from the Share sheet.

Once you have added pages, you access Reading List through the Bookmarks feature. When viewing Reading List, you can display either all the pages it contains or only those you have not read.

## Keep a Reading List of Web Pages

### Add a Web Page to Reading List

1. Press **Home**.

   The Home screen appears.

2. Tap **Safari** ( ).

   Safari opens and displays the last web page you were viewing.

3. Navigate to the web page you want to add to Reading List.

4. Tap **Share** ( ).

   The Share sheet appears.

5. Tap **Add to Reading List** (∞).

   Safari adds the web page to Reading List.

**Note:** Reading List stores the web page as it exists when you tap **Add to Reading List**, so when you return to the page, you see it exactly as it was when you stored it; you can also read the page offline. By contrast, tapping a bookmark displays the current version of the web page, which may be completely different from the version when you created the bookmark. For example, if you tap a bookmark to go to a news site's home page, you will see the latest stories.

## Open Reading List and Display a Page

**1** In Safari, tap **Bookmarks** (📖).

The Bookmarks panel opens.

**2** Tap **Reading List** (∞).

The Reading List tab appears.

**Ⓐ** You can tap **Show Unread** to display only unread pages. You can tap **Show All**, which replaces Show Unread, to display all the pages in Reading List.

**3** Tap the page you want to open.

**Ⓑ** The page opens.

**Ⓒ** You can tap **Bookmarks** (📖) to close the Bookmarks panel, or simply leave it open so that you can easily access other pages on your reading list.

**How do I remove an item from Reading List?**

To remove an item from Reading List, tap **Bookmarks** (📖) and then **Reading List** (∞). In the list of pages, swipe left on the button for the item you want to remove, and then tap the **Delete** button that appears.

# Share Web Pages with Others

When browsing the web, you will likely come across pages you want to share with other people. Safari makes it easy to share web page addresses via e-mail, instant messaging, Twitter, Facebook, and other apps. This example uses the Mail app.

When others share web pages with you via Twitter and similar apps, Safari adds them to the Shared Links list. You can open this list, browse the pages, and quickly display any pages you want to view.

## Share Web Pages with Others

### Share a Web Page with Others

**1** Press **Home**.

The Home screen appears.

**2** Tap **Safari** ( ).

Safari opens and displays the last web page you were viewing.

**3** Navigate to the web page you want to share.

**4** Tap **Share** ( ).

The Share sheet appears.

**5** Tap **Mail** ( ).

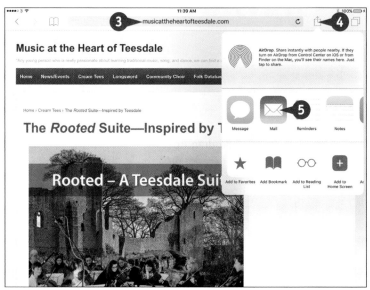

Your iPad starts a new message in the Mail app.

**A** The URL appears in the body of the message.

**6** Enter the recipient's address. You can tap **Add Contact** ( ) and choose the address for the message.

**7** Edit the suggested subject line as needed.

**8** Type any explanatory text needed.

**9** Tap **Send**.

Mail sends the message.

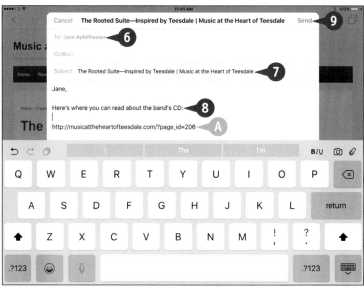

## Open a Page Someone Has Shared with You

**1** In Safari, tap **Bookmarks** (⌶).

The Bookmarks screen appears.

**2** Tap **Shared Links** (@).

The Shared Links list appears.

**Note:** If necessary, tap and drag up to scroll down to locate the link you want.

**3** Tap the link.

Safari displays the linked page.

**In what other ways can I share a web page?**
You can also share a web page address by including it in an instant message, by tweeting it to Twitter, or by posting it to Facebook. Another option is to use AirDrop to share the address with a nearby device. See Chapter 5 for instructions on using AirDrop.

# Fill In Forms Quickly with AutoFill

I f you fill in forms using your iPad, you can save time and typos by turning on the AutoFill feature. AutoFill can automatically fill in standard form fields, such as name and address fields, using the information from a contact card you specify. AutoFill can also store usernames and passwords to enter them for you automatically. If you want, you can also add one or more credit cards to AutoFill so that you can easily pay for items online.

## Fill In Forms Quickly with AutoFill

**1** Press **Home**.

The Home screen appears.

**2** Tap **Settings** (⚙).

The Settings screen appears.

**3** Tap **Safari** (🧭).

The Safari screen appears.

**Ⓐ** You can tap **Passwords** to display the Passwords screen, on which you can tap **Add Password** to add your credentials for a particular website.

**4** Tap **AutoFill**.

The AutoFill screen appears.

**5** Set the **Use Contact Info** switch to On (🔘) if you want to use AutoFill with contact info.

**6** Tap **My Info** to open the Contacts dialog, and then tap the appropriate contact card.

**7** Set the **Names and Passwords** switch to On (🔘) to use AutoFill for names and passwords.

**8** Set the **Credit Cards** switch to On (🔘) to enable storing credit card information.

**9** Tap **Saved Credit Cards**.

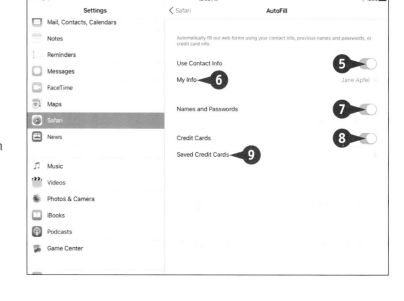

The Credit Cards screen appears.

**10** Tap **Add Credit Card**.

**Note:** The Description field in the Add Credit Card dialog is for your benefit. If you have multiple credit cards from the same issuer, give each card a clear description — for example, "Personal Account" or "Silver card with photo" — so you can distinguish them easily.

The Add Credit Card dialog opens.

**B** You can tap **Use Camera** and use your iPad's camera to photograph and recognize your credit card details.

**11** Enter your credit card details.

**12** Tap **Done**.

The Add Credit Card dialog closes, and the card appears on the Credit Cards screen.

**13** Tap **AutoFill**.

The AutoFill screen appears.

**14** Tap **Safari** (‹).

The Safari screen appears again.

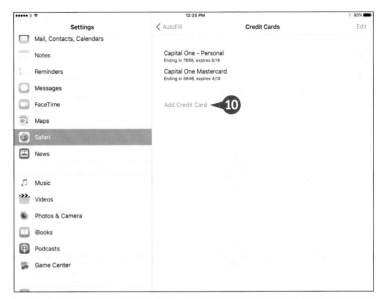

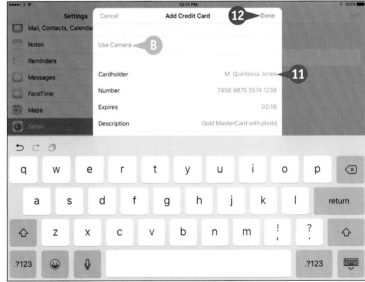

**Is it safe to store my passwords and credit card information?**

Storing this sensitive information is reasonably safe, because your iPad encrypts it securely. The main threat to this data is from someone picking up your iPad and being able to take actions using your passwords and make payments using your cards, so be sure to protect the device with Touch ID and a passcode or — better — a password. See Chapter 2 for instructions on setting a passcode or password.

In addition, Safari does not store the Card Verification Value number, or CVV number — the three- or four-digit number on the back of the card. Many online merchants and payment services require you to enter the CVV number as confirmation that you have the card.

# Tighten Up Safari's Security

To protect yourself against websites that try to infect computers with malevolent software — *malware* — or lure you into providing sensitive personal or financial information, you can turn on Safari's Fraudulent Website Warning feature, which warns you of blacklisted sites. You may also want to turn off the JavaScript programming language, which can be used to attack your iPad. You can also block pop-up windows, which some websites use to display unwanted information; choose which cookies to accept; and turn on the Do Not Track feature.

## Tighten Up Safari's Security

**1** Press **Home**.

The Home screen appears.

**2** Tap **Settings** (⚙).

The Settings screen appears.

**3** Tap **Safari** (🧭).

The Safari screen appears.

**4** Set the **Block Pop-ups** switch to On (🔘) to block unwanted pop-up windows.

**5** Set the **Do Not Track** switch to On (🔘) or Off ( ), as needed.

**Note:** Do Not Track requests websites not to track you but does not prevent them from tracking you.

**6** Tap **Block Cookies**.

The Block Cookies screen appears.

**7** Tap **Always Block**, **Allow from Current Website Only**, **Allow from Websites I Visit**, or **Always Allow**, as needed. See the tip for advice.

**8** Tap **Safari** (<).

The Safari screen appears again.

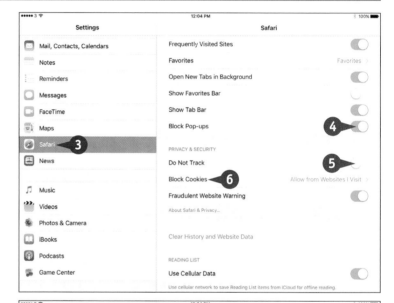

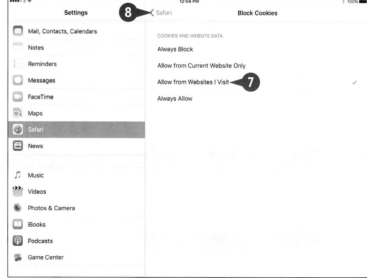

**9** Tap **Quick Website Search** and set the **Quick Website Search** switch to On (⬤) to enable yourself to include website names — such as "wiki" for wikipedia.org or "apple" for "apple.com" — in your searches.

**10** Set the **Preload Top Hit** switch to On (⬤) if you want Safari to preload the first search result page so it will load quickly.

**11** Set the **Fraudulent Website Warning** switch to On (⬤).

**12** To clear your browsing history, tap **Clear History and Website Data**.

The Clear History and Data dialog opens.

**13** Tap **Clear**.

**14** If you want to turn off JavaScript, tap **Advanced**. On the Advanced screen, set the **JavaScript** switch to Off ( ), and then tap **Safari** (<) to return to the Safari screen.

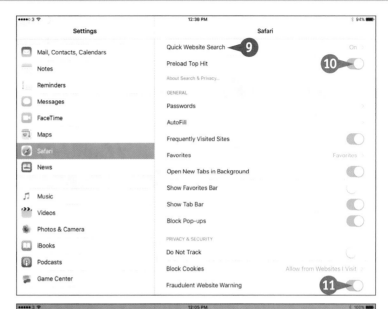

---

**TIP**

**What are cookies and what threat do they pose?**

A *cookie* is a small text file that a website places on a computer to identify that computer in the future. This is helpful for many sites, such as shopping sites in which you add items to a shopping cart, but when used by malevolent sites, cookies can pose a threat to your privacy. You can set Safari to block all cookies, but this prevents many legitimate websites from working properly. So blocking cookies from third parties and advertisers, but allowing cookies from sites you visit, is normally the best compromise.

# Read Your E-Mail Messages

After you have set up Mail, either by adding your iCloud account or by setting up accounts manually on the iPad, as described in Chapter 4, you are ready to send and receive e-mail messages using your iPad.

This section shows you how to read your incoming e-mail messages. You learn how to reply to messages and write messages from scratch later in this chapter.

## Read Your E-Mail Messages

1 Press **Home**.

The Home screen appears.

2 Tap **Mail** (icon).

The Mailboxes screen appears.

**Note:** If Mail does not show the Mailboxes screen, tap the button in the upper-left corner until the Mailboxes screen appears.

3 Tap the inbox you want to see.

Ⓐ To see all your incoming messages together, tap **All Inboxes**. Depending on how you use e-mail, you may find seeing all your messages at once helpful.

The inbox opens.

Ⓑ A blue dot to the left of a message indicates that you have not read the message yet.

Ⓒ A star to the left of a message indicates the message is from a VIP. See the second tip in this section for information about VIPs.

4 Tap the message you want to display.

The message appears.

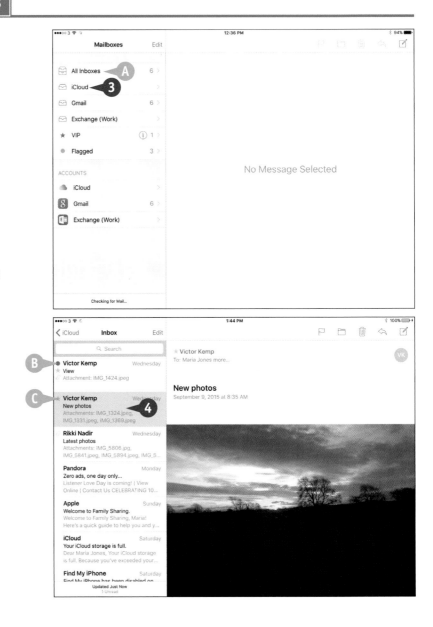

**5** Tap another message to display its contents.

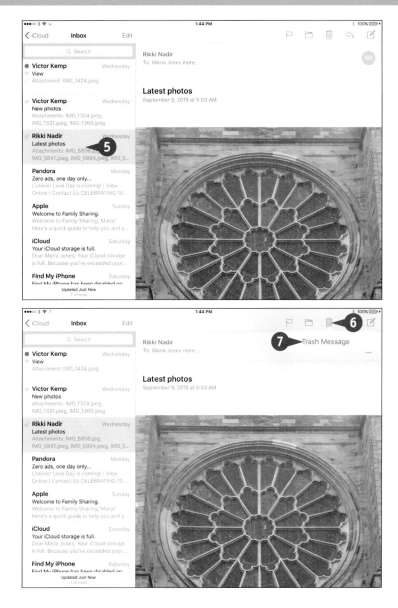

**6** If you want to delete the message, tap **Delete** (🗑).

**7** If the Trash Message confirmation dialog opens, tap **Trash Message**.

**Note:** If you want to reply to the message, see the next section, "Reply to or Forward an E-Mail Message." If you want to file the message in a folder, see the section "Organize Your Messages in Mailbox Folders."

**Note:** The badge on the Mail icon on the Home screen shows how many unread messages Mail has found so far.

---

## TIPS

**How do I view the contents of another mailbox?**
Tap **Back** (<) to return to the Mailboxes screen. You can then tap the mailbox you want to view.

**What is the VIP inbox on the Mailboxes screen?**
The VIP inbox is a tool for identifying important messages, no matter which e-mail account they come to. You mark particular contacts as being very important people to you, and Mail then adds messages from these VIPs to the VIP inbox. See Chapter 4 for instructions on adding VIPs.

# Reply to or Forward an E-Mail Message

After receiving an e-mail message, you often need to reply to it. You can choose between replying only to the sender of the message and replying to the sender and all the other recipients in the To field and the Cc field, if there are any. Any recipients in the message's Bcc field, whose names you cannot see, do not receive your reply. Other times, you may need to forward a message you have received to one or more other people.

## Reply to or Forward an E-Mail Message

**1** Press **Home**.

The Home screen appears.

**2** Tap **Mail** (✉).

The Mailboxes screen appears.

**Note:** When you launch Mail, the app checks for new messages. This is why the number of new messages you see on the Mailboxes screen may differ from the number on the Mail badge on the Home screen.

**3** Tap the inbox you want to see.

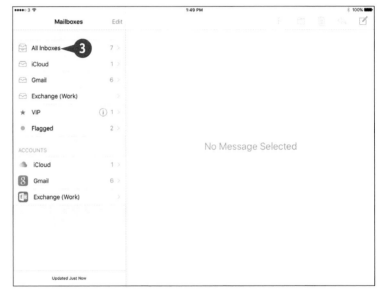

The inbox opens.

**4** Tap the message you want to open.

**5** Tap **Action** (↩).

**Note:** You can also reply to or forward a message by using Siri. For example, say "Reply to this message" or "Forward this message to Alice Smith," and then tell Siri what you want the message to say.

**6** Tap **Reply** or **Forward**, as appropriate.

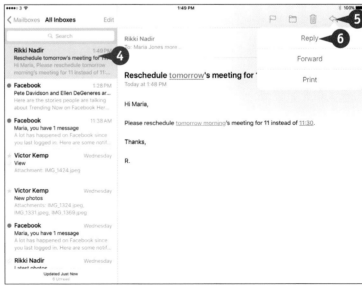

## Reply to the Message

**1** In the Action menu, tap **Reply**.

**Note:** To reply to all recipients, tap **Reply All**. Reply to all recipients only when you are sure that they need to receive your reply. Often, it is better to reply only to the sender.

The reply message appears.

**2** Type your reply to the message.

**3** Tap **Send**.

Mail sends the message.

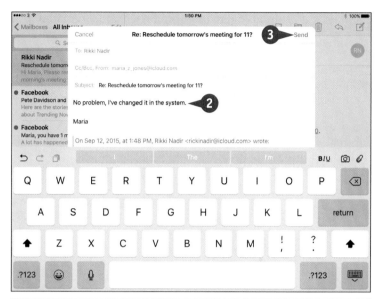

## Forward the Message

**1** In the Action menu, tap **Forward**.

The forwarded message appears.

**2** Type the recipient's name or address.

Alternatively, tap **Add Contact** (⊕) and choose the recipient in your Contacts dialog.

**3** Type a message if needed.

**4** Tap **Send**.

Mail sends the message.

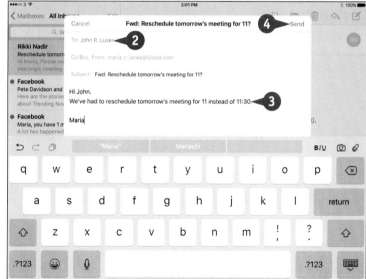

**Can I reply to or forward only part of a message?**

Yes. The quick way to do this is to select the part of the message you want to include before tapping **Action** (↩). Mail then includes only your selection. Alternatively, you can start the reply or forwarded message, and then delete the parts you do not want to include.

# Organize Your Messages in Mailbox Folders

To keep your inbox or inboxes under control, you should organize your messages into mailbox folders.

You can quickly move a single message to a folder after reading it, or you can select multiple messages in your inbox and move them all to a folder in a single action.

## Organize Your Messages in Mailbox Folders

### Move a Single Message to a Folder

1 Press **Home**.

The Home screen appears.

2 Tap **Mail** (▢).

The Mailboxes screen appears.

3 Tap the inbox you want to see.

The inbox opens.

4 Tap the message you want to read.

The message opens.

5 Tap **Move** (▢).

The list of folders appears in the left pane.

6 Tap the folder you want to move the message to.

Mail moves the message.

The next message in the inbox appears, so that you can read it and file it if necessary.

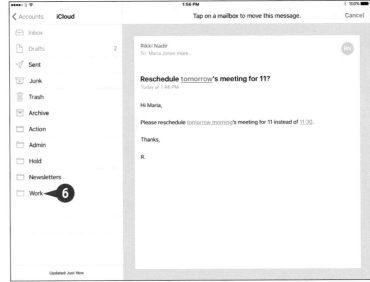

## Move Multiple Messages to a Folder

1 In the inbox or another mail folder, tap **Edit**.

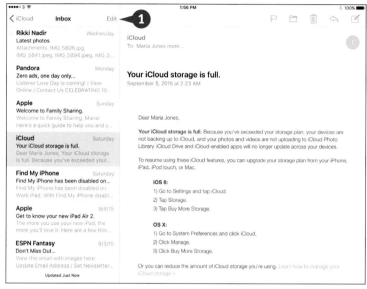

An empty selection button appears to the left of each message, and the Mark button, Move button, and Trash button appear.

2 Tap the selection button ( changes to ✓) next to each message you want to move.

A Mail displays the messages as a stack.

3 Tap **Move**.

The list of folders appears in the left pane.

4 Tap the folder you want to move the messages to.

Mail moves the messages.

Your inbox then appears again, so that you can work with other messages.

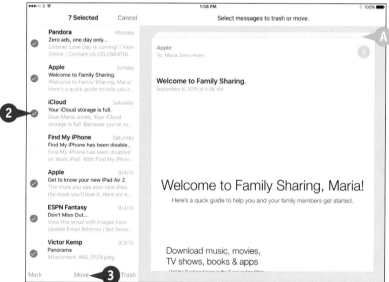

**Can I move messages from an inbox in one account to a folder in another account?**

Yes. In the inbox, tap **Edit**, and then tap the selection button ( changes to ✓) for each message you want to affect. Tap **Move** and then tap **Accounts**. In the Accounts list, tap the account that contains the destination folder for the messages, and then tap the folder.

# Write and Send E-Mail Messages

Your iPad is great for reading and replying to e-mail messages you receive, but you will likely also need to write new messages. When you do, you can use the data in the Contacts app to address your outgoing messages quickly and accurately. If the recipient's address is not one of your contacts, you can type the address manually. You can attach one or more files to an e-mail message to send those files to the recipient. This works well for small files, but many mail servers reject files larger than several megabytes in size.

## Write and Send E-Mail Messages

**1** Press **Home**.

The Home screen appears.

**2** Tap **Mail** (icon).

The Mailboxes screen appears.

**3** Tap **New Message** (icon).

The New Message dialog opens.

**A** If you have set up a signature for this account, Mail inserts the signature at the end of the new message.

**4** Tap **Add Contact** (⊕).

The Contacts dialog opens.

**Note:** You can change the Contacts list displayed by tapping **Groups**, making your choice in the Groups dialog, and then tapping **Done**.

**B** If the person you are e-mailing is not a contact, type the address in the To field. You can also start typing here and then select a matching contact from the list that the Mail app displays.

**5** Tap the contact.

198

**C** The contact's name appears in the To field.

**Note:** You can add other contacts to the To field by repeating steps **4** and **5**.

**6** If you need to add a Cc or Bcc recipient, tap **Cc/Bcc, From**.

The Cc, Bcc, and From fields expand.

**7** Tap the Cc field or Bcc field, and then follow steps **4** and **5** to add a recipient.

**D** To change the e-mail account you are sending the message from, tap **From**, and then tap the account to use.

**E** To receive notifications for replies to this e-mail thread, tap **Notify** (🔔) and then tap **Notify Me** (🔔 changes to 🔔).

**8** Tap **Subject**, and then type the message's subject.

**9** Tap below the Subject line, and then type the body of the message.

**10** Tap **Send**.

Mail sends the message.

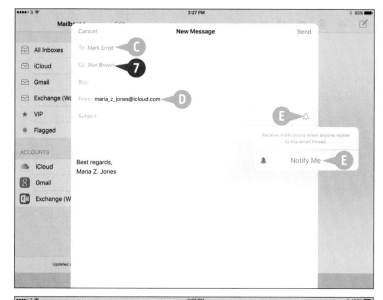

## TIP

### How do I attach a file to a message?

Tap and hold open space in the body area of the message to display the command bar. To insert a photo or video, tap **Insert Photo or Video** on the command bar, and then follow the prompts to select the photo or video. To attach a file from iCloud Drive, tap **Add Attachment** on the command bar, and then select the file.

Alternatively, you can start the message from the app that contains the file. For example, to send a photo, open the Photos app. Select the photo, tap **Share** (⬆), and then tap **Mail** (✉). Mail starts a message with the photo attached. You then address the message and send it.

# View Files Attached to Incoming Messages

E-mail is not just a great way to communicate; you can also use it to transfer files quickly and easily. When you receive an e-mail message with a file attached to it, you can often quickly view the file from the Mail app. After viewing the file, you can choose the app in which you want to open the file.

## View Files Attached to Incoming Messages

**1** Press **Home**.

The Home screen appears.

**2** Tap **Mail** (✉).

The Mailboxes screen appears.

**3** Tap the appropriate inbox.

The inbox opens.

**A** A paper clip icon (🔗) indicates an attachment.

**4** Tap the message.

The message opens.

**5** Tap the attachment's button.

**Note:** If you want to open the attachment in a particular app without first viewing it in the Viewer, tap and hold the attachment's button. When the Share sheet opens, tap the app in which you want to open the file.

The attached file opens in Mail's Viewer feature.

**Note:** The Viewer feature provides basic tools for viewing widely used document types, such as PDF files, Microsoft Word documents, and Microsoft Excel workbooks. If the Viewer app cannot open a file, your iPad suggests a suitable app if it has one.

**6** Tap **Share** (📤).

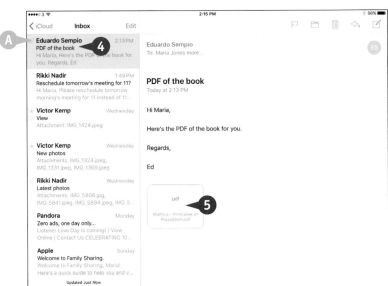

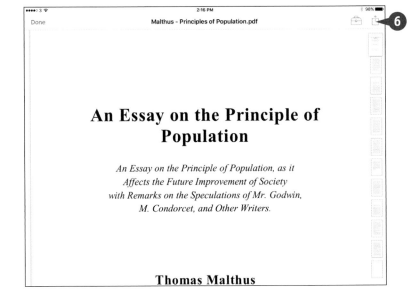

The Share sheet opens.

**Note:** The options on the Share sheet vary depending on the file type and the apps installed on your iPad.

⑦ Tap the app in which you want to open the document. For example, tap **Copy to iBooks** (📖).

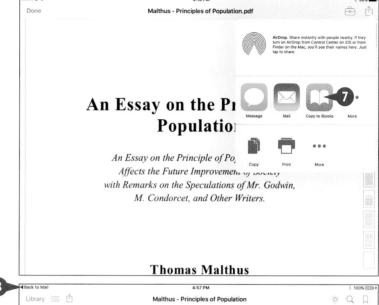

Ⓑ The file opens in the app you chose.

**Note:** After you open an attached file in an app, your iPad stores a copy of the file in that app's storage. You can then open the file again directly from that app.

⑧ Tap **Back to Mail** when you want to return to the Mail app.

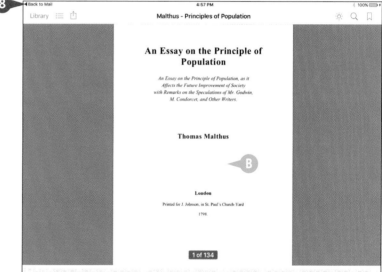

---

**TIP**

**How can I delete an attached file from an e-mail message I have received?**
As of this writing, you cannot directly delete an attached file from an e-mail message you have received in Mail on the iPad. You can delete only the message along with its attached file. If you use an e-mail app such as Mail in OS X or web-based e-mail such as iCloud.com to manage the same e-mail account, you can remove the attached file using that app. When you update your mailbox on your iPad, the iPad deletes the attached file but leaves the message.

# CHAPTER 8

# Keeping Your Life Organized

Your iPad comes with the Contacts app for managing your contacts, the Calendars app for organizing your schedule, the Reminders app for tracking tasks, the Maps app for directions, and the Clock app for timekeeping.

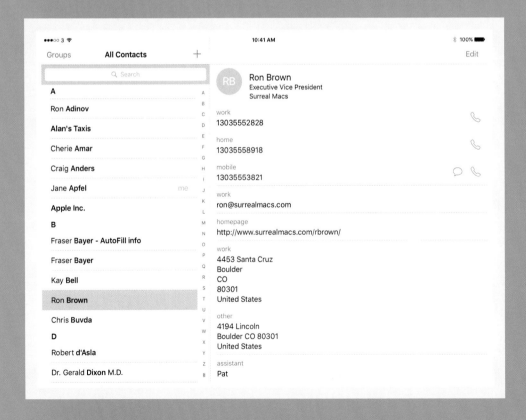

# Browse or Search for Contacts

The Contacts app gives you easy access to the contacts that you have synced to your iPad from an online service, such as iCloud, or that you have created directly on the iPad.

To see which contacts your iPad contains, or to find a particular contact, you can browse through the contacts. You can either browse through your full list of contacts or choose to display only particular groups. You can also locate contacts by searching for them.

## Browse or Search for Contacts

### Browse Your Contacts

**1** Press **Home**.

The Home screen appears.

**2** Tap **Contacts** (👤).

The Contacts list appears.

**Note:** If All Contacts appears, you are viewing all contacts. If Contacts appears, you are viewing only some groups of contacts.

**A** To navigate the screen of contacts quickly, tap the letter that you want to jump to. To navigate more slowly, scroll up or down.

**3** Tap the contact whose information you want to view.

The contact's details appear.

**4** If necessary, tap and drag up to scroll down the screen to display more information.

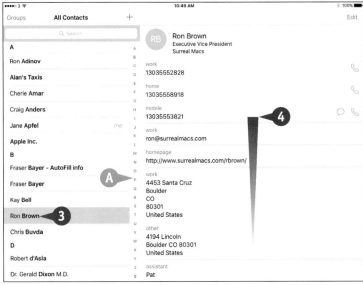

## Choose Which Groups of Contacts to Display

**1** From the Contacts list, tap **Groups**.

The Groups screen appears.

**2** Tap **Show All Contacts**.

Contacts displays a check mark next to each group.

**Note:** When you tap **Show All Contacts**, the Hide All Contacts button appears in place of the Show All Contacts button. You can tap **Hide All Contacts** to remove all the check marks.

**3** Tap a group to remove its existing check mark or apply a check mark.

**4** Tap **Done**.

The Contacts list appears, showing the contacts in the groups you selected.

## Search for Contacts

**1** In the Contacts list, tap **Search** (🔍).

The Search screen appears.

**2** In the Search box, type the name you want to search for.

**3** From the list of matches, tap the contact you want to view.

The contact's information appears.

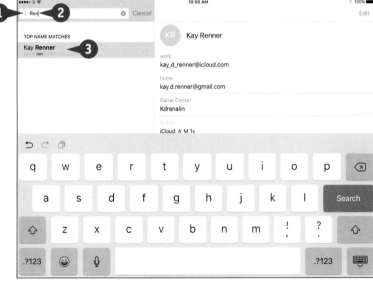

---

### TIPS

**How do I make my iPad sort my contacts by first names instead of last names?**
Press **Home**. Tap **Settings** and then tap **Mail, Contacts, Calendars**. In the Contacts area, tap **Sort Order**, then tap **First, Last**.

**How do I combine two contact records for the same person?**
Tap one of the contact records to open it, and then tap **Edit** to switch to Edit Mode. At the bottom of the screen, tap **link contacts**. In the dialog that opens, tap the contact record you want to link, and then tap **Link**. Tap **Done** to switch off Edit Mode.

# Create a New Contact

Normally, you put contacts on your iPad by syncing them from existing records on your computer or on an online service such as iCloud. But when necessary, you can create a new contact directly on your iPad — for example, when you meet someone you want to remember.

You can then sync the contact record back to your computer, adding the new contact to your existing contacts.

## Create a New Contact

**1** Press **Home**.

The Home screen appears.

**2** Tap **Contacts** (👤).

The Contacts list appears.

**3** Tap **Add** (+).

The New Contact screen appears, with the on-screen keyboard displayed.

**4** Type the first name.

**5** Type the last name.

**6** Add other information as needed by tapping each field and then typing the information.

**7** To add a photo of the contact, tap **add photo**.

The Photo dialog opens.

**8** To use an existing photo, tap **Choose Photo** and follow this example. To take a new photo, tap **Take Photo** and see the tip.

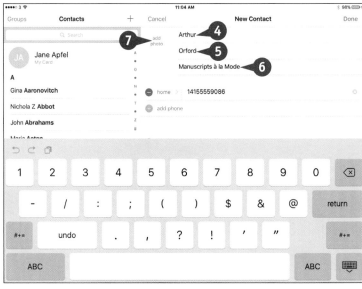

The Photos dialog opens.

**9** Tap the album that contains the photo you want to use.

The album's contents appear.

**10** Tap the appropriate photo.

The Move and Scale screen appears.

**11** Position the part of the photo you want to use in the middle.

**Note:** Pinch in with two fingers to zoom the photo out. Pinch out with two fingers to zoom the photo in.

**12** Tap **Choose**.

The photo appears in the contact record.

**13** Tap **Done** when you finish editing the contact record.

The contact appears in your Contacts list.

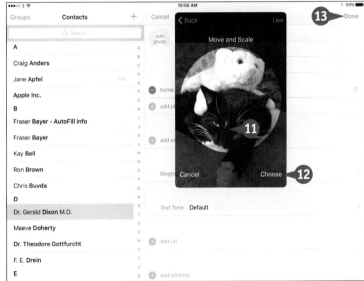

## TIP

**How do I take a new photo of my contact?**

In the Photo dialog, tap **Take Photo**. The screen shows the image from the rear camera on the iPad. Compose the photo, and then tap **Take Photo** (⭕). The Move and Scale screen then appears. Position the photo as needed, scale it if necessary, and then tap **Use Photo**.

# Share Contacts via E-Mail and Messages

Often in business or your personal life, you will need to share your contacts with other people. Your iPad makes it easy to share a contact record either via e-mail or via iMessage, the instant-messaging service offered by Apple.

The iPad shares the contact record as a virtual business card in the widely used vCard format. Most phones and personal-organizer software can easily import vCard files.

Share Contacts via E-Mail and Messages

### Open the Contact You Want to Share

**1** Press **Home**.

The Home screen appears.

**2** Tap **Contacts** (  ).

The Contacts list appears.

**3** Tap the contact you want to share.

The contact's details appear.

**4** Tap **Share Contact**.

The Share sheet opens.

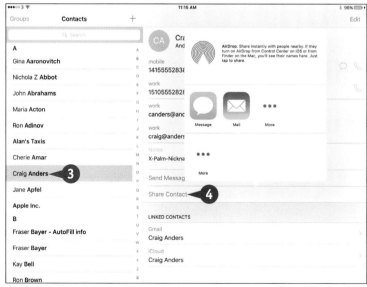

## Share a Contact via E-Mail

**1** On the Share sheet, tap **Mail**.

**A** A new message titled Contact appears in the Mail app, with the contact record attached as a vCard file.

**2** Address the message by typing the address or by tapping and choosing a contact as the recipient.

**3** Edit the default subject line if necessary.

**4** Type a message.

**5** Tap **Send** to send the message.

## Share a Contact via Messages

**1** On the Share sheet, tap **Message**.

**B** The New Message screen appears, with the contact record attached to the message.

**2** Address the message by typing the name or number or by tapping and choosing a contact as the recipient.

**Note:** After you add the address, Messages changes the message type as needed. For example, the New Message screen may change its name to New MMS, indicating a Multimedia Messaging Service message, or to New Group MMS for a message with multiple recipients.

**3** Type a message.

**4** Tap **Send** to send the message.

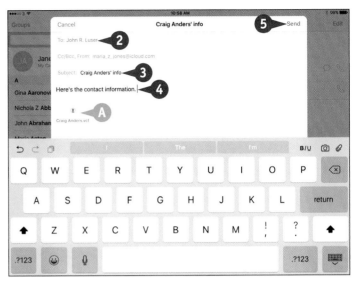

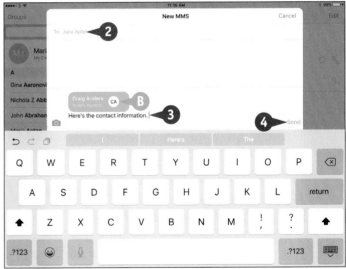

---

### TIPS

**Why is the recipient's address on the New Message screen red instead of blue?**

The address appears in red if the recipient's address is not registered with the iMessage service. Tap and hold the recipient's name until a dialog opens, and then tap **Remove**.

**How do I add a vCard I receive in an e-mail message to my contacts?**

In the Mail app, tap the button for the vCard file. At the bottom of the dialog that opens, tap **Create New Contact**. If the vCard contains extra information about an existing contact, tap **Add to Existing Contact**, and then tap the contact.

# Browse Existing Events in Your Calendars

Your iPad Calendar app gives you a great way of managing your schedule and making sure you never miss an appointment.

After setting up your calendars to sync using iTunes, iCloud, or another calendar service, as described in Chapter 1, you can take your calendars with you everywhere and consult them whenever you need to. You can view all your calendars or only the ones you choose.

## Browse Existing Events in Your Calendars

**1** Press **Home**.

The Home screen appears.

**2** Tap **Calendar** ( ).

The Calendar screen appears.

**3** Tap **Month** to see Month view, in which each day appears in a box on a calendar chart.

**A** Month view shows a one-line entry with the time of each event that will fit in the box.

**4** Tap an event.

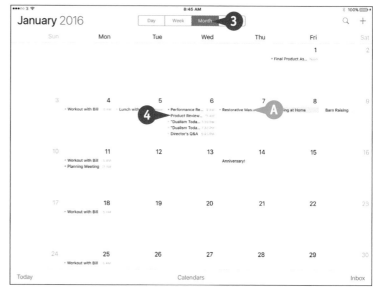

A dialog opens, showing the event's details.

**B** You can tap **Edit** to open the event so you can change its details.

**Note:** You can drag up and down to change the month that appears.

**5** Tap outside the dialog to close it.

**6** Tap **Week**.

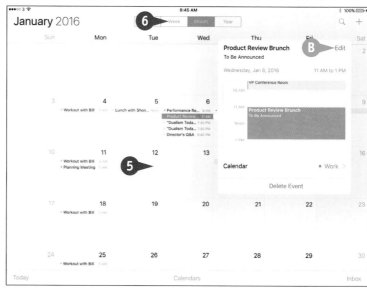

The Calendar switches to Week view.

**C** Your events appear on a grid that shows the days as columns and the hours as rows.

**Note:** In Week view, you can scroll left, right, up, or down to change the days and hours shown.

**Note:** In Week view and Day view, you can move an event by tapping and holding it until its color darkens, and then dragging it to where you want it.

**7** Tap **Day**.

The Calendar switches to Day view.

**D** You can tap another day to display that day.

**E** The left pane shows a vertical timeline for the day.

**F** The right pane shows the details of the selected event.

**G** You can tap **Edit** to edit the event.

**8** Tap **Today**.

Calendar displays the events for the current day.

## TIPS

**How can I quickly find an event?**
Tap **Search** (🔍) in the upper-right corner of the Calendar screen, and then type your search term. When Calendar displays a list of matches, tap the event you want to view.

**How do I control which calendars' events appear?**
Tap **Calendars** at the bottom of the screen. In the Show Calendars dialog, tap to place a check mark next to each calendar you want to see, or tap **Show All Calendars** or **Hide All Calendars**. After making your choices, tap **Done**.

# Create New Events in Your Calendars

Normally, you will probably create most new events in your calendars on your computer, and then sync them to your iPad. But when you need to create a new event using the iPad, you can easily do so.

You can create either a straightforward, one-shot event or an event that repeats on a schedule. And you can choose which calendar the event belongs to.

## Create New Events in Your Calendars

**1** Press **Home**.

The Home screen appears.

**2** Tap **Calendar** (☷).

The Calendar app opens.

**3** Tap **Week** to switch to Week view.

**4** Tap and hold the appropriate time slot.

The New Event dialog opens.

**5** Type the title of the event.

**6** Tap **Location**.

The Location dialog opens.

**7** Type or tap the location of the event.

The location appears.

**Ⓐ** For an all-day event, set the **All-day** switch to On (⬤).

**8** Tap **Alert**.

The Alert dialog opens.

**9** Tap the timing for the alert — for example, **30 minutes before**.

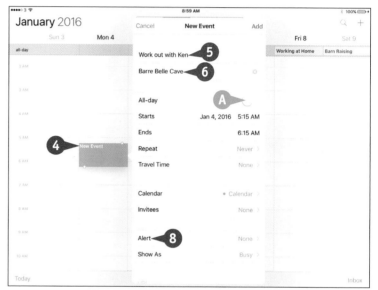

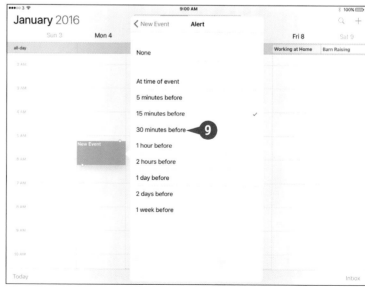

The New Event dialog appears again.

**Note:** You can assign a second alert to the event by tapping **Second Alert** after choosing the first alert. A second alert can be a useful safety net for events you must not miss.

**10** Tap **Starts**.

The time controls appear.

**11** Drag the date and time controls to set the start time.

**12** Tap **Ends**.

**13** Set the end time.

**B** If you need to change the time zone, tap **Time Zone**, type the city name, and then tap the time zone.

**14** Tap **Calendar**.

The Calendar dialog opens.

**15** Tap the calendar to which you want to assign the event.

The New Event dialog reappears.

**16** Tap **Done**.

The event appears on your calendar.

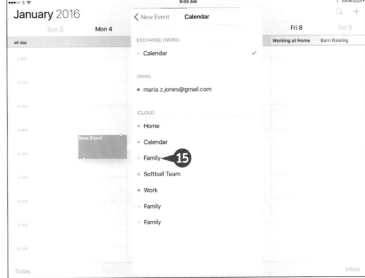

---

**TIP**

**How do I set up an event that repeats, say, every 2 weeks?**
In the New Event dialog, tap **Repeat**. In the Repeat dialog, tap **Every 2 Weeks** to place a check mark next to it, and then tap **Done**.

# Work with Calendar Invitations

ost likely, you will receive invitations to events that others create. When you receive an event invitation attached to an e-mail message, you can choose whether to accept the invitation or decline it. If you accept the invitation, you can add the event automatically to a calendar of your choice and set an alert for it.

## Work with Calendar Invitations

### Respond to an Invitation from an Alert

**1** When an invitation alert appears, tap **Options**.

**Note:** To control whether you receive alerts for invitations, press **Home**, and then tap **Settings** (⚙). In the Settings app, tap **Notifications** (🔲), and then tap **Calendar** (📅). Tap **Invitations** to display the Invitations screen. In the Alert Style When Unlocked area, tap **Alerts** to receive alerts in dialogs or tap **Banners** to display banners instead.

The event's dialog opens.

**2** Tap **View**.

**Ⓐ** You can also tap **Accept** to accept the invitation, **Decline** to turn it down, or **Maybe** to accept tentatively.

214

The Calendar app appears.

**Ⓑ** The event appears on the calendar.

The dialog for the event opens automatically.

**Ⓒ** You can tap **Calendar** and choose the calendar to which you want to add the event.

**Ⓓ** You can tap **Alert** and use the Event Alert dialog to set the alert time you want — for example, tap **30 minutes before**.

**③** Tap **Accept**, **Maybe**, or **Decline** to give your response.

## Respond to an Invitation from the Inbox

**Ⓔ** In your calendar, the Inbox button shows the number of invitations.

**①** Tap **Inbox**.

The Inbox dialog opens.

**②** To respond to an invitation immediately, tap **Accept**, **Maybe**, or **Decline**, as needed.

**Note:** To see the details of an invitation, tap its button in the Inbox dialog. A dialog with the invitation's details opens. From this dialog, you can accept the invitation, decline it, or return a "maybe."

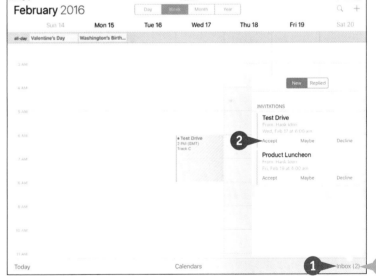

---

**TIP**

**What is the Travel Time item in an invitation?**
Tap **Travel Time** to display the Travel Time screen. You can then set the **Travel Time** switch to On ( ◯ ) to have Calendar automatically add travel time for you to get to the event. Calendar blocks off the travel time so that you will not create or accept other events when you should be traveling to or from the event.

# Track Your Commitments with Reminders

The Reminders app gives you an easy way to note and track your commitments. Reminders comes with a built-in list called Reminders, but you can create as many other lists as you need — for example, Errands, Shopping, or Household. You can create a reminder with no due time. Alternatively, you can tie each reminder to a due time, arriving at or leaving a location, or both, and have your iPad remind you of each reminder at the appropriate time or place.

## Track Your Commitments with Reminders

### Open the Reminders App

**1** Press **Home**.

The Home screen appears.

**2** Tap **Reminders** (  ).

The Reminders screen appears.

**Note:** When you complete a task, tap the circle ( ) to the left of the reminder ( changes to ). If you need to reinstate the task, tap ( changes to ).

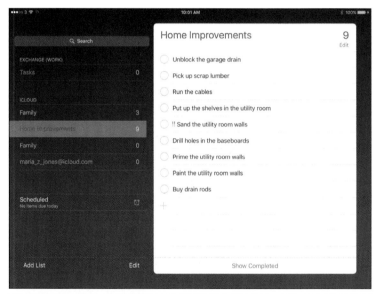

### Create a New Reminder

**1** In the Reminders app, tap the first blank line below the last reminder in the list.

Reminders starts a new reminder and displays the on-screen keyboard.

**2** Type the text of the reminder.

**A** If you do not want to set any further details for the reminder, tap **Done**.

**3** Tap **Information** ( ).

**Note:** To create a reminder using Siri, press **Home** for a couple of seconds until Siri beeps, and then say the reminder aloud. For example, say "Remind me at 8AM tomorrow to take the project files to the office."

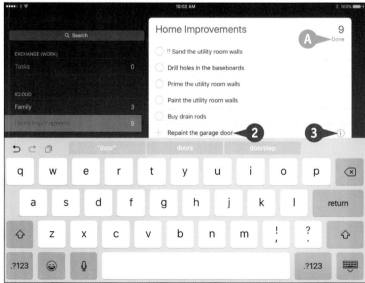

The Details dialog opens.

**4** Set the **Remind me on a day** switch to On (⬤).

The Alarm button appears.

**5** Tap **Alarm**.

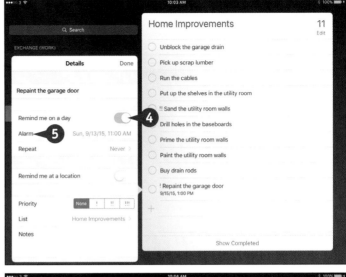

Date and time controls appear.

**6** Select the date and time for the reminder.

**7** If you need to create a repeating reminder, tap **Repeat** and choose the repeat schedule in the Repeat dialog. For example, touch **Every Day** or **Every Week**.

**8** To assign a priority, tap **!**, **!!**, or **!!!**. To remove the priority, tap **None**.

**9** To add notes, tap **Notes** and type the text.

**10** Tap **Done**.

The Details dialog closes.

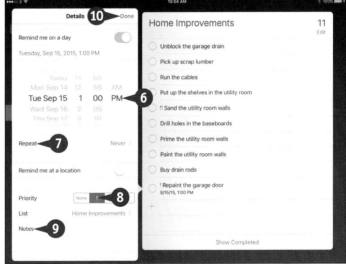

---

**TIP**

**How do I sync the reminders on my iPad with the ones on my Mac?**

Use your iCloud account to sync your iPad reminders with your Mac reminders.

On your iPad, press **Home** to display the Home screen, and then tap **Settings** (⚙) to display the Settings screen. Tap **iCloud** (☁) to display the iCloud screen, and then set the **Reminders** switch to On (⬤).

On your Mac, click **Apple** () and then click **System Preferences** to open System Preferences. Click **iCloud** (☁) to display the iCloud pane, and then click the **Reminders** check box (☐ changes to ☑).

You can also sync reminders via Exchange; for example, for your work tasks.

continued ▶

You can organize your reminders into different lists so that you can look at a single category of reminders at a time. For example, you may find it useful to create a Work list that enables you to focus on your work-related reminders.

After creating lists, you can easily switch among them. You can also move a reminder from one list to another as needed. And when you no longer need a particular reminder, you can delete it.

## Track Your Commitments with Reminders (continued)

### Create Different Lists of Reminders

**1** On the Reminders screen, tap **Add List**.

**2** Type the name for the new list.

**3** Tap the color button for the list.

**4** Tap **Done**.

Reminders adds the new list.

**Note:** To delete a Reminders list quickly, tap it in the lists pane and swipe left; then tap **Delete** and tap **Delete** again in the confirmation dialog. Alternatively, tap **Edit** at the bottom of the lists pane, tap **Delete**, and then tap **Delete** again.

**Note:** Deleting a Reminders list also deletes all the reminders it contains.

### Switch Among Your Reminders Lists

**1** On the Reminders screen, tap the list you want to display.

**B** The list appears.

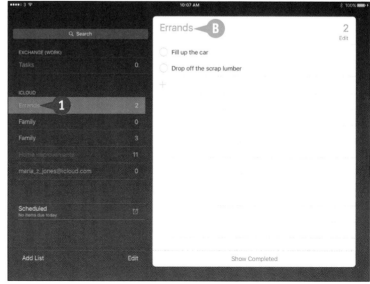

## Change the List to Which a Reminder Is Assigned

**1** In a Reminders list, tap the reminder.

The Information button (ⓘ) appears.

**2** Tap **Information** (ⓘ).

The Details dialog opens.

**3** Tap **List**.

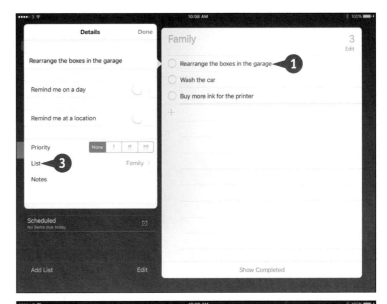

The Change List dialog opens.

**4** Tap the list to which you want to assign the reminder.

The Details dialog opens.

**5** Tap **Done**.

The Details dialog closes.

The reminder moves to the list you chose.

**Note:** You can delete a reminder by tapping **Edit** on its list page, tapping next to the reminder, and then tapping **Delete**. Alternatively, tap the reminder in its list, swipe left, and then tap **Delete**.

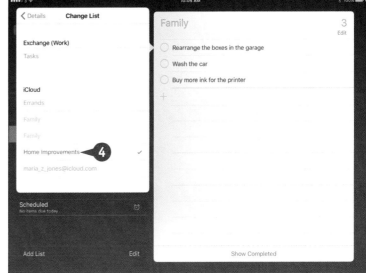

---

### TIP

**Can I change the default list that Reminders puts my reminders in?**
Yes. Press **Home** to display the Home screen, and then tap **Settings** (⚙) to display the Settings screen. Tap **Reminders** (    ) in the left column to display the Reminders screen, tap **Default List** to display the Default List screen, and then tap the list you want to make the default. On the Reminders screen, you can also tap **Sync** and choose how many reminders to sync — for example, **Reminders 2 Weeks Back** or **All Reminders**.

# Take Notes

Your iPad is a great device for taking notes wherever you go. The Notes app enables you to create notes stored in an online account, such as your iCloud account, and sync them across your devices. Alternatively, you can store notes on your iPad itself, which is useful if you don't have reliable Internet connectivity or if you distrust online storage.

You can create straightforward notes in plain text, but you can also add formatting, check boxes, photos, and sketches.

## Take Notes

### Open the Notes App, Choose the Account, and Create a Note

1 Press **Home**.

The Home screen appears.

2 Tap **Notes** ( ).

The Notes app opens.

A The Notes pane shows the notes in the account you are currently using.

B The note on which you were last working appears.

C You can tap **Full Screen** ( ) to expand the current note to full-screen, hiding the Notes pane. Tap **Back** ( ) or **Notes** to display the Notes pane again.

3 Tap **Back** ( ).

The Folders pane appears.

D The Recently Deleted folder contains notes you have recently deleted. Notes remain here for 30 days and then are deleted.

E You can create a new folder in your iCloud account by tapping **New Folder**.

4 Tap the account or folder in which you want to create the new note.

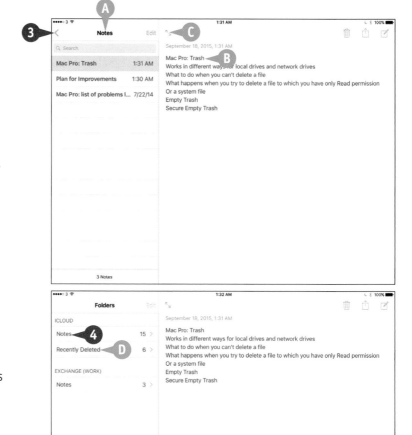

The Notes pane appears, showing the notes in that account or folder.

**5** Tap **New** (✏️).

A new note opens.

**6** Type the title or first paragraph of the note.

**Note:** The first paragraph of the new note receives the style specified by the New Notes Start With setting. To change this setting, press **Home**, tap **Settings** (⚙️), and then tap **Notes** (📝).

**7** Tap **return** and continue typing the note.

**F** The note's entry in the Notes pane shows the first line and part of the next line.

**8** To apply a style to the current paragraph, tap **Style** (Aa).

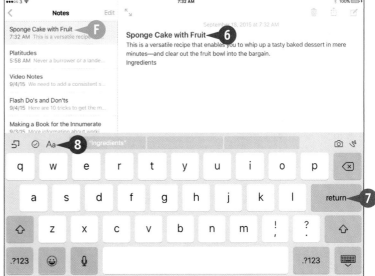

## TIPS

**What does the button with the curving arrow do?**
Tap this button, **More Actions** (↰), to display a pop-up command bar with three buttons. Tap **Undo** (↶) to undo an action. Tap **Redo** (↷) to redo an action you have undone. Tap **Paste** (📋) to paste in the contents of the Clipboard.

**Can I use styles and formatting in all my notes?**
Styles are available only in notes you store on your iPad or in iCloud. Basic formatting — boldface, italic, and underline — works for notes on Google, Exchange, and IMAP accounts as well as notes in iCloud.

continued ▶

The Notes app includes six built-in styles that enable you to format your notes with a title, headings, body text, bulleted lists, dashed lists, and numbered lists. By using these styles to format notes instead of using direct formatting, such as bold and italic, you can create structured notes that you can easily use in a word processing app.

You can also insert round check boxes to create lists from which you can check off completed items.

## Take Notes (continued)

The Style panel opens.

**9** Tap the style you want to apply.

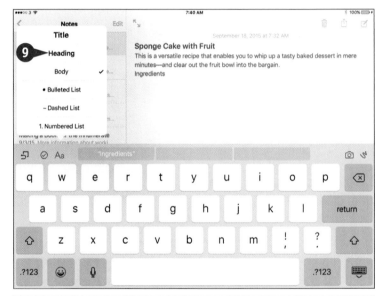

The Style panel closes.

**G** The paragraph takes on the style.

**10** Tap **Check Box** (⊘).

**H** A round check box appears in the text.

**11** Type the text to accompany the check box.

**12** Tap **return**.

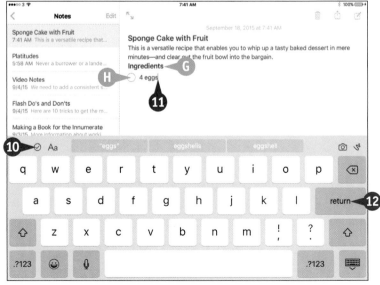

Another round check box appears at the beginning of the next paragraph, continuing the list.

**13** When you want to stop using check boxes, tap **return** twice in succession.

**Note:** You can also stop using check boxes by tapping **Check Box** (⊘) on a paragraph that contains a check box.

**I** To add a photo, tap **Photo** (📷). You can then tap **Photo Library** to use an existing photo or tap **Take Photo or Video** to use the camera.

**14** To add a drawing, tap **Drawing** (✎).

The Drawing screen appears, showing the drawing tools.

**15** Tap the pen you want to use.

**16** Tap the color.

**17** Draw lines or shapes.

**J** You can tap **Ruler** to display a ruler.

**K** To erase part of a drawing, tap **Eraser** and then tap what you want to remove. To erase all the drawing, tap **Erase All**.

**18** Tap **Done**.

The drawing appears in the note.

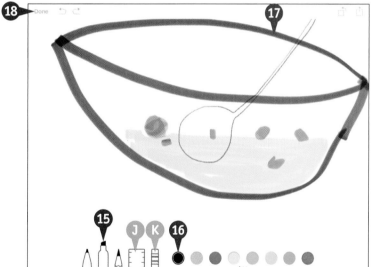

## TIPS

**What else can I add to notes?**
For notes stored on your iPad or in iCloud, you can insert maps and web addresses — URLs — as well as pictures and drawings.

**How do I move a note from one account or folder to another?**
In the Notes pane, swipe left on the note you want to move. The Move button and Delete button appear on the right of the note. Tap **Move** to display the Folders pane. You can then tap the folder to which you want to move the note. You can tap **New Folder** and create a new folder to which you want to move the note.

# Find Your Location with the Maps App

The Maps app can pinpoint your location by using known Wi-Fi networks or — on cellular iPads — by using GPS (Global Positioning System) satellites or cellular towers. You can view your location on a road map or a satellite picture, either with or without place names. You can switch among map types to find the most useful one. To help you get your bearings, the Tracking feature in the Maps app can show you which direction you are facing.

## Find Your Location with the Maps App

**①** Press **Home**.

The Home screen appears.

**②** Tap **Maps** (🧭).

The Maps screen appears.

**Ⓐ** A blue dot shows your current location. The expanding circle around the blue dot shows that Maps is determining your location.

**Note:** It may take a minute for Maps to work out your location accurately. While Maps determines the location, the blue dot moves, even though the iPad remains stationary.

**③** Tap and pinch in with two fingers.

**Note:** You can tap and pinch out with two fingers to zoom in.

The map zooms out, showing a larger area.

**④** Tap **Information** (ⓘ).

The Map Options dialog opens.

**⑤** Tap **Satellite**.

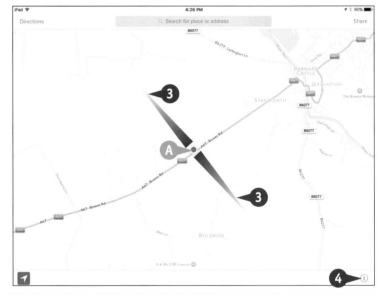

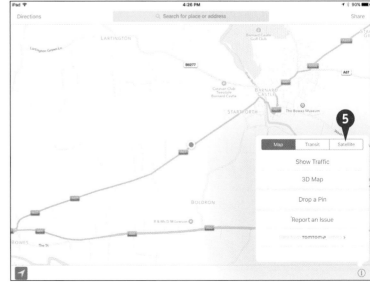

The Satellite view appears.

**B** You can tap **Hide Labels** to hide the place names.

**6** Tap **Show Traffic**.

The dialog closes.

**C** Traffic information appears where it is available.

**7** Tap **Location** (⊲ changes to ◤) to turn on the Location service.

**8** Tap **Location** (◤ changes to ◢).

**D** The Compass arrow appears (●). The red arrow indicates north.

**E** The map turns to show the direction the iPad is facing, so that you can orient yourself.

**TIP**

**What does the blue sector in the location circle mean?**
The blue sector shows the direction the iPad is facing. Use this sector to help yourself align the map with the landscape.

# Find Directions with the Maps App

The Maps app on your iPad can give you directions to where you want to go. Maps can also show you current traffic congestion to help you identify the most viable route for a journey.

Maps displays driving directions by default, but you can also display walking and, in some cities, mass transit directions.

## Find Directions with the Maps App

1 Press **Home**.

The Home screen appears.

2 Tap **Maps** (▣).

The Maps app opens.

3 Tap **Directions**.

The Directions dialog opens.

Ⓐ You can tap **Home** (🏠), **Work** (🏢), or **Favorites** (♥) to use one of your preset locations.

4 Tap **Start**, and type the start location for the directions.

**Note:** If the starting location or ending location is an address in the Contacts app, start typing the name, and then tap the match in the list.

5 Type the end location.

Ⓑ You can tap **Switch Places** (↕) to switch the start location and end location.

6 Tap **Route**.

Maps displays the driving routes.

Ⓒ The green pin marks the start.

Ⓓ The red pin marks the end.

Ⓔ You can tap a time button to view a different route. The time button changes to blue to indicate it is active.

7 Tap **Start**.

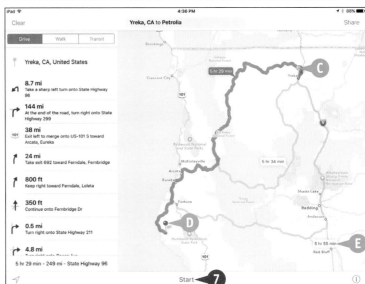

The first screen of directions appears.

**8** Tap, scroll, and zoom as needed to follow the directions.

**F** If you want to see the entire route on the map, tap **Overview**.

**9** Tap **List Steps** (≣).

**G** The Directions panel appears, showing a complete list of the directions.

**H** You can tap a direction to display it on the map.

**10** Tap on the map outside the Directions panel.

The Directions panel closes.

---

**TIPS**

**How do I get directions for walking?**

After getting the directions, tap **Walk** at the top of the left pane to display the distance and time for walking the route. Be aware that walking directions may be inaccurate. Before walking the route, check that it does not send you across pedestrian-free bridges or through rail tunnels.

**How do I get Transit directions?**

After getting the directions, tap **Transit** at the top of the left pane to display public transit options. Tap **Information** (ⓘ) for the route you would like to view. You can then tap a step in the route to zoom in on it.

# Explore with 3D Flyovers

Maps is not only great for finding out where you are and for getting directions to places, but it can also show you 3D flyovers of the places on the map.

After switching on the 3D feature, you can zoom in and out, pan around, and move backward and forward.

## Explore with 3D Flyovers

**1** Press **Home**.

The Home screen appears.

**2** Tap **Maps** (🗺️).

The Maps screen appears.

**3** Display the area of interest in the middle of the screen. For example, tap and drag the map, or search for the location you want.

**4** Tap **Information** (ⓘ).

The Map Options dialog opens.

**5** Tap **3D Map**.

The screen switches to 3D view.

**6** Pinch out with two fingers to zoom in.

**Note:** You can pinch in with two fingers to zoom out.

**7** Tap and drag to scroll the map.

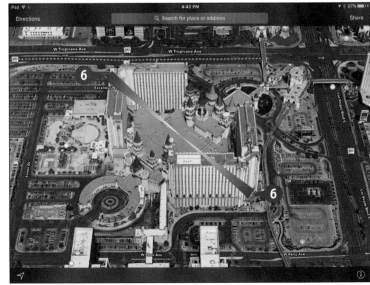

**8** Place two fingers on the screen and twist clockwise or counterclockwise to rotate the view.

Ⓐ The Compass arrow () appears. The red arrow indicates north. You can tap this icon to restore the direction to north.

**Note:** Pan and zoom as needed to explore the area.

**9** Tap and drag up with two fingers.

The viewing angle decreases.

**Note:** Tap and drag down with two fingers to make the viewing angle steeper.

**10** Tap **Information** (ⓘ).

The Map Options dialog opens.

**11** Tap **2D Map**.

The two-dimensional view reappears.

**TIP**

**What does 3D View do when I am not using the Satellite map?**

When you tap to switch on 3D View with the regular map or the Transit map displayed rather than the Satellite map, Maps tilts the map at an angle, as you might do with a paper map. In cities, building shapes appear when you zoom in on the map, enabling you to see the layout without using the full detail of the satellite photos.

# Using the Maps App's Favorites and Contacts

When you want to return to a location easily in the Maps app, you can create a favorite for the location. Similarly, you can add a location to your contacts, so that you can access it either from the Contacts app or from the Maps app. You can either create a new contact or add the location to an existing contact. You can also return quickly to locations you have visited recently but not marked with a favorite or a contact.

## Using the Maps App's Favorites and Contacts

**1** Press **Home**.

The Home screen appears.

**2** Tap **Maps** (◉).

The Maps screen appears.

**3** Find the place for which you want to create a favorite. For example, tap and drag the map, or search for the location you want.

**4** Tap and hold the place.

If the place has a map listing, Maps displays an information label. If not, Maps drops a pin on the place and displays a Dropped Pin label.

**Note:** To get rid of a pin you have dropped, tap the pin to display its pop-up label, and then tap the label. In the Location dialog that opens, tap **Remove Pin**.

**5** Tap **More** ( > ) on the label.

The Location dialog opens.

**Note:** You can quickly get directions to or from this location by tapping **Directions to Here** or **Directions from Here** in the Location dialog.

**6** Tap **Share** (⬆).

The Share sheet opens.

**7** Tap **Add to Favorites** (★).

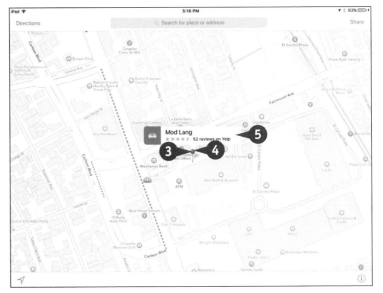

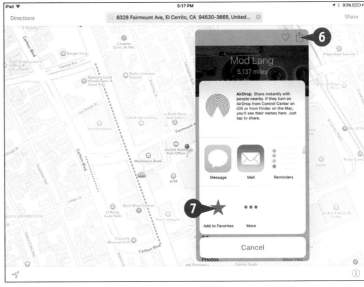

230

The Add to Favorites dialog opens.

**8** Type the name for the favorite. Alternatively, you can accept the default name, if there is one.

**9** Tap **Save**.

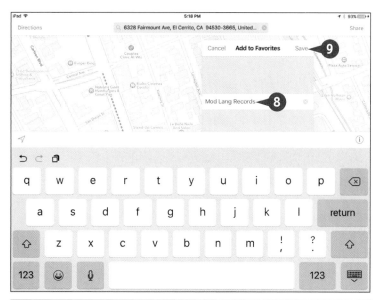

The Add to Favorites dialog closes.

The Location dialog remains open.

**10** To create a new contact record for this location, tap **Create New Contact**. In the New Contact dialog that opens, type the details for the contact, and then tap **Done**.

**11** To add this location to an existing contact record, tap **Add to Existing Contact**. On the Contacts screen that appears, tap the contact to which you want to add the location.

---

**TIP**

**How do I go to a location for which I have created a favorite or a contact?**

In the Maps app, tap the address box to display the Recents dialog. You can then tap a recently visited place in the list or tap **Favorites** to display the Favorites dialog. This dialog has three tabs: Favorites, Recents, and Contacts. Tap the appropriate tab to show its contents, and then tap the favorite, contact, or recent place you want to display.

# Using Clock, Stopwatch, Timer, and World Clock

The Clock app on your iPad provides four helpful time-keeping features. The World Clock feature enables you to keep track of the time easily in different cities; you can display a clock full screen to use your iPad as a timepiece. The Alarm feature lets you set as many alarms as you need, each with a different schedule and your choice of sound. The Stopwatch feature allows you to time events to the hundredth of a second. The Timer feature enables you to count down a set amount of time and play a sound when the timer ends.

## Open the Clock App and Set Up the World Clock

To open the Clock app, press **Home** and then tap **Clock** (⊙) on the Home screen. The app displays the screen for the feature you last used. You can switch among the four features by tapping **World Clock**, **Alarm**, **Stopwatch**, or **Timer** at the bottom of the screen.

Tap **World Clock** (⊕ changes to ⊕) at the bottom of the screen to display the World Clock screen. The World Clock shows a dark face for a clock where the local time is between 6:00PM and 5:59AM and a white face for a clock where the local time is between 6:00AM and 5:59PM.

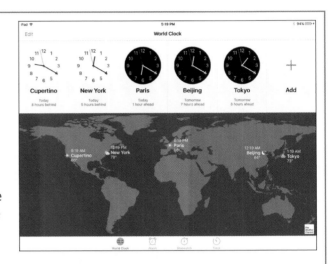

To add cities, tap **Add** (+) and then either type the start of the city name or simply browse the list. Tap the city you want to add, and it appears at the bottom of the list on the World Clock screen.

You can edit the list of cities by tapping **Edit**. To remove a city, tap **Delete** (⊖), and then tap **Delete**. To change the order, tap a handle (≡) and drag up or down. Tap **Done** when you finish editing.

## Display a Clock Full-Screen

To display a clock full-screen, tap **World Clock** (⊕ changes to ⊕) and then tap the clock you want to show.

Swipe left or right or touch the dots at the bottom of the screen to change the clock displayed.

Tap **World Clock** (<) when you want to return to the World Clock screen.

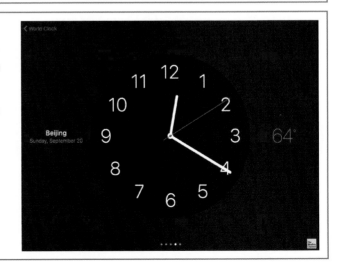

## Set Alarms

Tap **Alarm** (⏰ changes to ⏰) at the bottom of the screen to display the Alarm screen, which shows the current alarms with switches for enabling and disabling them.

Tap **Add** (+) to start creating a new alarm. In the Add Alarm dialog, spin the dials to set the time. To create a repeating alarm, tap **Repeat** and then tap the days in the Repeat dialog. Tap **Back** (<) to return to the Add Alarm dialog, then tap **Label**, type a descriptive name for the alarm, and tap **Done**. Tap **Sound** and choose the sound to play, and set the **Snooze** switch to On (⬤) or Off ( ), as needed. Tap **Save** to save the alarm.

## Time Events with the Stopwatch

Tap **Stopwatch** (⏱ changes to ⏱) at the bottom of the screen to display the Stopwatch screen. You can then tap **Start** to start the stopwatch running.

If you need to mark lap times, tap **Lap** at the appropriate points. The elapsed lap times appear at the bottom of the screen. The current lap time appears below the main time readout.

Tap **Stop** to stop the stopwatch. You can then tap **Start** to restart the stopwatch or tap **Reset** to reset it so it is ready for its next use.

## Use the Timer

Tap **Timer** (⏲ changes to ⏲) at the bottom of the screen to display the Timer screen. Spin the Hours dial and the Minutes dial to set the amount of time you want to count down. Tap the current sound name below the dials to display the When Timer Ends dialog, tap the sound you want to play or the **Stop Playing** action, and then tap **Set**. You can then tap **Start** to start the timer.

If you need to interrupt the timer, tap **Cancel** or **Pause**. Otherwise, when the timer sound plays, tap the prompt to stop it.

The Stop Playing action enables you to play music for a period of time and have it stop automatically — for example, to lull you to sleep.

# Using Apple Pay

If your iPad is an iPad Air 2, iPad Pro, or an iPad mini 3 or a later model, you can use Apple's payment service to make payments online using your iPad. Earlier iPad models do not have this capability, because it requires authentication using the Touch ID feature, which these models do not have.

Apple's payment service is called Apple Pay. You can use it at a wide variety of online stores for convenience and security. If you have an iPhone 6 or a later model, you can also use Apple Pay to make contactless payments at payment terminals.

## Understand How Apple Pay Works

The Apple Pay service links with the four major payment networks — Visa, MasterCard, American Express, and Discover — and enables you to use debit cards and credit cards issued on these networks by a wide variety of banks.

Apple Pay uses the Near Field Communications, or NFC, chip built into the iPhone 6 and later iPhone models to make contactless payments with card readers. On the iPhone, a chip called the Secure Element stores your payment information in an encrypted format for security.

At this writing, no iPad model has an NFC chip, so you cannot make contactless payments using an iPad. But

on iPad models that include the Touch ID feature, you can use Apple Pay to make payments online quickly, easily, and securely in Apple Pay–compatible apps.

## Set Up Your Means of Payment

Before you can make a payment with Apple Pay, you must set up your means of payment. To do so, you add the details of your debit card or credit card to Apple Pay.

When you first set up your iPad, iOS prompts you to add a credit card or debit card to Apple Pay. You can add other cards by using the Settings app. Press **Home** to display the Home screen, and then tap **Settings** (⚙) to display the Settings screen. Tap **Wallet & Apple Pay** (▣) to display the Wallet & Apple Pay screen, tap **Add Credit or Debit Card**, and then follow the prompts. You can either use the iPad's rear camera to recognize

the card's details or tap **Enter Card Details Manually** and type in the details.

The iPad may also prompt you to add the credit card or debit card associated with your iTunes account to Apple Pay.

## Make a Payment Online with Your iPad

After setting up Apple Pay, you can use it to make payments online using your iPad. You can make payments in various apps, including the Safari web browser. You can make payments to any retailer that accepts Apple Pay.

When an app displays a button with the Apple Pay logo on a payment screen, you can tap that button to use Apple Pay. On the subsequent screen, you use one of the fingers you have registered for Touch ID on **Home** to confirm the purchase and authenticate your identity.

## Make a Payment at a Payment Terminal with an iPhone or Apple Watch

If you have an iPhone 6 or a later model, such as an iPhone 6s or iPhone 6s Plus, you can use Apple Pay to make payments easily at payment terminals located in retailers, cafés and restaurants, and places such as stations or airports.

Before you can make a payment, you must set up your means of payment on the iPhone. Apple Pay does not sync credit and debit cards from one iOS device to another, so you must add to Apple Pay on the iPhone each card you want to use for Apple Pay. Press **Home** to display the Home screen, and then tap **Settings** (⚙) to display the Settings screen. Tap **Wallet & Apple Pay** (▭) to display the Wallet & Apple Pay screen, tap **Add Credit or Debit Card**, and then follow the prompts.

To make a payment, you simply bring your iPhone up to the payment terminal, verify the amount displayed on-screen, and place one of the fingers you have registered with Touch ID on **Home** to approve the transaction and authenticate your identity.

If you have an Apple Watch, you can use it to make payments at payment terminals. Because your Apple Watch is an accessory to your iPhone, Apple Watch picks up the cards you have added to your iPhone; you do not need to add them to Apple Watch separately.

# Using iCloud Drive

iCloud Drive is online storage that enables you to store your files securely "in the cloud" — in other words, on the Internet — so that you can access them from anywhere. You can upload your files to iCloud Drive using your Mac and then access them using your iPad, your iPhone, or other devices.

## Turn on iCloud Drive on Your Mac

Before you can use iCloud Drive on your Mac, you must turn it on. To do so, first click **Apple** (⬢) and **System Preferences** to open the System Preferences app, then click **iCloud** (☁) to display the iCloud pane.

Click **iCloud Drive** (☐ changes to ☑) to enable iCloud Drive. Then click **Options**. The Options dialog opens.

Click **Documents**. The Documents tab appears.

Click each check box (☐ changes to ☑, or ☑ changes to ☐) to specify which apps may store documents and data in iCloud.

You can click **Look Me Up By Email** to display the Look Me Up by Email tab, and then choose which apps can look you up by your Apple ID.

Click **Done** to close the Options dialog. You can then click **System Preferences** on the menu bar and click **Quit System Preferences** to close the System Preferences app.

## Put Files on iCloud Drive from Your Mac or PC

If you have files on your Mac or PC that you want to make available to yourself anywhere, so that you can access them from any Mac or PC or from your iPad or other iOS device, or other iOS device, upload them to iCloud Drive.

To upload files to iCloud Drive on the Mac, you use the Finder. First, click open space on the Desktop to activate the Finder, and then press ⌘+N to open a new Finder window. Click **iCloud Drive** in the Favorites section of the sidebar to display the contents of iCloud Drive.

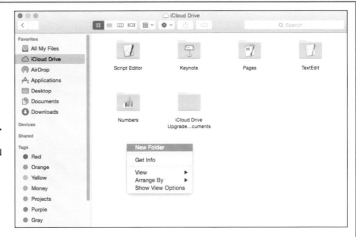

You can then create folders on iCloud Drive and copy files and folders to or from iCloud Drive using standard Finder techniques. For example, to create a new folder, Control+click, click **New Folder** on the context menu, type the name for the folder over the default name, and press Return.

To upload files to iCloud Drive on Windows, you use File Explorer or Windows Explorer, depending on which version of Windows you have. Open a File Explorer or Windows Explorer window to the iCloud Drive folder, in which you can use standard commands to create folders and copy and paste files.

## Put iCloud Drive on the Home Screen and Access iCloud Drive

On your iPad, you can use the iCloud Drive app to access your storage space on iCloud.

Various iCloud-enabled apps can connect directly to iCloud Drive to save files and to open files. In these apps, iCloud Drive appears in dialogs such as the Open dialog and the Save As dialog.

For easy access to iCloud Drive, you can put the iCloud Drive icon on the Home screen. To do so, press **Home**, tap **Settings** (⚙) to open the Settings app, and then tap **iCloud** (☁).

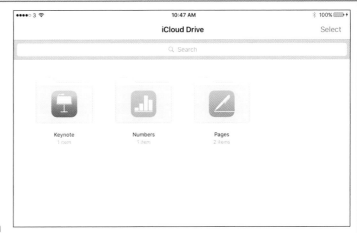

On the iCloud screen, tap **iCloud Drive** (☁) to display the iCloud Drive screen, and then set the **Show on Home Screen** switch to On (◯).

After adding iCloud Drive to the home screen, you can press **Home** and tap **iCloud Drive** (☁) to open the iCloud Drive app. You can then tap an app's folder to display the items it contains. From there, you can select an item and download it to your iPad.

# CHAPTER 9

# Playing Music, Videos, and Games

In addition to being a powerful handheld computer, your iPad is a full-scale music and video player and gaming device.

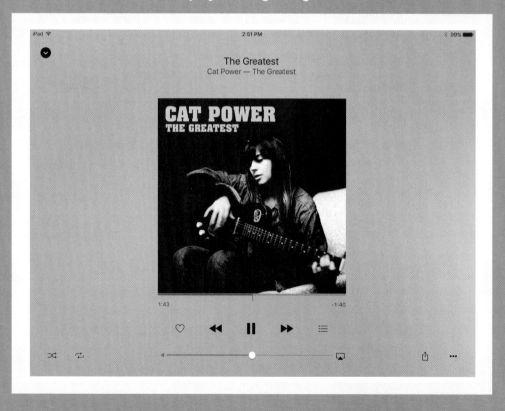

# Navigate the Music App and Set Preferences

The Music app enables you to enjoy music you have loaded on your iPhone, music you have stored on Apple's iTunes Match service, and music on Apple's Beats Radio and Apple Music services. This chapter shows the Music app with an Apple Music subscription active.

The Music app packs a wide range of functionality into its interface. If you have an Apple Music subscription, you will normally want to start with the For You feature, which enables you to set your musical preferences.

## Navigate the Music App and Set Preferences

1 Press **Home**.

The Home screen appears.

2 Tap **Music** ( ♪ ).

The Music app opens.

3 Tap **For You** (♡ changes to ♥).

The Tell Us What You Like screen appears, showing an array of floating circles, each representing a different music type.

4 Tap a circle to indicate you like that type.

The circle becomes larger.

Ⓐ You can tap **Reset** to reset your choices and start again.

5 Double-tap a circle to indicate you love the type.

The circle becomes much larger.

6 Tap and hold a circle to remove a type you do not like.

7 Tap **Next**.

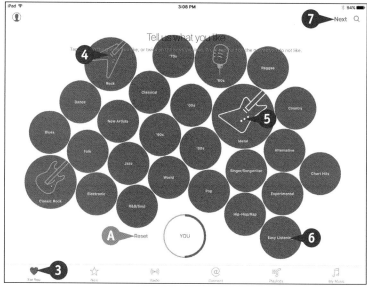

The Choose Three or More of Your Favorites screen appears.

Ⓑ You can tap **More artists** to display other artists.

⑧ Tap an artist you like.

⑨ Double-tap an artist you love.

⑩ Tap and hold a circle to remove an artist.

⑪ Tap **Done**.

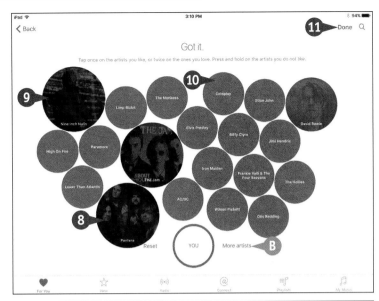

The For You screen shows suggested music.

Ⓒ If you want to change the artists the Music app chooses for you, tap **Account** (⨀). In the Account panel, tap **Choose Artists for You** to display the Tell Us What You Like screen. You can then select artists or tap **Reset** and start again.

⑫ Tap **New** (☆ changes to ★).

## TIP

**How does the Search function work?**

The Search function enables you to search both your own music and the Apple Music service. Tap **Search** (🔍) to display the Search screen and then type your search terms in the box at the top of the screen. Tap the **Apple Music** tab to see matching searches you can perform on Apple Music; you can then tap a search to perform it. Tap the **My Music** tab to see matching items in your music, broken down into categories such as Artists, Albums, or Songs; tap an item to go to it.

continued ▶

The Radio feature allows you to listen to Apple's Beats Radio station and a wide variety of other stations, while the Connect feature lets you connect to artists — or their social-media representatives — online.

From the Playlists screen, you can quickly access the playlists that come built into the Music app. You can also create and edit your own playlists. From the My Music screen, you can explore and play your own music.

## Navigate the Music App and Set Preferences (continued)

The New screen appears, showing suggested new music.

**D** You can tap **All Genres** and then tap a specific genre.

**E** You can tap **Radio** ((•)) changes to (•)) to listen to radio. See the section "Listen to iTunes Radio," later in this chapter, for details.

**13** Tap **Connect** (@ changes to @).

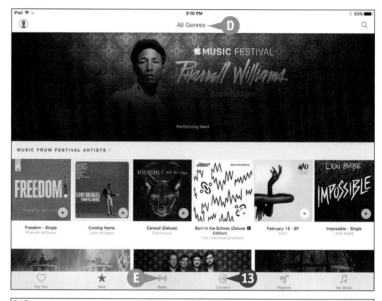

The Connect screen appears, showing artists and curators with whom you can connect.

**F** You can tap a post to display its full contents.

**14** Tap **Playlists** (≣♪ changes to ≣♪).

The Playlists screen appears.

(G) The Smart Playlist symbol (☼) marks a Smart Playlist, one that selects songs automatically based on rules you define, such as types of music or beats per minute.

(H) The playlist symbol (♫) marks a regular playlist.

(I) You can tap a playlist to display its contents.

(15) Tap **My Music** (♫ changes to ♫).

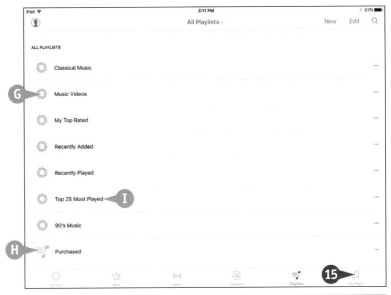

The My Music screen appears. See the next section, "Play Music Using the Music App," for details.

(J) You can tap the pop-up menu at the top to switch among music collections: Artists, Albums, Songs, Genres, Composers, and Compilations.

(K) You can set the **Only Offline Music** switch to On (◯ changes to ◉) to display only the music on your iPad. This is useful when you want to avoid streaming audio over the Internet connection.

**TIP**

**How do I put my music on my iPad from my computer?**
To copy music from your computer to your iPad, use iTunes. See the section "Choose Which Items to Sync from Your Computer" in Chapter 1 for details.

# Play Music Using the Music App

After loading music on your iPad, as described in the section "Choose Which Items to Sync from Your Computer" in Chapter 1, you can play it back using the Music app.

You can play music by song or by album, as described in this section. You can play songs in exactly the order you want by creating a custom playlist, as described in the section "Create a Music Playlist," later in this chapter. You can also play by artist, by genre, or by composer.

## Play Music Using the Music App

**1** Press **Home**.

The Home screen appears.

**2** Tap **Music** ( ♫ ).

The Music app opens.

**3** Tap **My Music** ( ♫ changes to ♫ ).

**Note:** The For You tab and the New tab appear only if you have an Apple Music subscription.

The My Music screen appears.

**4** Tap the pop-up menu. This shows the current category, such as Artists.

The pop-up menu opens.

**5** Tap the button by which to sort. This example uses **Albums**.

The list of albums appears.

**Note:** Scroll up or down the screen as needed to reach the album you want to play.

**A** You can tap the letter that starts the name of the item you want to play. That section of the list appears.

**B** Tap above the letter A in the navigation list to go back to the top of the screen.

**6** Tap the album to display the songs from it that are on your iPad.

**7** Tap a song.

The song starts playing.

**8** Tap **Shuffle** to turn on shuffling (⤨ changes to ⤨). Tap **Shuffle** to turn off shuffling (⤨ changes to ⤨).

**C** You can tap **Love** (♡ changes to ❤) to indicate you love the song.

**Note:** The Music app uses your Love designations to hone its recommendations for you.

**9** Tap **Now Playing**, the button that shows the current song's details.

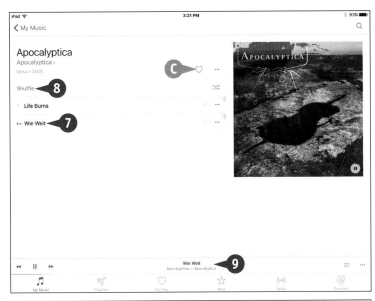

The Now Playing screen shows the album cover and play controls.

**10** Tap and drag the playhead — the vertical white line — to change the position in the song.

**11** To repeat the current list, tap **Repeat** (⟳ changes to ⟳). To repeat the current song only, tap **Repeat** (⟳ or ⟳ changes to ⟳).

**12** Tap **Up Next** (☰) to display the Up Next panel, which shows the songs set to play next. From here, you can tap another song to start it playing, tap **Add** to add other songs, or tap **Clear** to clear the list.

**13** Tap **Back** (⌄) to display the previous screen.

**TIP**

**How can I control the Music app's playback when I am using another app?**
You can quickly control the Music app from Control Center. Tap and swipe up from the bottom of the screen to open Control Center, and then use the playback controls on the left side.

# Play Videos Using the Videos App

To play videos — such as movies, TV shows, or music videos — you use the Videos app. You can play back a video on the iPad screen, which is handy when you are traveling; on a TV to which you connect the iPad; or on a TV connected to an Apple TV box. Using a TV is great when you need to share a movie or other video with family, friends, or colleagues.

## Play Videos Using the Videos App

**1** Press **Home**.

The Home screen appears.

**Note:** You can also play most videos that are included on web pages. To do so, press **Home**, tap Safari ( ), navigate to the page, and then tap the video.

**2** Tap **Videos** ( ).

The Videos screen appears.

**3** Tap the category of videos you want to view, such as **Home Videos**.

The videos in that category appear.

**4** Tap the video you want to play.

The video starts playing.

**Note:** Your iPad plays video in the orientation it was shot or produced — typically landscape orientation. So if you are holding the iPad in its upright, portrait orientation, turn it on its side for viewing the video.

**5** When you need to control playback, tap the screen.

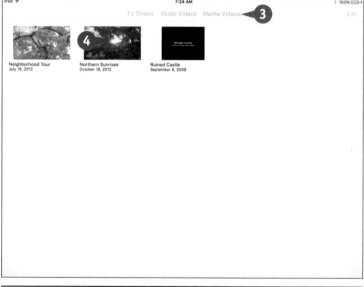

The playback controls appear, and you can pause the video, move forward, or take other actions.

Ⓐ You can drag the playhead to move quickly forward or backward through the movie.

Ⓑ For some videos, you can tap **Full Screen** (⬜ changes to ⬛, or ⬛ changes to ⬜) to switch between full-screen and letterboxed views.

Ⓒ You can drag the **Volume** slider to change the volume.

Ⓓ You can tap **Picture-in-Picture** (⬛) to switch to Picture-in-Picture view. Picture-in-Picture (⬛) appears only if your iPad supports it.

⑥ Tap **Done** when you want to stop playing the video.

The video's information screen appears.

Ⓔ You can tap another video category to display that category.

⑦ Tap **Back** (<).

The category screen from which you opened the video appears.

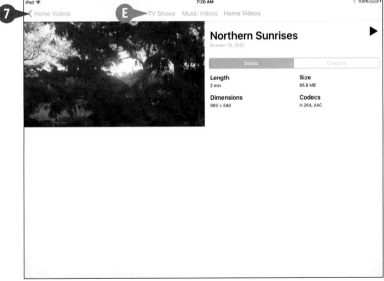

---

**How do I play back videos on my television from my iPad?**
If you have an Apple TV or AirPlay-compatible device, use AirPlay, as explained in the next section, "Play Music and Videos Using AirPlay." Otherwise, use the Apple Lightning Digital AV Adapter and an HDMI cable to connect your iPad to a TV.

# Play Music and Videos Using AirPlay

Using the AirPlay feature, you can play music from your iPad on remote speakers connected to an AirPlay-compatible device such as an AirPort Express or Apple TV. Similarly, you can play video from your iPad on a TV or monitor connected to an Apple TV. Even better, you can use the iOS feature called AirPlay Mirroring to display an iPad app on a TV or monitor. For example, you can display a web page in Safari on your TV screen.

## Play Music and Videos Using AirPlay

### Play Music on External Speakers Using AirPlay

1. In the Music app, start playing the song you want to hear.

2. Tap and swipe up from the bottom of the screen.

   Control Center opens.

3. Tap **AirPlay** (🔲).

   The AirPlay dialog opens.

4. Tap the speakers or Apple TV you want to use.

5. Tap outside the AirPlay dialog.

   The AirPlay dialog closes.

   The AirPlay button shows the device you selected.

   The music starts playing through the AirPlay device.

6. Tap in the Music app above Control Center.

   Control Center closes, and the Music app appears full screen.

248

## Play a Video from Your iPad to Your TV's Screen

**1** In the Videos app, open the video you want to play.

**2** Tap and swipe up from the bottom of the screen.

Control Center opens.

**3** Tap **AirPlay** (⬜).

**4** Tap the AirPlay device to use.

The video content appears on the TV or monitor connected to the AirPlay device. The Videos app displays a message that the content is playing on an AirPlay device.

## Display an iPad App on Your TV's Screen

**1** With the app open (Keynote in this example), navigate to the content you want to display.

**2** Tap and swipe up from the bottom of the screen to open Control Center.

**3** Tap **AirPlay** (⬜).

**4** Tap the AirPlay device.

**5** Set the **Mirroring** switch to On (⬜).

**6** Tap outside the AirPlay dialog.

The TV or monitor mirrors the iPad screen.

**7** Tap in the app above Control Center to close Control Center.

---

## TIPS

**Why does the AirPlay button not appear in Control Center?**
The AirPlay button appears only when your iPad is connected to a wireless network to which AirPlay devices are attached. If you use multiple wireless networks, make sure your iPad is connected to the right network.

**Can I launch AirPlay without opening Control Center?**
Yes — if an app displays an AirPlay icon, tap that icon to launch AirPlay from within that app.

# Create a Music Playlist

Instead of playing individual songs or playing a CD's songs from start to finish, you can create a playlist that contains only the songs you want in your preferred order. Playlists are a great way to enjoy music on your iPad. You can either create a standard playlist by putting the songs in order yourself or use the Genius Playlist feature to have the Music app create the playlist for you. See the next section, "Configure iPad Audio Settings," for instructions on enabling the Genius feature.

## Create a Music Playlist

**1** Press **Home**.

The Home screen appears.

**2** Tap **Music** ( ♫ ).

The Music screen appears.

**3** Tap **Playlists** ( ≡♫ changes to ≡♪ ).

The Playlists screen appears.

**A** When browsing playlists, you can tap the pop-up menu and then tap **All Playlists** to view all your playlists, tap **Apple Music Playlists** to view your Apple Music playlists, or tap **My Playlists** to view your personal playlists.

**4** Tap **New**.

The New Playlist screen appears.

**5** Type the name for the playlist.

**6** Optionally, type a description for the playlist.

**7** Tap **Add Songs** ( ⊕ ).

The Add Music screen appears.

**8** Tap the category by which you want to browse: **Artists**, **Albums**, **Songs**, **Music Videos**, **Genres**, **Composers**, **Compilations**, or **Playlists**. This example uses **Songs**.

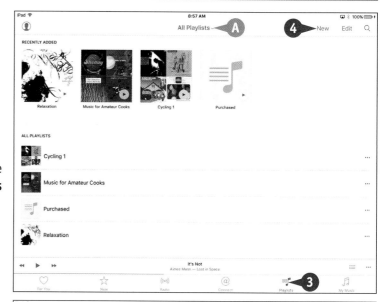

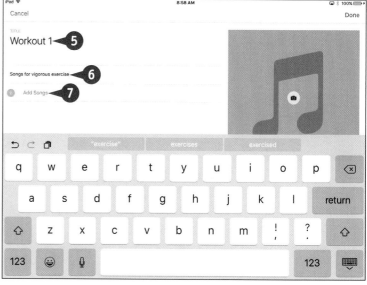

The Songs screen appears.

**9** Tap **Add** ( + ) for each song you want to add, or simply tap the song's button ( + changes to ✓).

**10** Tap **Done**.

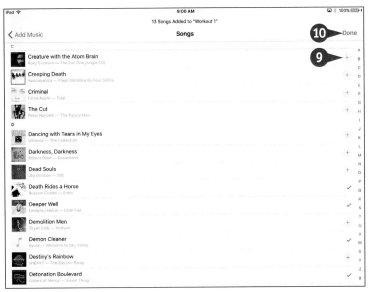

The playlist appears.

**11** Tap and drag a song up or down to move it.

**B** To remove a song, you can tap **Delete** (⊖) and then tap the textual **Delete** button.

**C** To add songs, you can tap **Add Songs** (⊕).

**12** Tap **Done** when you finish editing the playlist.

The playlist appears.

**13** Tap a song to start the playlist playing.

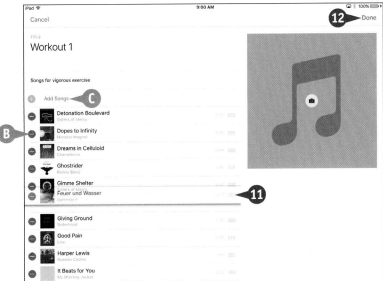

## TIP

**How do I delete a playlist?**

In the Music app, tap **Playlists** (▤ changes to ▤) to display the Playlists screen. Tap **Edit** to open the screen for editing. You can then tap **Delete** (⊖) to the left of the playlist and then tap the textual **Delete** button.

You can delete only playlists you have created on your iPad. To remove a playlist you have synced from iTunes, deselect the playlist in iTunes and sync again.

# Configure iPad Audio Settings

To make your music sound the way you want it, you can apply an Equalizer, or EQ, preset. The EQ offers presets that help to accentuate music including Rock, Hip Hop, Jazz, Piano, and Vocal Latin. The EQ even includes Spoken Word and Vocal Booster presets.

EQ presets change the sound quality as soon as you apply them. Some settings are more noticeable than others. Which EQ preset is best depends on your music, your speakers or headphones, and your ears.

## Configure iPad Audio Settings

**1** Press **Home**.

The Home screen appears.

**2** Tap **Settings** (⚙).

The Settings screen appears.

**3** Tap **Music** ( ♪ ).

The Music settings appear.

**4** Set the **Sound Check** switch to On (⬤) to have iTunes play songs at the same volume level, or to Off ( ) to play each song at its own level.

**5** Tap **EQ**.

The EQ options appear.

**Note:** The EQ options are audio presets that you can choose to customize audio playback on your iPad.

**6** Tap an EQ option to select it.

**Note:** Playing music with an EQ preset uses a little more battery power than playing without a preset, but not usually enough to worry about.

**7** Tap **Music** (<).

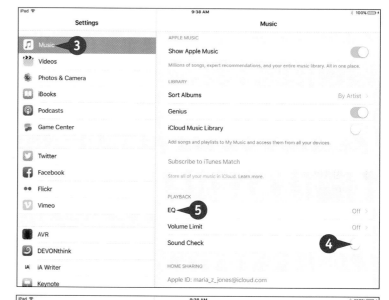

The Music screen appears again.

**8** Tap **Sort Albums** to display the Sort Albums screen; tap **By Artist** or **By Title** to specify how to sort the album; and then tap **Music** (<) to return to the Music screen.

**9** Set the **Genius** switch to On ( ) if you want to use the Genius feature, which automatically creates playlists for you.

**10** Tap **Volume Limit** to set a maximum volume at which audio will play on your iPad.

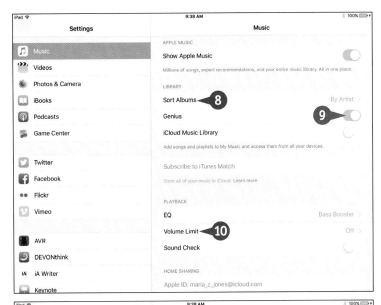

The Volume Limit screen appears.

**11** Drag the slider to the desired level.

**12** Tap **Music** (<).

The Music screen appears once more.

## TIPS

**Can I keep the volume limit from being changed after I set it?**

Yes. Set the volume limit as described in this section, and then apply restrictions. In the Settings app, tap **General** ( ), and then tap **Restrictions**. Tap **Enable Restrictions**, and then enter a passcode to lock the restrictions. On the Restrictions screen, tap **Volume Limit**. On the Volume Limit screen, tap **Don't Allow Changes**.

**Should I use the Sound Check feature?**

This is entirely up to you, so try Sound Check and see if it suits you. Sound Check reduces the variations in volume between songs at the expense of dynamic range, so music tends to lose impact when Sound Check is on.

# Listen to iTunes Radio

The Radio feature in the Music app enables you to listen to Apple's Beats 1 global radio station and to preset, curated stations that play on demand. You can also create custom stations based on music you like, quickly access music on the iTunes Store, and share songs and stations with others.

You can listen to iTunes Radio for free. Apple's main music service, Apple Music, requires a subscription. This is either a $9.99-per-month individual subscription or a $14.99-per-month family subscription, which covers up to six people.

## Listen to iTunes Radio

**1** Press **Home**.

The Home screen appears.

**2** Tap **Music** ( ♫ ).

The Music app opens.

**3** Tap **Radio** (( (•) ) changes to (◉)).

The Radio screen appears.

**A** You can tap **Listen Now** to listen to the Beats 1 station, which appears at the top of the screen.

**B** The Recently Played list appears below Beats 1.

**4** Tap and drag up to scroll down.

The Featured Stations list appears.

**C** You can tap **Play** (▶) to start a station playing.

**5** Tap and drag up to scroll down further.

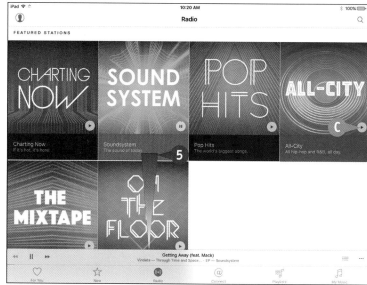

The list of genre stations appears.

**6** Tap the station you want to play.

The station starts playing.

The station appears on the Now Playing button.

**D** You can tap **Pause** (❚❚) to pause playback.

**E** You can tap **Skip** (▶▶) to skip to the next track.

**7** Tap **Now Playing**.

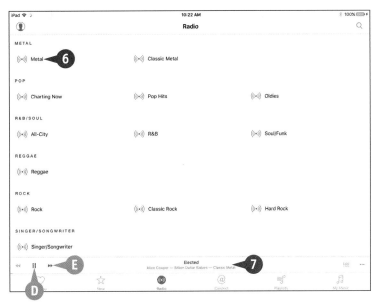

The Now Playing screen appears.

**F** You can tap **Back** (⌄) to return to the Radio screen.

**G** You can drag the playhead to move through the song.

**H** You can drag the volume control to change the volume.

**8** To take other actions, tap **More** (⋯).

The More dialog opens.

**I** You can tap **Add to a Playlist** to add the song to a playlist.

**J** You can tap **Show in iTunes Store** to display the song in the iTunes Store app.

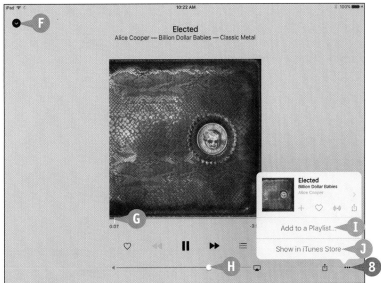

---

**TIP**

**Why can I not skip this unlistenable song?**
iTunes Radio lets you skip a maximum of six songs between ads. But if you have a subscription to the iTunes Match service from Apple, you can skip as many songs as you want.

# Enjoy Podcasts and Learn with iTunes U

**Y**ou can use your iPad to watch or listen to podcasts, video or audio programs released via the Internet. You can find podcasts covering many different topics by using the free Podcasts app from Apple. Podcasts can be entertaining, educational, or both.

Similarly, you can use the iTunes U app to access podcasts containing free educational content. iTunes U also acts as a portal to other types of content, including paid material. You may need to download iTunes U from the App Store.

## Enjoy Podcasts and Learn with iTunes U

**1** Press **Home**.

The Home screen appears.

**2** Tap **Podcasts** (⦿).

The Podcasts app opens, showing either the My Podcasts screen or the Unplayed screen.

**A** At first, when you have added no podcasts, you see an informational message.

**3** Tap **Featured** (☆ changes to ★) or **Top Charts** (☰ changes to ☰). This example uses **Featured**.

The Featured screen appears.

**B** You can tap **Categories** and then tap the category of podcasts you want to see.

The category's screen appears.

**Note:** You can also search for podcasts by tapping **Search** (🔍 changes to 🔍) and then typing search terms in the Search box on the Search screen.

**4** Tap a podcast that interests you.

The information screen for the podcast appears.

⑤ Tap **Subscribe** if you want to subscribe to the podcast, downloading future updates automatically.

⑥ Tap **Download** (⬇) to download an episode of the podcast.

⑦ Tap **Unplayed** (▶ changes to ▶) or **My Podcasts** (🎙 changes to 🎙). This example uses **Unplayed**.

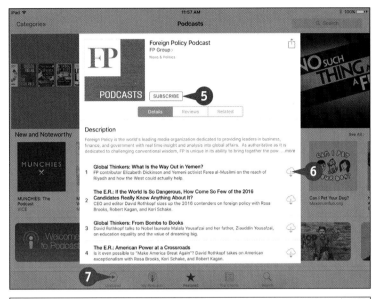

The Unplayed screen appears, showing the unplayed episodes of podcasts.

Your library appears, now showing the podcast or podcasts you have added.

⑧ Tap the episode you want to play.

The episode starts playing.

**Note:** If the episode's description expands when you tap it, tap again to start the episode playing.

## TIP

### How do I use iTunes U?

iTunes U works in a similar way to the Podcasts app. Press **Home**, and then tap **iTunes U** to launch the app. Tap **Featured**, **Charts**, **Browse**, or **Search** to display the associated screen, and then use it to find a lecture that interests you. After that, tap **Library** to display the Library screen, and then tap the item you want to play.

# Sign In to Game Center

Game Center is a social gaming feature included in OS X and in iOS, the operating system for the iPhone, iPad, and iPod touch. Game Center enables you to take part in a wide range of single-player and multiplayer games.

To start using Game Center, you sign in using your Apple ID. If you do not yet have an Apple ID, you can create one for free within minutes by tapping Create New Apple ID at the bottom of the Game Center setup screen.

## Sign In to Game Center

**1** Press **Home**.

The Home screen appears.

**2** Tap **Game Center** ( ).

The Game Center setup screen appears.

**3** Type your Apple ID.

**4** Type your password.

**5** Tap **Sign In**.

The Create a Nickname screen appears.

**6** Type the nickname you want to use for Game Center.

**Note:** Your Game Center nickname must be unique. If it is not, the setup routine prompts you to choose another nickname.

**7** Tap **Next**.

The Privacy screen appears.

**8** Set the **Public Profile** switch to On ( ) if you want everyone to be able to see you. Set this switch to Off ( ) if you want to be hidden from other players.

**9** Tap **Next**.

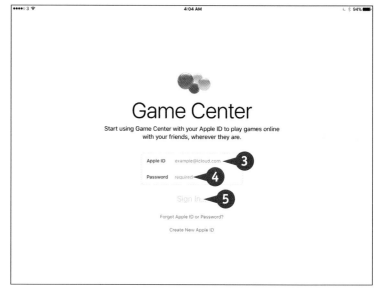

The Friend Recommendations screen appears.

**10** Set the **Contacts** switch to On (⬤) if you want to upload your iCloud contacts to Game Center and get personalized friend recommendations. Otherwise, set this switch to Off (  ).

**11** Set the **Facebook** switch to On (⬤) if you want to upload your Facebook contacts to Game Center so you can get personalized friend recommendations. Otherwise, set this switch to Off (  ).

**12** Tap **Next**.

The Me screen appears.

**A** You can tap **add photo** to add a photo to your account. Adding a photo of yourself can help your friends recognize you.

**B** You can tap **Enter status** and type your current status for others to see.

You can start using Game Center as explained in the next section, "Add and Play Games with Game Center."

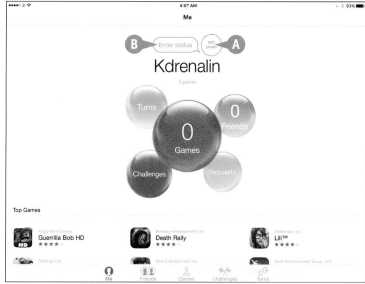

## TIPS

**Should I set the Public Profile switch to On or Off?**

Generally it is better to err on the side of caution and set the **Public Profile** switch to Off (  ) while you are familiarizing yourself with Game Center. After you have explored Game Center, you can decide whether to make yourself publicly visible on it.

**Should I upload my Facebook and iCloud contacts to Game Center?**

Uploading your contacts can be a great way to get started quickly with Game Center. But here, too, you may prefer to take a gradual approach and explore Game Center before uploading your contacts.

# Add and Play Games with Game Center

After setting up your account, as explained in the previous section, "Sign In to Game Center," you can play games with Game Center.

If your iPad already contains games that work with Game Center, the games will be ready to play when you launch Game Center. You can add further games by opening the App Store application from Game Center and downloading either free or purchased games.

## Add and Play Games with Game Center

**1** Press **Home**.

The Home screen appears.

**2** Tap **Game Center** (🎮).

Game Center logs you in.

The Me screen appears.

**3** Tap **Games** (♟ changes to ♟).

**A** From the Me screen, you can also tap **Games** to reach the Games screen.

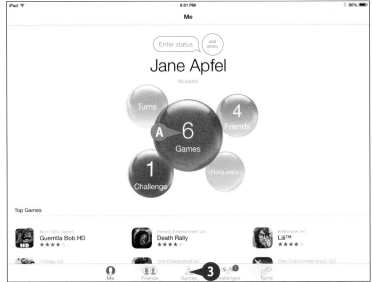

The Games screen appears.

**B** The Recommended list shows games you do not have.

**Note:** In the Recommended list, "Based on" means that the recommendation is based on a game you have, not on the game mentioned.

**C** The My iOS Games list shows the games you have.

**D** To launch a game you have, you can tap it in the My iOS Games list.

**4** Tap a game that interests you.

The game's screen appears.

**5** Tap **Free** or the price button if you want to buy the game.

The Install button appears in place of the Free button or price button.

**6** Tap **Install**.

The Apple ID Password dialog appears.

**7** Type your password.

**8** Tap **OK**.

Your iPad downloads and installs the app.

**9** After the installation finishes, tap **Open**.

The game launches, and you can start playing.

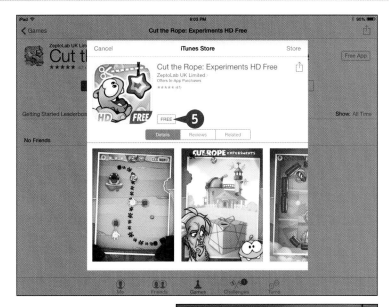

TIP

**How can I tell which games work with Game Center?**

All the games you can access through Game Center work with Game Center.

When you are browsing games in the App Store, tap **Details** and scroll down in the Supports area. Make sure the Game Center name appears in this area.

# Add Friends and Play Games with Them

To get the most out of Game Center, you can add friends to your Friends list and challenge them to play games with you. Similarly, other people can invite you to be friends and to play games. When other people send you invitations, you respond accordingly.

## Add Friends and Play Games with Them

### Send a Friend Request

1. Press **Home**.

   The Home screen appears.

2. Tap **Game Center** (🎮).

   Game Center opens.

   The Me screen appears.

3. Tap **Friends** (👥 changes to 👥).

   The Friends screen appears.

4. Tap **Add** (+).

5. Enter the friend's Game Center nickname or e-mail address.

6. Type a message. Usually, it is a good idea to write something to help your friend identify you.

7. Tap **Send**.

   Game Center sends the friend request.

**Note:** When your friend accepts the request, Game Center notifies you and adds the friend as a Game Center friend.

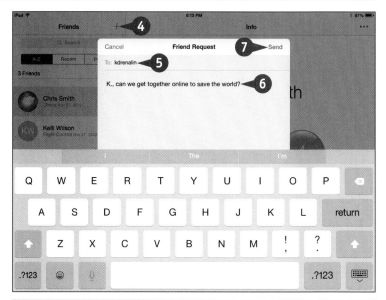

### Send a Challenge

1. In Game Center, tap **Friends** (👥 changes to 👥).

   The Friends screen appears.

2. Tap the friend you want to challenge.

   The friend's Games list appears, showing the games you and your friend both have.

3. Tap the game for the challenge.

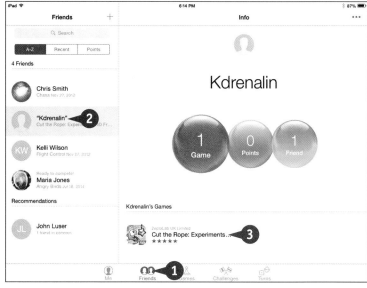

The game's screen appears.

**4** Tap the score or achievement for which you want to issue the challenge.

The Info dialog opens.

**5** Tap **Send Challenge**.

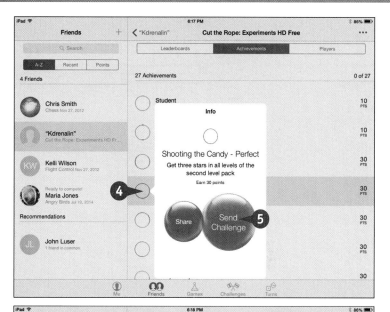

The Challenge dialog opens.

**6** Type a message.

**7** Tap **Send**.

Game Center sends the challenge.

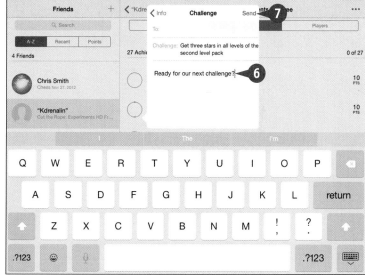

---

**TIP**

**How do I stop someone from being a friend?**
Tap **Friends** (🙂 changes to 👥) to display the Friends screen, and then tap the friend in the Friends list. Tap **More** (•••) to display the More dialog, and then tap **Unfriend**.

# CHAPTER 10

# Working with Photos and Books

In this chapter, you learn to use the Photos app to view and share photos. You also learn to use the iBooks app to read e-books and PDF files.

# Browse Photos Using Years, Collections, and Moments

You can use the Photos app to browse the photos you have taken with the camera in your iPad, photos you have synced using iTunes or via the iCloud Shared Streams feature, and photos you saved from instant messages, e-mail, web pages, and social media.

You can browse your photos by date and locations using the smart groupings that Photos creates. Each Year grouping contains Collections; and the Collections grouping contains Moments, which contain your photos.

## Browse Photos Using Years, Collections, and Moments

**1** Press **Home**.

The Home screen appears.

**2** Tap **Photos** (✿).

The Photos app opens.

**3** Tap **Photos** (▢ changes to ▪).

The Photos screen appears, showing the Years list.

**4** Tap the year you want to open.

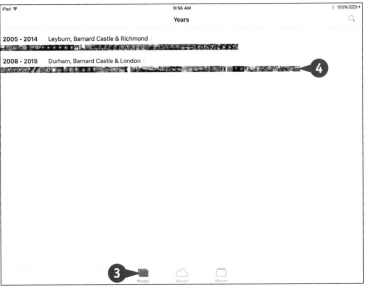

The Collections screen for the year appears.

**Note:** Scroll up or down as needed to see other collections. You can scroll from one year to another.

**5** Tap the collection you want to open.

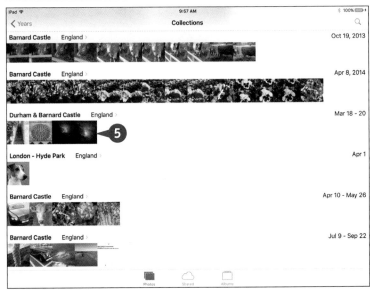

The Moments screen for the collection appears.

Ⓐ You can tap **Share** to display the Share pop-up panel.

Ⓑ Tap **Share this moment** to share all the photos in the moment via a means that you choose on the Share sheet.

Ⓒ Tap **Play Slideshow** to start a slide show containing the photos in the moment.

❻ Tap the photo you want to view.

The photo opens.

Ⓓ You can tap **Edit** to edit the photo, as explained in Chapter 11.

Ⓔ You can tap **Share** (⬆) to share the photo, as explained later in this chapter.

❼ Tap and swipe left or right to display other photos in the moment.

Another photo appears.

❽ Tap **Moments** (‹).

The Moments screen appears.

❾ Tap **Collections** (‹).

The Collections screen appears.

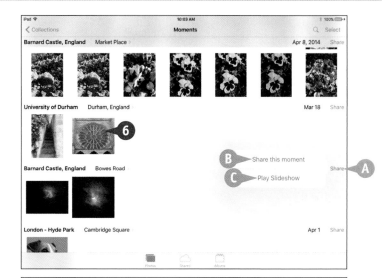

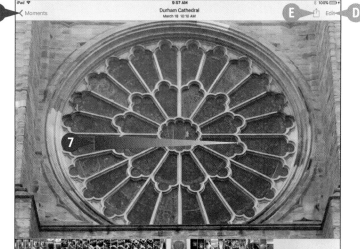

❿ Tap **Years** (‹).

The Years screen appears, and you can navigate to another year.

---

## TIP

**How can I move a photo to a different year?**

To move a photo to a different year, you need to change the date set in the photo's metadata. You cannot do this with the Photos app, but you can change the date with a third-party app such as Pixelgarde, which is free from the App Store at this writing. Alternatively, if you sync the photos from your computer, you can change the date in the photo on your computer. For example, in the Photos app on OS X, select the photo or photos, click **Photos** on the menu bar, and then click **Adjust Date and Time**.

# Browse Shared Photos

The Photos app on your iPad includes support for sharing photo albums on iCloud. This feature enables you to share photos easily with others and enjoy the photos they are sharing. In this section, you learn how to add other people's shared albums to the Photos app on your iPad by accepting invitations. You also learn how to browse through the photos they are sharing.

Later in this chapter, you learn to share your own photos via shared albums.

## Browse Shared Photos

**1** When you receive an invitation to a photo stream, open the e-mail message in Mail.

**2** Tap **Subscribe**.

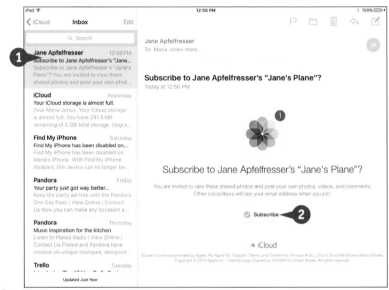

The Photos app becomes active, and the iCloud Photo Sharing screen appears.

The new album appears on the iCloud Photo Sharing screen.

**Note:** The Activity item in the upper-left corner of the iCloud Photo Sharing screen shows new activity on your shared albums. Tap **Activity** to see the latest photos posted on all your shared albums.

**A** The badge indicates there are new items for you.

**B** You can tap **Back to Mail** to return to the Mail app.

**3** Tap the new album.

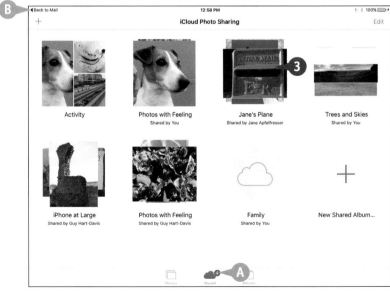

The new album's screen appears.

④ Tap a photo.

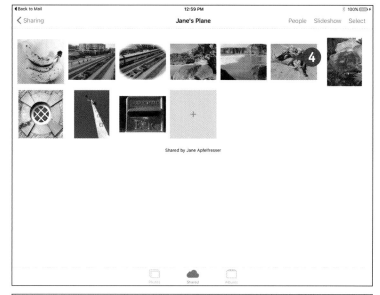

The photo opens.

⑥ You can tap **Add a comment** to add a comment on the photo.

⑩ You can tap **Share** (⬆) to share the photo with others.

**Note:** You can swipe left or right to display other photos.

⑤ Tap the album's name (❮).

The album's screen appears.

⑥ Tap **Back** (❮).

The iCloud Photo Sharing screen appears, and you can navigate to another album.

## TIP

**How do I remove a shared album?**

In the Photos app, tap **Shared** (☁ changes to ☁) to display the iCloud Photo Sharing screen. Tap **Edit** to turn on Editing Mode, and then tap **Remove** (⊗) at the upper-left corner of the album you want to remove. Tap the **Unsubscribe** button in the Unsubscribe dialog that opens.

# Browse Photos Using Albums

Along with browsing by collections and browsing shared photo albums, you can browse your photos by albums. The Camera app on your iPad automatically maintains several albums, storing each photo you take in the Camera Roll album, each video in an album called Videos, and each time-lapse video in an album called Time-Lapse. You can also create other albums manually from your photos or sync existing albums from your computer.

## Browse Photos Using Albums

**1** Press **Home**.

The Home screen appears.

**2** Tap **Photos** (🌸).

The Photos app opens.

**3** Tap **Albums** (☐ changes to ▣).

The Albums screen appears.

**Note:** Camera Roll is the album in which iOS places the photos you take; photos you save from web pages, e-mail messages, instant messages, and social media; and photos you save after opening them from other people's albums and editing them.

**4** Tap the album you want to open. This example uses the Favorites album.

The album's screen appears, showing a thumbnail of each photo.

**5** Tap the photo you want to view.

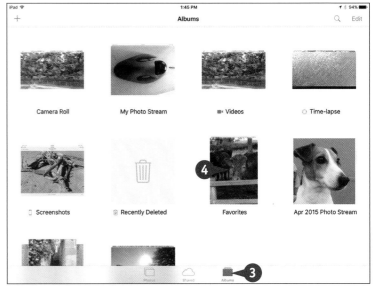

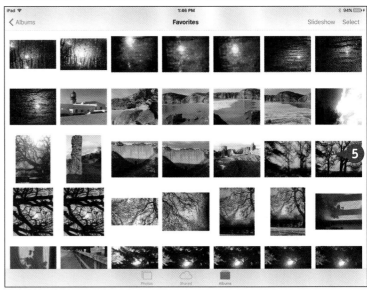

The photo opens.

**6** Tap a photo on the Thumbnails bar.

**Note:** You can also swipe left to display the next photo or right to display the previous photo.

The photo you tapped appears.

**7** Tap the album's name ($<$) in the upper-left corner of the screen.

The album appears.

**8** Tap **Albums** ($<$).

The Albums screen appears, and you can tap another album to display it.

**How can I move through a long list of photos quickly?**
You can move through the photos quickly by using momentum scrolling. Tap and flick up with your finger to set the photos scrolling. As the momentum drops, you can tap and flick up again to scroll further. Tap and drag your finger in the opposite direction to stop the scrolling.

# Create Albums

Not only can you sync photo albums you have created on your computer to your iPad, but you can also create albums directly on your iPad. The process is similar to creating a playlist within the Music app in that you start a new album, name it, and then select the photos you want to include in it. You can create albums to store a collection of photos with a similar theme and include only the photos that you want to view.

## Create Albums

1. Press **Home**.

   The Home screen appears.

2. Tap **Photos** (✿).

   The Photos app opens.

3. Tap **Albums** (□ changes to ▪).

   The Albums screen appears.

4. Tap **New** (+).

The New Album dialog opens.

5. Type the name for the new album.

6. Tap **Save**.

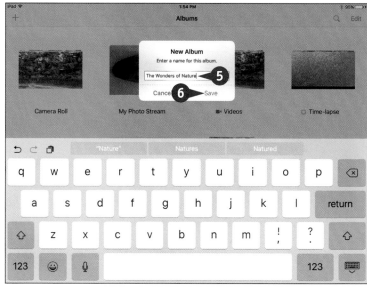

The Photos category automatically opens.

**7** Tap each photo that you want to add to the album.

A check mark appears in the bottom-right corner of each photo that you pick.

**Note:** You can select multiple adjacent photos in one move by tapping and holding, and then sliding your finger across the photos you want to select.

**Note:** Tap **Select All** to add all photos to the album. This may not be a sensible choice if you have many photos in your library.

**8** Tap **Done**.

Photos adds the selected photos to the album.

**A** The album appears on the Albums screen. You can tap the album if you want to open it and view its contents.

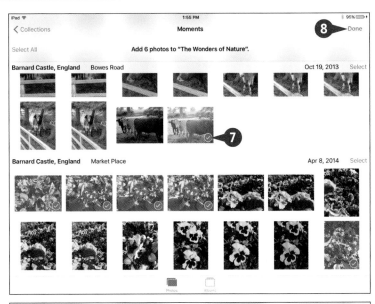

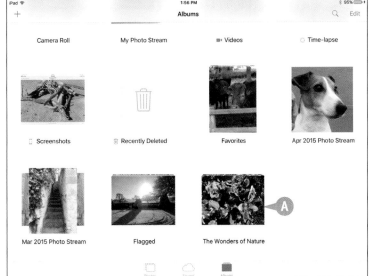

---

### TIP

**How do I delete albums from my iPad?**
On the main Photos screen, tap **Albums** (⬜ changes to ⬛), and then tap **Edit**. A Delete icon (⊗) appears in the upper-left corner of the albums you created on your iPad; tap this icon to delete the album. You cannot use this method to delete albums that you have synced from your computer. To remove those albums, choose not to sync those albums to your iPad and then run another sync.

# Share Photos Across Your Devices and Computers

I f you have an iCloud account, you can use the My Photo Stream feature to share your photos among your iOS devices and your computer.

After you turn on My Photo Stream on your iPad, other iOS devices, and your Macs, Photo Stream automatically syncs your 1,000 most recent photos among the devices and your computers.

## Share Photos Across Your Devices and Computers

### Turn On My Photo Stream on Your iPad

1 Press **Home**.

The Home screen appears.

2 Tap **Settings** (⚙).

The Settings screen appears.

3 Tap **iCloud** (☁).

The iCloud screen appears.

4 Tap **Photos** (❀).

The Photos screen appears.

Ⓐ You can set the **iCloud Photo Library** switch to On (◯) to store your entire library in iCloud.

5 Set the **My Photo Stream** switch to On (◯).

6 Set the **Upload Burst Photos** switch to On (◯) if you want to upload every photo in bursts you shoot.

7 If you want to share photo streams with others, set the **iCloud Photo Sharing** switch to On (◯). See the next section, "Share Photo Albums with Other People," for details.

8 Tap **iCloud** (‹).

The iCloud screen appears again.

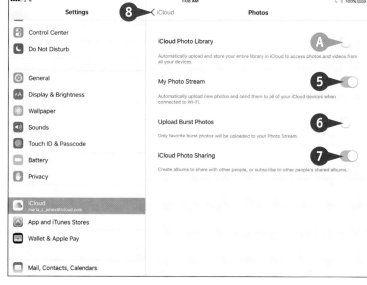

274

## Set Your Mac to Upload Photos to Your Photo Stream

**1** Right-click or **Control**+click **System Preferences** (⚙) on the Dock.

The shortcut menu opens.

**2** Click **iCloud**.

The System Preferences app opens.

The iCloud pane appears.

**3** Click **Photos** (☐ changes to ☑).

**4** Click **Options**.

The iCloud Photo Options dialog opens.

**5** Click **iCloud Photo Library** (☐ changes to ☑) to use iCloud Photo Library.

**6** Click **My Photo Stream** (☐ changes to ☑).

**7** If you want to share photo streams with others, click **iCloud Photo Sharing** (☐ changes to ☑).

**8** Click **Done**.

**9** Click **System Preferences**.

**10** Click **Quit System Preferences**.

Your Mac is now configured to import your recent photos from your devices that do not use iCloud Photo Library and to send its new photos to the My Photo Stream on those devices.

**How do I configure Photo Stream in Windows?**

In Windows 10, click **Start** to display the Start menu, click **All Apps**, click the **iCloud** folder, and then click **iCloud** to display iCloud Control Panel. Click **Photos** (☐ changes to ☑). Click **Options** to display the Photos Options dialog box. Click **My Photo Stream** (☐ changes to ☑) and **iCloud Photo Sharing** (☐ changes to ☑). Click **Change** and select the folder. Click **OK**, and then click **Apply**.

# Share Photo Albums with Other People via iCloud

After turning on the Photo Sharing feature in the Settings app, you can create shared photo albums, invite people to subscribe to them, and add photos. See the previous section, "Share Devices Across Your Devices and Computers," to turn on the Photo Sharing feature.

You can also control whether subscribers can post photos and videos, decide whether to make the album publicly available, and choose whether to receive notifications when subscribers comment on your photos or post their own.

## Share Photo Albums with Other People via iCloud

**1** Press **Home**.

The Home screen appears.

**2** Tap **Photos** (✿).

The Photos app opens.

**3** Tap **Shared** (☁ changes to ☁).

The Shared screen appears.

**4** Tap **Add** (+).

The iCloud dialog opens.

**5** Type the name for the album.

**6** Tap **Next**.

Another iCloud dialog opens.

**7** Tap **Add Contact** (⊕) to display the Contacts screen, and then tap the contact to add.

**8** Repeat step **7** to add other contacts as needed. You can also type contact names.

**9** Tap **Create**.

The iCloud Photo Sharing screen appears.

**10** Tap the new stream.

The stream's screen appears.

**11** Tap **Add** (+).

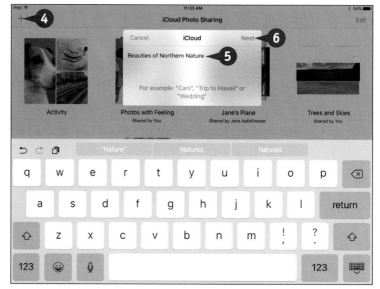

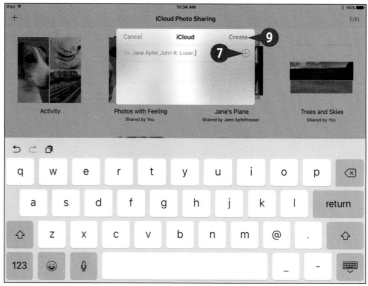

The Moments screen appears, with the selection controls displayed.

**Note:** You can add photos from other views. For example, tap **Albums** (⬚ changes to ▬) to browse by albums.

⑫ Tap each photo you want to add.

⑬ Tap **Done**.

⑭ In the iCloud dialog that appears, type any text you want to post with the photos.

⑮ Tap **Post**.

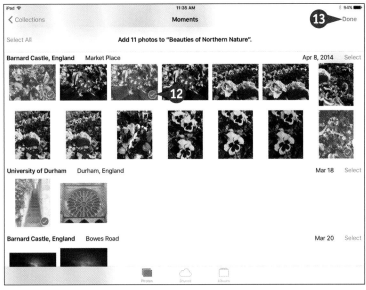

⑯ On the album's screen, tap **People**.

The Edit Shared Album panel appears.

Ⓐ To invite others to the stream, tap **Invite People**.

⑰ Set the **Subscribers Can Post** switch to On (⬤) or Off ( ), as needed.

⑱ Set the **Public Website** switch to On (⬤) or Off ( ) to control whether to make the stream publicly accessible on the iCloud.com website.

⑲ Set the **Notifications** switch to On (⬤) or Off ( ), as needed.

⑳ Tap outside the Edit Shared Album panel to close it.

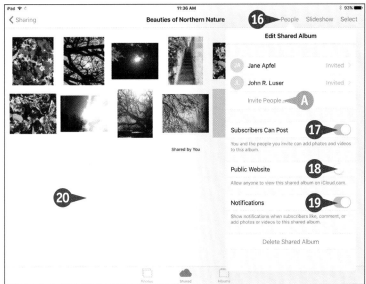

**TIP**

**If I make a shared album public, how do people find the website?**

In the Edit Shared Album panel, when you set the **Public Website** switch for a shared album to On (⬤), a Share Link button appears. Tap **Share Link** to display the Share sheet, and then tap the means of sharing you want to use — for example, **Message** (⬤), **Mail** (⬤), **Twitter** (⬤), or **Facebook** (⬤).

# Share Photos via E-Mail and Messaging

From the Photos app on your iPad, you can quickly share photos via e-mail or instant messaging. You can send either a single photo or multiple photos in a message. You can include multiple photos either by using the Share sheet to add other photos to the one you have already selected or by selecting multiple photos before displaying the Share sheet.

## Share Photos via E-Mail and Messaging

### Select the Photo and Display the Share Sheet

1 In the Photos app, browse to the photo you want to share. Use the techniques explained in the three previous sections.

2 Tap **Share** ( ).

The Share sheet appears.

3 To include another photo from the same source, tap the photo's selection button ( changes to ). Scroll left or right as needed to find the photos you want.

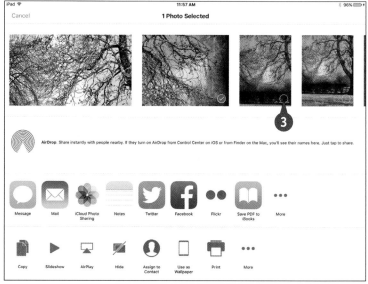

### Select Multiple Photos

1 In the Photos app, display the collection of photos. For example, tap **Albums** ( changes to ) to display the Albums screen, and then tap the appropriate album.

2 Tap **Select** in the upper-right corner of the screen.

The Photos app switches to Selection Mode.

3 Tap each photo to include ( appears on each photo).

4 Tap **Share** ( ).

The Share sheet appears.

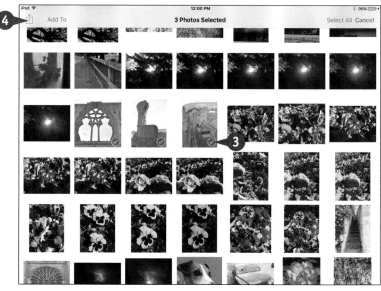

## Share the Photo via Messaging

**1** In the Share sheet, tap **Message**.

Your iPad creates a new message in the Messages app with the photo attached to the message.

**2** Tap **To** and address the message.

**3** Tap in the body area, and then type any text needed.

**4** Tap **Send**.

The Messages app sends the message.

## Share the Photo via E-Mail

**1** On the Share sheet, tap **Mail**.

**2** Tap **To** and address the e-mail message.

**3** Tap **Subject** and type the subject for the e-mail message.

**4** Tap in the body area, and then type any text needed.

**5** Tap **Cc/Bcc, From**.

The CC area, Bcc area, From area, and Image Size options appear.

**6** Tap **Small**, **Medium**, **Large**, or **Actual Size**, as needed.

**7** Tap **Send**.

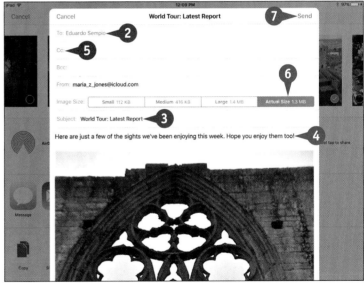

---

### TIP

**What is the best size to use when sending photos via e-mail?**

This depends on what the recipient will do with the photo. If the recipient needs to edit or print the photo, choose **Actual Size**. If the recipient will merely view the photo on-screen, choose **Large** or **Medium**. The **Small** size works for contact card images, but its picture quality is too low for most other uses.

# Play Slide Shows of Photos

Your iPad can not only display your photos but also play them as a slide show. You can select an existing group of photos, such as an album, or make a custom selection from moments. You can also choose to repeat the slide show or run the photos in random order. Then, when you start the slide show, you can choose which transition to use and add music. To make the most of your slide shows, you can choose the slide timing in the Photos screen in Settings.

## Play Slide Shows of Photos

**1** Press **Home**.

The Home screen appears.

**2** Tap **Photos** (✿).

The Photos screen appears.

**3** Navigate to the photo with which you want to start the slide show. For example, tap **Photos** (☐ changes to ▦), tap the appropriate year, tap the appropriate collection, and then tap the moment that contains the photo.

The moment or other photo collection opens.

**4** Tap the photo you want to use at the beginning of the slide show.

The photo opens.

**5** Tap **Share** (📤).

The Share sheet appears.

**6** Tap each photo you want to include in the slide show (○ changes to ✓).

**7** Tap **Slideshow** (▶).

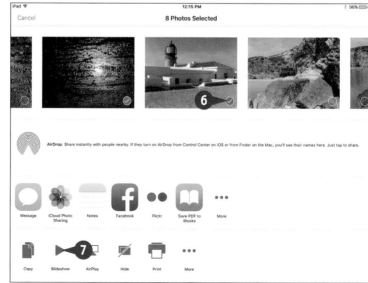

The slide show starts playing with default settings.

**8** Tap the screen.

The controls appear.

**Ⓐ** You can tap **AirPlay** (◰) to play the slide show to an Apple TV.

**Ⓑ** You can tap **Pause** (❚❚) to pause the slide show while you choose options.

**9** Tap **Options**.

The Options dialog opens.

**10** Drag the slider to set the playback speed.

**11** Set the **Repeat** switch to On (◯) if you want the slide show to repeat.

**12** Tap **Theme**.

The Themes dialog opens.

**13** Tap the theme you want to use.

**14** Tap **Music**.

The Music dialog opens.

**15** Tap the music you want, or tap **None** if you prefer no music.

The Music dialog closes, and the Options dialog reappears.

**16** Tap the screen.

The Options dialog closes.

**Ⓒ** If you paused the slide show, tap **Play** (▶).

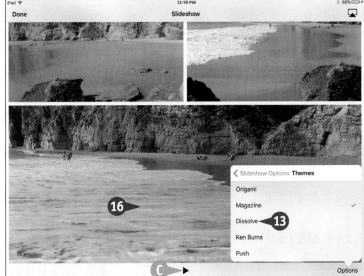

---

**TIP**

**How can I play my photos on a TV or projector?**
To play your photos on a bigger screen, you have two options. First, you can use AirPlay to play photos on a TV or monitor connected to an Apple TV. Second, you can use the Apple Lightning Digital AV Adapter and an HDMI cable to connect your iPad to a TV.

# Read Digital Books with iBooks

U sing the iBooks app, you can read e-books that you load on the iPad from your computer, read e-books that you download for free or purchase from online stores, or read PDF files you transfer from your computer.

If you have already loaded some e-books, you can read them as described in this section. If iBooks contains no books, press the Store button to visit the iBooks Store, which offers both free books and books for which you must pay.

## Read Digital Books with iBooks

**1** Press **Home**.

The Home screen appears.

**2** Tap **iBooks** (📖).

The Books screen appears.

**A** If Books does not appear in the upper-middle area of the iBooks screen, tap the pop-up menu button (▼). In the Collections dialog that appears, tap **Books** to display the list of books.

**B** You can tap **List** (≡) to display the books as a list instead of as a grid.

**3** Tap the book you want to open.

The book opens.

**Note:** When you open a book, iBooks displays your current page. When you open a book for the first time, iBooks displays the book's cover, first page, or default page.

**4** Tap anywhere on the screen to hide the reading controls. Tap again to display them once more.

**5** Tap the right side of the page to display the next page.

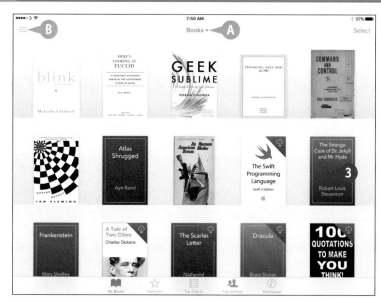

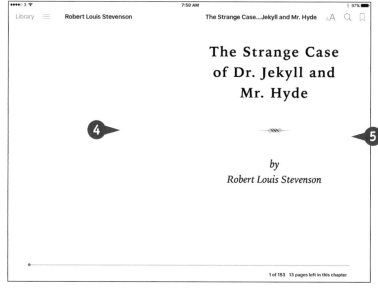

**Note:** To display the previous page, tap the left side of the page. Alternatively, tap the left side of the page and drag to the right.

**6** To look at the next page without fully revealing it, tap the right side and drag to the left. You can then either drag further to turn the page or release the page and let it fall closed.

**7** To jump to another part of the book, tap **Table of Contents** (☰).

**Note:** Alternatively, you can drag the indicator at the bottom of the screen to move quickly through the book.

The table of contents appears.

**8** Tap the part of the book you want to display.

**Note:** To search in the book, tap **Search** (🔍). On the Search screen, type the search term, and then tap the match you want to display.

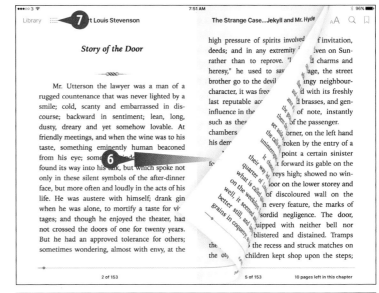

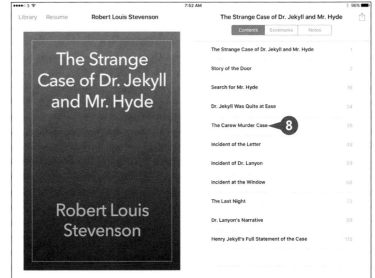

## TIP

**How do I change the font iBooks uses?**
Tap the screen to display the controls, and then tap **Font Settings** (ₐA). In the Font Settings dialog, tap **Smaller** or **Larger** to change the font size. Tap **Fonts** to display the font list, and then tap the font you want to use.

In the Font Settings dialog, you can also tap one of the colored circles to apply a theme, such as the Sepia theme or the Night theme. You can set the **Auto-Night Theme** switch to On (⬤) to have iBooks automatically apply the Night theme when ambient light is low. And you can set the **Scrolling View** switch to On (⬤) to display the book as a long scrolling page instead of individual pages that you turn.

# CHAPTER 11

# Taking Photos and Videos

The Camera app on the iPad enables you to take both still photos and videos, and the Photo Booth app helps you take fun photos. You can also edit your photos on the iPad, edit your videos using the Trim feature, and share your photos and videos with others.

# Take Photos with the Camera App

Your iPad includes a high-resolution camera in its back for taking still photos and videos, plus a lower-resolution camera in the front for taking photos and videos of yourself and for making video calls.

To take photos using the cameras, you use the Camera app. For the rear camera, this app includes a digital zoom feature for zooming in and out, a feature for taking HDR (high dynamic range) photos, and a grid that you can use for composing your photos.

## Take Photos with the Camera App

1 Press **Home**.

The Home screen appears.

2 Tap **Camera** (📷).

The Camera app opens, showing whatever is positioned in front of the lens.

3 Aim the iPad so that your subject appears in the middle of the photo area.

**Note:** If you need to take tightly composed photos, get a tripod and a tripod mount that fits the model of iPad you have. You can find various models on Amazon, eBay, and photography sites.

4 Place two fingers together on the screen and pinch outward to zoom in or pinch together to zoom out.

The zoom slider appears.

5 Tap **Zoom In** (➕) to zoom in or **Zoom Out** (➖) to zoom out. Tap as many times as needed up to 5× zoom.

Ⓐ You can also zoom by tapping and dragging the zoom slider.

**6** Tap where you want to focus.

The focus changes.

**Note:** By default, the Camera app focuses on the middle of the screen, because that is where your subject is most likely to be. If what you see on the screen appears blurred, try tapping the subject to change the focus.

**7** Tap **Take Photo** ().

**Note:** On many iPad models, you can tap and hold **Take Photo** (○) to take a burst of photos.

The Camera app takes the photo and displays a thumbnail.

**8** Tap the thumbnail.

The photo appears.

**B** From the photo screen, you can navigate as discussed in Chapter 10. Tap a thumbnail to display its photo, swipe your finger to the left to display the next photo, or swipe to the right to display the previous photo.

**C** You can tap **Delete** (🗑) to delete the photo.

**9** Tap **Done** to go back to the Camera app.

**TIP**

**How do I switch to the front-facing camera?**

Tap **Switch Cameras** (📷) to switch from the rear-facing camera to the front-facing camera. The image that the front-facing camera is seeing appears on-screen, and you can take pictures as described in this section. Tap again when you want to switch back to the rear-facing camera.

# Take HDR Photos and Square Photos

To help you capture photos with lush, vibrant color, the Camera app includes a feature called *high dynamic range*, HDR for short. HDR combines several photos into a single photo with adjusted color balance and intensity.

By default, both the front and rear cameras take photos in a rectangular, 4:3 aspect ratio. You can crop any photo to a different aspect ratio, as explained later in this chapter. But when you need to take a photo that is perfectly square, you can use the Square feature instead.

## Take HDR Photos and Square Photos

### Take an HDR Photo

**1** Press **Home**.

The Home screen appears.

**2** Tap **Camera** (📷).

The Camera app opens, showing whatever is positioned in front of the lens.

**3** Tap **HDR** (HDR).

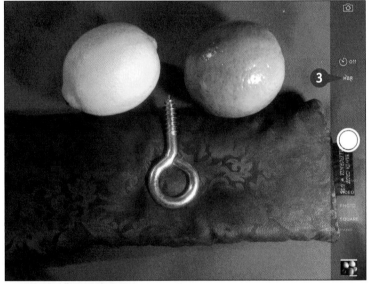

**A** HDR changes to HDR.

**B** The HDR flag appears at the bottom of the screen.

**4** Tap **Take Photo** (◯).

Camera takes a photo.

**Note:** HDR photos have a larger file size than regular photos.

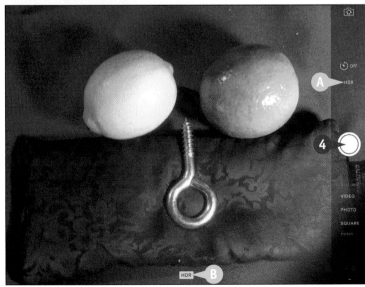

## Take a Square Photo

**1** In the Camera app, tap **Square**.

**Note:** Square photos are useful for adding to contact records and similar needs.

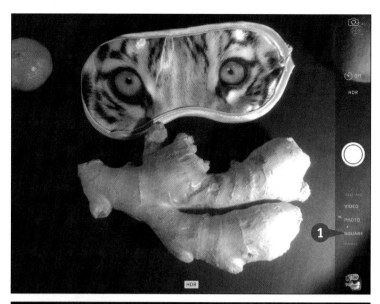

**C** Camera reduces the frame to a square by displaying black borders at the sides.

**2** Tap **Take Photo** (⭕).

Camera takes a photo.

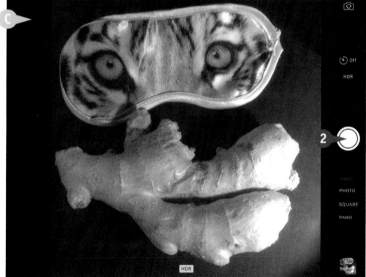

**When should I use the HDR feature?**

Turn on HDR when you need to get the best color and lighting balance for a stationary subject. The Camera app needs longer to take an HDR photo than to take a regular photo, so HDR is not suitable for subjects that are moving or otherwise changing. For example, use HDR for photographing landscapes or houses, but do not use it for photographing sports, people, or live animals. HDR can be especially useful in bright sunlight, which can make automatic light-metering more difficult.

# Using the Self-Timer and the Grid

he Camera app includes a self-timer feature that enables you to set the app to take a burst of photos 3 seconds or 10 seconds after you tap the Take Photo button. By using the self-timer, you can include yourself in group shots or simply minimize camera shake when taking photos of still subjects.

The Camera app also includes a Grid feature that you can turn on to help you compose your pictures. You can display the grid at any point when you will find it useful, or simply display the grid all the time.

## Using the Self-Timer and the Grid

### Open the Camera App and Take a Timed Photo

**1** Press **Home**.

The Home screen appears.

**2** Tap **Camera** (📷).

The Camera app opens.

**3** Tap **Timer** (⏱).

The Timer settings appear.

**4** Tap **3s** or **10s** to set the number of seconds for delay.

The delay appears next to the Timer icon.

**5** Compose the photo.

**6** Tap **Take Photo** (◯).

The Camera app displays an on-screen countdown.

When the countdown ends, the app takes a burst of photos.

**Note:** The timer remains set until you change it.

## Turn the Grid On or Off

**1** Press **Home**.

The Home screen appears.

**2** Tap **Settings** (⚙).

The Settings screen appears.

**3** Tap **Photos & Camera** (✳).

The Photos & Camera screen appears.

**4** Set the **Grid** switch to On (●) or Off (   ), as needed.

Ⓐ To control whether the Camera app keeps the normal photo when taking HDR photos, set the **Keep Normal Photo** switch to On (●), the default setting, or Off (   ).

## Compose Photos Using the Grid

**1** Press **Home**.

The Home screen appears.

**2** Tap **Camera** (📷).

The Camera app opens.

**3** Use the grid to position your subject and align the iPad.

**4** Tap **Take Photo** (◯).

The Camera app takes the photo.

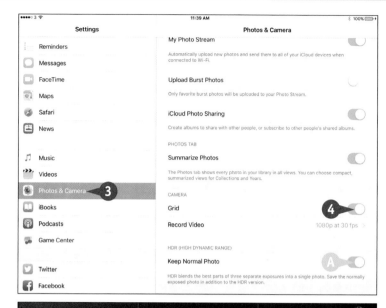

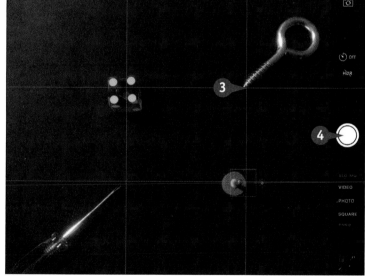

## TIP

**How does the Grid feature help with photo composition?**

Apart from enabling you to align vertical lines and horizontal lines quickly and accurately, the grid can help you implement the Rule of Thirds. This rule suggests placing the major point of interest on one of the dividing lines or intersections in the picture.

# Take Time-Lapse Movies

The Camera app's Time-Lapse feature enables you to take time-lapse movies easily: All you need to do is point the camera lens at your subject, select the Time-Lapse feature, start taking the movie — and then stop it at the appropriate point. This feature is great for shooting movies of sunrises and sunsets, changing weather patterns, or wildlife.

To take effective time-lapse movies, use a tripod or another type of holder to keep your iPad still and aimed in the right direction.

## Take Time-Lapse Movies

① Set up the iPad on the tripod or holder.

② Press **Home**.

The Home screen appears.

③ Tap **Camera** (📷).

The Camera app opens.

④ Aim the lens at your subject.

⑤ Scroll the Camera options down if necessary and then tap **Time-Lapse**.

The view changes to that of the video camera.

⑥ Tap **Take Time-Lapse Movie** (🔘).

The Camera app starts filming.

**7** When the time has elapsed, tap **Stop Recording** (◉).

**8** Tap the thumbnail for the movie.

The movie opens.

**9** Tap **Play** (▶).

The movie starts playing.

**Note:** The Camera app stores your time-lapse movies in both the Videos album and in the Time-Lapse album. In the Videos album, you can easily identify the time-lapse movies by the Time-Lapse symbol (❋) on their thumbnails.

**How much space do time-lapse movies take up?**
Time-lapse movies take around 5MB to 10MB per minute at the 1080p resolution.

**How do I control the number of frames the Time-Lapse feature shoots?**
At this writing, you cannot control the number of frames beyond choosing when to start and stop shooting the movie. The Time-Lapse feature has no configurable settings. The Camera app automatically adjusts the focus and the exposure as necessary to cope with changing subjects and lighting conditions.

# Take Fun Photos with Photo Booth

Your iPad includes the Photo Booth app, which you can use to take photos using special effects such as Thermal Camera, X-Ray, or Kaleidoscope.

On your iPad, you can use Photo Booth with either the front camera — the one on the screen side — or the rear camera, so you can apply the effects to subjects other than yourself if you choose. Photo Booth stores the photos you take in the Camera Roll album, so they appear together with the photos you take with the Camera app.

## Take Fun Photos with Photo Booth

1 Press **Home**.

The Home screen appears.

2 Tap **Photo Booth** (📷).

Photo Booth opens, showing the front camera on your iPad.

3 Tap the effect you want to use. This example uses **Kaleidoscope**.

Photo Booth displays the camera's input full screen with the effect applied.

**4** Compose your features to suit the effect.

**5** Tap **Take Photo** (⭕).

Photo Booth takes the photo.

**6** Tap **Switch Cameras** (📷).

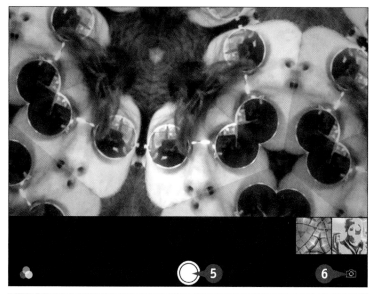

Photo Booth switches to the rear camera.

**7** Tap **Filters** (◉).

The screen for choosing effects appears.

**8** Tap the effect you want. This example uses **Thermal Camera**.

The effect appears on-screen.

**9** Compose your photo.

**10** Tap **Take Photo** (⭕).

Photo Booth takes the photo.

**How do I share the photos I take in Photo Booth?**

Photo Booth stores the photos in the Camera Roll album, just as the Camera app does, so you can share them like any other photos. Press **Home** and tap **Photos** (❋) to open the Photos app, and then tap **Albums** and **Camera Roll** to open the Camera Roll album. You can then tap a photo to open it, and tap **Share** (📤) to open the Share sheet.

# Crop, Rotate, and Straighten Photos

I f you have a photo where the subject is sideways or upside down, you can use the Rotate feature in the Photos app to rotate the photo so it is the right way up. If the photo is the right way up but is not straight, you can straighten it. This works both for photos you take on the iPad and for photos you copy to the iPad. Before taking the following steps, press **Home** to display the Home screen, and then tap **Photos** (●) to launch the Photos app.

## Crop, Rotate, and Straighten Photos

**1** Open the photo that you want to rotate.

**Note:** You may need to tap the screen to reveal the controls at the top of the screen. These options disappear after a brief period of inactivity.

**2** Tap **Edit**.

**Note:** If the This Photo Is Not Editable dialog opens when you tap **Edit**, tap **Duplicate and Edit** to create a duplicate photo in your Camera Roll album and open it for editing.

The editing controls appear.

**3** Tap **Crop** (▦).

The Photos app automatically applies any straightening that it detects the photo needs.

Ⓐ You can tap **Reset** to undo the automatic straightening.

Ⓑ You can move the rotation dial to adjust the straightening.

Ⓒ You can tap **Rotate** () to rotate the photo 90 degrees counterclockwise. Tap again to rotate to 180 degrees; tap a third time to rotate to 270 degrees.

**Note:** You can tap **Cancel** and then tap **Discard Changes** to abandon the edit.

④ Tap and drag a corner crop handle or a border to adjust the cropping.

⑤ Tap **Done**.

Photos saves your changes to the photo.

**Note:** When you rotate an image, the original image in the album is changed. You can revert the image back to its original state while in Edit view by tapping **Revert** and then tapping **Revert to Original**.

---

**TIP**

**How can I crop a photo to a specific size ratio?**
You can crop a photo to a specific aspect ratio, such as 3:2 or Square, by tapping **Aspect Ratio** (▱) and then tapping the appropriate ratio in the dialog that opens.

# Enhance Photos

To instantly improve the appearance of a photo, use the Enhance feature. Enhance analyzes the brightness and color balance of the photo and attempts to improve them by lightening or darkening the photo, raising the contrast, and boosting dull colors.

Before taking the following steps, press **Home** to display the Home screen, and then tap **Photos** (✱) to launch the Photos app.

## Enhance Photos

**1** Open the photo that you want to enhance.

**2** Tap **Edit**.

**Note:** You may need to tap the screen to reveal the menu options at the top of the screen. These options disappear after a brief period of inactivity.

The Edit Photo screen appears.

**3** Tap **Enhance** (🪄).

Photos enhances the image.

**Note:** Tap **Enhance** (🪄) to toggle Enhance off and on so you can judge the effect.

**4** Tap **Done**.

**Note:** When you enhance an image, the original image in the album is changed. You can revert the image back to its original state while in Edit view by tapping **Revert** and then tapping **Revert to Original**.

# Reduce Red-Eye in Photos

Red-eye is a photographic effect that occurs when the camera's flash reflects off the back of the subject's eyes, causing the eyes to glow red. You can reduce or remove red-eye by using the Red-Eye feature in the Photos app.

Before taking the following steps, press **Home** to display the Home screen, and then tap **Photos** (✱) to launch the Photos app.

## Reduce Red-Eye in Photos

**1** Open the photo for which you want to reduce red-eye.

**2** Tap **Edit**.

**Note:** You may need to tap the screen to display the controls.

The Edit Photo screen appears.

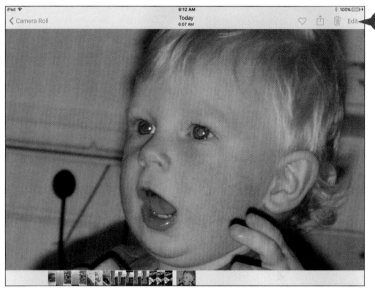

**3** Tap **Red-Eye** (⊘).

**4** Tap each red eye in the photograph.

Photos tries to remove the red-eye.

**Note:** You can tap each red eye again to undo your changes.

**5** Tap **Done**.

**Note:** When you remove red-eye from an image, the original image in the album is changed. You can revert the image back to its original state while in Edit view by tapping **Revert**, and then tapping **Revert to Original**.

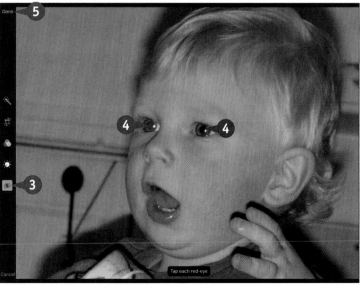

# Apply Filters to Photos

You can use the Filter feature in the Photos app to change the look of a photo by applying a filter such as Mono, Tonal, Chrome, Transfer, or Instant. If you like the effect, you can save the photo with the effect applied.

Photos applies the filter as an effect overlaid on the photo rather than by making it an integral part of the photo. This means you can subsequently remove the filter, returning the photo to its previous state. Alternatively, you can apply another filter, giving the photo a different look.

## Apply Filters to Photos

**1** Press **Home**.

The Home screen appears.

**2** Tap **Photos** ( ).

The Photos app opens.

**3** Navigate to the photo and tap it.

The photo appears.

**4** Tap **Edit**.

The editing controls appear.

**5** Tap **Filters** ( ).

Ⓐ The Filters bar appears.

❻ Tap the filter you want to apply.

Photos displays the filter effect on-screen.

❼ Tap **Done**.

Photos saves the change to the photo.

**How do I remove a filter from a photo?**

Open the photo, and then tap **Edit** to switch to Edit Mode. Tap **Filters** (◐) to display the Filters bar, and then tap **None**. Tap **Done** to apply the change.

After opening an edited photo for further editing, you can also tap **Revert**, and then tap **Revert to Original** to restore the photo to its original state. Reverting to the original photo removes any other edits you have made, as well as removing the filter you have applied.

A long with capturing still photos, the cameras on your iPad can capture high-quality, full-motion video. The rear camera records 1080p video, while the front camera records 720p video. A single video can use only one resolution.

To capture video, you use the Camera app. You launch the Camera app as usual, and then switch it to Video Mode. After taking the video, you can view it on the iPad screen.

## Capture Video

**1** Press **Home**.

The Home screen appears.

**Note:** To change the video resolution, tap **Settings** (⚙), tap **Photos & Camera** (✿), tap **Record Video**, and then tap the resolution.

**2** Tap **Camera** (📷).

The Camera screen appears, showing the image the lens is seeing.

Ⓐ Some iPad models can also shoot video in slow motion. Tap **Slo-Mo** to access this feature.

**3** Tap **Video**.

The video image and video controls appear.

**4** Aim the camera at your subject.

**5** Tap **Record** (⦿).

The camera starts recording.

Ⓑ The time readout shows the time that has elapsed.

**6** To finish recording, tap **Stop Recording** (⦿).

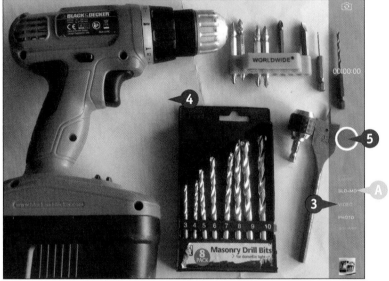

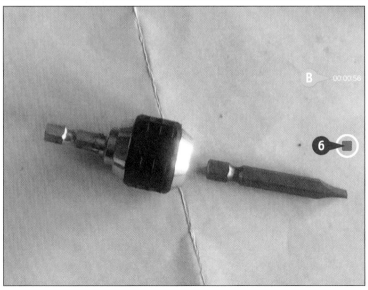

The Camera app stops recording and displays a thumbnail of the video's first frame.

**7** Tap the thumbnail.

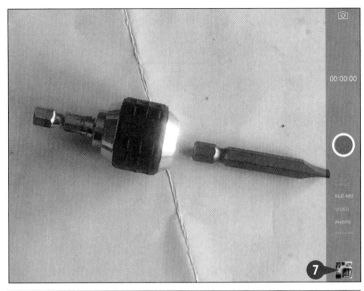

The video appears.

**8** Tap **Play** (▶).

The video starts playing.

**Note:** Tap anywhere on the screen to display the video controls.

**Note:** If you want to trim the video, follow the procedure described in the next section, "Edit Videos with the Trim Feature," before tapping **Done**.

**9** When you finish viewing the video, tap **Done**.

The Camera app appears again.

**Note:** Video takes up a lot of space on your iPad, so delete any videos that are not worth keeping.

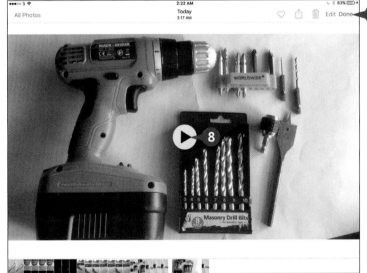

## TIPS

**Why does the picture and picture shape change when I switch to the video camera?**

The picture may appear to zoom in because the video camera uses a longer focal length than the still camera. The picture shape changes because the video camera uses a different aspect ratio, 16:9, than the still camera, which uses 4:3.

**What does the bar of miniature pictures at the top of the video playback screen do?**

The navigation bar gives you a quick way of moving forward and backward through the movie. Tap the vertical playhead bar, and then drag to the right or to the left, either when the movie is playing or when it is paused.

# Edit Videos with the Trim Feature

hen you capture video, you normally shoot more footage than you want to keep. You then edit the video to keep only the footage you need.

The Camera and Photos apps on your iPad share a straightforward Trim feature that you can use to trim the beginning and end of a video clip. For greater precision in editing, or to make a movie out of multiple clips, you can use the iMovie app, which you can download from the App Store; it is free for all new iOS devices.

## Edit Videos with the Trim Feature

**1** Press **Home**.

The Home screen appears.

**2** Tap **Photos** ( ).

The Photos screen appears.

**3** Tap **Albums** ( changes to ).

The Albums list appears.

**4** Tap **Videos**.

The videos appear.

**5** Tap the thumbnail for the video you want to trim.

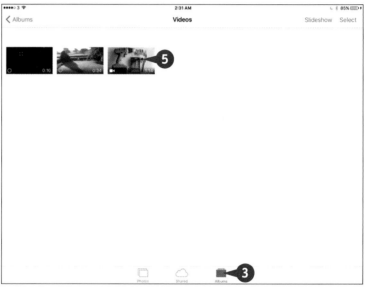

The video opens.

**6** Tap **Edit**.

Photos opens the video for editing.

**7** Tap the left handle and drag it to the right until you see the frame at which you want to start the clip.

**8** Tap the right handle and drag it to the left until you see the frame at which you want to end the clip.

**9** Tap **Done**.

The Trim dialog appears.

**10** Tap **Trim Original** if you want to trim the original clip. Tap **Save as New Clip** to create a new clip from the trimmed content, leaving the original clip unchanged.

Photos trims the video and then displays it.

**11** Tap **Play** (▶) to view the video and verify it is correctly trimmed.

**12** Tap **Videos** (‹).

The Videos screen appears.

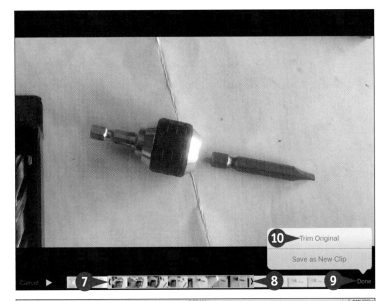

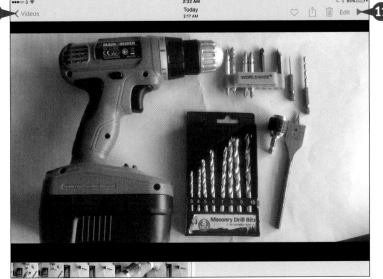

**TIP**

**Are there other ways of trimming my videos?**
Yes. If you have the Apple iMovie app on your iPad, you can trim your videos in it. You can also create movies from your video clips, add effects and titles, and share them online.

If you have a Mac, you can trim your videos more precisely, and make many other changes, by importing the clips into iMovie on the Mac and then working with them there. In Windows, you can use a program such as Adobe Premiere Elements.

After taking photos and videos with your iPad camera, or after loading photos and videos on the iPad using iTunes, you can share them with other people.

Chapter 5 shows you how to share photos via AirDrop, Twitter, and Facebook, and Chapter 10 explains how to share photos via e-mail and Messages. This section explains how to assign a photo to a contact, use a photo as wallpaper, and print a photo.

## Share Your Photos and Videos

### Select the Photo or Video to Share

1 Press **Home**.

The Home screen appears.

2 Tap **Photos** (⬡).

The Photos app opens.

3 Navigate to and tap the photo or video you want to share.

4 Tap **Share** (⬆).

The Share sheet opens.

5 Tap the appropriate button — **Use as Wallpaper** (▢), **Assign to Contact** (●), or **Print** (🖨) — and then follow the instructions in the next sets of steps.

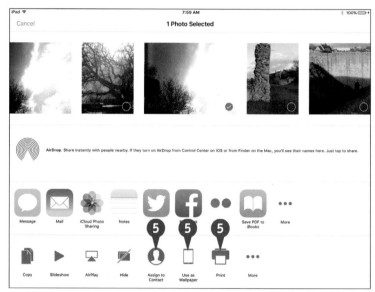

### Set a Photo as Wallpaper

1 On the Share sheet, tap **Use as Wallpaper** (▢).

2 Move the photo to display the part you want.

3 If necessary, pinch in to shrink the photo or pinch out to enlarge it.

4 Tap **Perspective Zoom** to toggle perspective zoom between On and Off.

5 Tap **Set Lock Screen**, **Set Home Screen**, or **Set Both**, as needed.

## Assign a Photo to a Contact

**1** On the Share sheet, tap **Assign to Contact** (👤).

The Contacts list appears.

**2** Tap the contact you want to assign the photo to.

The Move and Scale screen appears.

**3** Move the photo so that the face appears centrally.

**4** If necessary, pinch in to shrink the photo or pinch out to enlarge it.

**5** Tap **Use**.

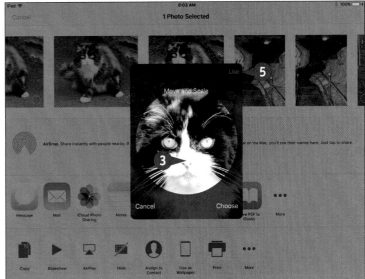

**How do I print a photo?**

To print a photo, you need access to an AirPrint–compatible printer. Display the photo you want to print, and then tap **Share** (🔼) to display the Share sheet. Tap **Print** (🖨) to display the Printer Options dialog. If the Printer readout does not show the correct printer, tap **Select Printer**, and then tap the printer. Adjust the number of copies as needed, and then tap **Print** to print the photo.

# CHAPTER 12

# Troubleshooting Your iPad

To keep your iPad running well, you should learn essential troubleshooting moves for the iPad itself and for iTunes. You can also update your iPad software and track the device if it goes missing.

# Close an App That Has Stopped Responding

Normally, the apps on your iPad run without problems, but if an app stops responding, you can force it to close. Usually, you can easily tell when an app has stopped responding, because the screen does not change and your taps and gestures on the screen get no reaction. But if you are not certain that an app has stopped responding, allow the app a few seconds to recover before you force it to close.

## Close an App That Has Stopped Responding

**1** When an app stops responding, press **Home** twice in quick succession. The app in this example is Mail.

**Note:** You can also swipe up the screen with four or five fingers to display the app-switching screen. For this to work, gestures must be enabled. Press **Home**, tap **Settings** (⚙), tap **General** (⚙), and then set the **Multitasking Gestures** switch to On (⚪).

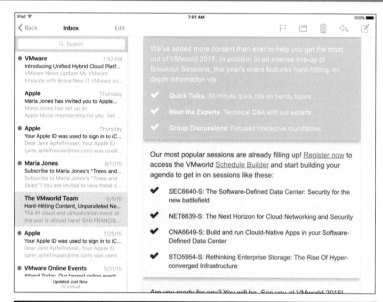

The app-switching screen appears, showing a carousel of running apps.

**A** The latest app — the app that has stopped responding — appears on the right of the screen.

**2** Tap and drag the app that has stopped responding up off the list of apps.

iOS closes the app.

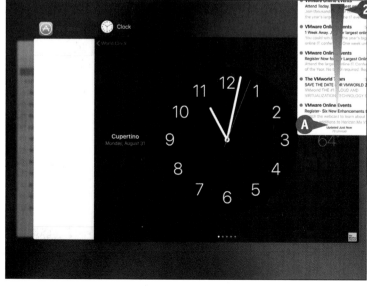

The app disappears from the list.

③ Tap the Home screen icon on the list.

The Home screen appears.

④ Tap the icon of the app that you closed.

**Note:** You may need to display another Home screen to reach the app's icon.

The app launches again, and you can resume using it.

**TIP**

**How else can I regain control of my iPad when it will not display the app-switching screen?**

If your iPad does not display the app-switching screen when you press **Home** twice in rapid succession, shut down the iPad. Hold down **Sleep/Wake** until the Slide to Power Off prompt appears, and then drag the slider across. If the Slide to Power Off prompt does not appear, continue to hold down **Sleep/Wake** until the iPad shuts down. You can then press **Sleep/Wake** again to restart the iPad.

# Update the Software on Your iPad

pple periodically releases new versions of iOS for the iPad to fix problems, improve performance, and add new features. To keep your iPad running quickly and smoothly, and to add any new features, update the device's software when a new version becomes available.

Your iPad notifies you automatically when a new version of the iPad software is available; if you sync your iPad with a computer, iTunes notifies you, too. You can also check manually for new software versions.

## Update the Software on Your iPad

### Start an Update from an iTunes Prompt

1 Connect your iPad to your computer via the USB cable.

When an update is available, iTunes displays a dialog prompting you to update your iPad.

Ⓐ You can click **Later** to postpone the update.

Ⓑ Before clicking Later, you can click **Do not ask me again** (☐ changes to ✅) to prevent iTunes from prompting you about this update again.

2 Click **Update**.

The update process starts.

### Start an Update Manually

1 Connect your iPad to your computer via the USB cable.

2 Click **iPad** (☐).

The iPad-management screen appears.

3 Click **Summary**.

The Summary screen appears.

Ⓒ The readout indicates an update is available.

4 Click **Update**.

## Complete the Update

After you start the update running, a dialog opens to confirm the update.

**1** Click **Update**.

iTunes extracts the software, backs up your iPad, updates the iPad software, and verifies the update.

The iPad restarts one or more times.

The iPad's button then reappears on the navigation bar in iTunes.

**2** Click **iPad** (☐) on the navigation bar.

The iPad-management screen appears.

**3** Click **Summary**.

The Summary screen appears.

**4** Verify the version number in the Software Version readout in the iPad area.

**D** You can subsequently click **Check for Update** to check for updated software manually.

**5** Disconnect your iPad from the USB cable. You can now start using the iPad as usual.

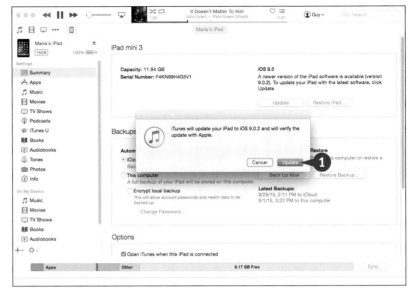

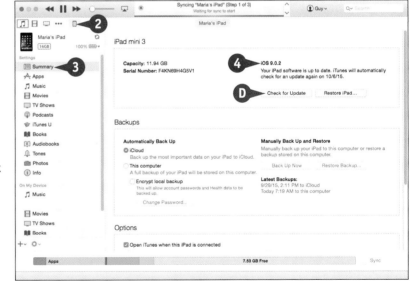

## TIP

**Can I update my iPad software without using a computer?**

Yes. You can update your iPad "over the air" by using a wireless network. Press **Home**, tap **Settings** (⚙), tap **General** (⚙), and then tap **Software Update** to check for new software. If a new version appears, tap **Download and Install**. If your iPad has cellular connectivity, you can also update using the cellular network, but because the update may involve transferring hundreds of megabytes of data, it is faster and less expensive to use a wireless network.

# Extend Your iPad's Runtime on the Battery

You can extend the runtime of your iPad on its battery by reducing the demands on the battery. You can dim the screen so that it consumes less power. You can set your iPad to go to sleep quickly. You can turn off Wi-Fi and Bluetooth when you do not need them, and you can turn off the power-hungry GPS feature on a cellular iPad when you do not need to track your iPad with the Find My iPad feature.

## Extend Your iPad's Runtime on the Battery

### Dim the Screen

1 Press **Home**.

The Home screen appears.

2 Tap **Settings** (⚙).

The Settings screen appears.

3 Tap **Display & Brightness** (AA).

The Display & Brightness screen appears.

4 Tap the **Brightness** slider and drag it to the left to dim the screen.

Ⓐ Set the **Auto-Brightness** switch to On (◯) if you want the iPad to adjust the brightness automatically to suit the ambient light conditions.

### Turn Off Wi-Fi and Bluetooth

1 On the Settings screen, tap **Wi-Fi** (📶).

The Wi-Fi screen appears.

2 Set the **Wi-Fi** switch to Off ( ).

3 Tap **Bluetooth** (*).

**Note:** If you have a cellular iPad, turning off Wi-Fi may cause data transfer over the cellular connection.

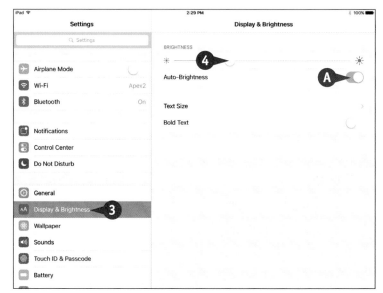

The Bluetooth screen appears.

④ Set the **Bluetooth** switch to Off (　).

**Note:** You can enable or disable Wi-Fi and Bluetooth quickly from Control Center. You can also adjust the display brightness, but you cannot control Auto-Brightness.

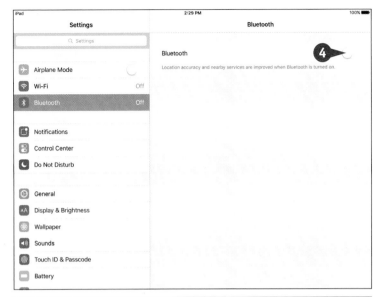

## Turn Off the GPS Feature

① On the Settings screen, tap **Privacy** (　).

The Privacy screen appears.

② Tap **Location Services** (　).

The Location Services screen appears.

③ Set the **Location Services** switch to Off (　).

The Location Services dialog opens.

④ Tap **Turn Off**.

⑤ Tap **Privacy** (＜).

The Privacy screen appears.

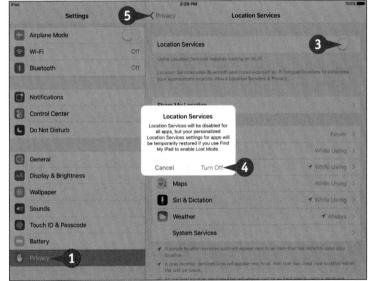

---

**TIPS**

**How can I make my iPad put itself to sleep quickly?**
You can set a short time for the Auto-Lock setting. To do so, press **Home**. Tap **Settings** (　), tap **General** (　), and then tap **Auto-Lock**. Tap a short interval — for example, **2 Minutes**.

**What is the best way to charge my iPad quickly?**
Use the iPad Power Adapter or an Apple-certified equivalent power adapter. These adapters charge your iPad much more quickly than a standard USB socket. Be careful with uncertified third-party power adapters, because these may cause electrical problems.

# Back Up and Restore Your iPad Using iTunes

You can back up your iPad either to your computer or to iCloud. Backing up your iPad to your computer using iTunes creates a full backup of the iPad on your computer, enabling you to restore your data and settings to the iPad — or to a new iOS device — if your iPad becomes corrupted or damaged. If you encrypt the backup, iTunes saves your passwords, enabling you to restore them as well.

## Back Up and Restore Your iPad Using iTunes

**1** Connect your iPad to your computer via the USB cable.

**2** Click **iPad** (⬚) on the navigation bar in iTunes.

The iPad-management screen appears.

**3** Click **Summary**.

The Summary screen appears.

**4** Click **This computer** (○ changes to ●).

**5** Click **Back Up Now.**

**A** The Latest Backup readout shows the date and time of your most recent backup.

**6** Click **Restore Backup.**

**Note:** If a message appears saying *Find My iPad must be turned off before* iPad *can be restored*, tap **Settings** (⚙) on the iPad, tap **iCloud** (☁), tap **Find My iPad** (◉), and set the **Find My iPad** switch to Off (◯ changes to ◯ ).

**7** In the Restore From Backup dialog, click the pop-up menu (◉) and then click the backup to use.

**8** Click **Restore.**

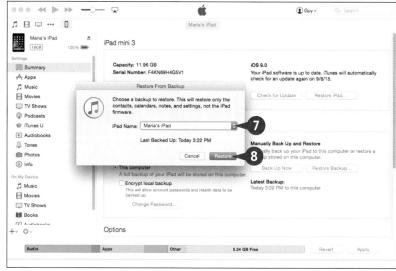

Ⓑ iTunes restores the data from the backup, showing a progress readout as it does so.

**Note:** Do not disconnect the iPad during the restore process. Doing so can leave the iPad in an unusable state.

iTunes displays a message saying that the settings for your iPad have been restored.

⑨ Click **OK** or wait for the countdown timer to close the dialog automatically.

Your iPad restarts.

iTunes automatically syncs your iPad.

⑩ After the sync completes, disconnect the iPad from your computer.

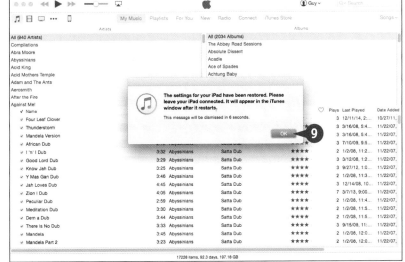

---

**TIP**

**How can I protect confidential information in my iPad backups?**

On the Summary screen in iTunes, click **Encrypt local backup** (☐ changes to ☑). In the Set Password dialog, type the password, and then click **Set Password**. iTunes then encrypts your backups using strong encryption.

In the Set Password dialog on the Mac, you can click **Remember this password in my keychain** (☐ changes to ☑) to store the password securely in your account's keychain.

# Back Up and Restore Your iPad Using iCloud

Instead of backing up your iPad to your computer, you can back it up to iCloud. If your iPad suffers a software or hardware failure, you can restore its data and settings from backup.

You can choose which items to back up to iCloud. You do not need to back up apps, media files, or games you have bought from the iTunes Store, because you can download them again.

## Back Up and Restore Your iPad Using iCloud

**1** Press **Home**.

The Home screen appears.

**2** Tap **Settings** (⚙).

The Settings screen appears.

**3** Tap **iCloud** (☁).

The iCloud screen appears.

**4** Choose the data you want to synchronize with iCloud by setting the **Mail** (✉), **Contacts** (👤), **Calendars** (📅), **Reminders** (⋮), **Safari** (🧭), **Notes** (—), and **News** (📰) switches to On (◉) or Off (○), as needed.

**5** Tap **Find My iPad** (◉) and then set the **Find My iPad** switch to On (◉) or Off (○), as needed.

**6** Tap **iCloud Drive** (☁).

The iCloud Drive screen appears.

**7** Set the **iCloud Drive** switch to On (○) to enable apps to store data in iCloud.

**8** Set each iCloud-capable app's switch to On (◉) or Off (○), as needed.

**9** Tap **iCloud** (<).

The iCloud screen appears.

**10** Tap **Photos** (🌼).

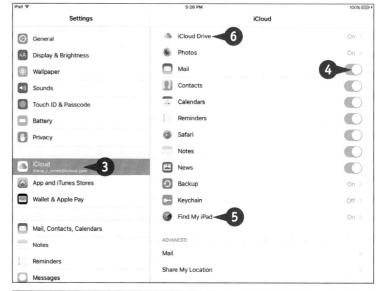

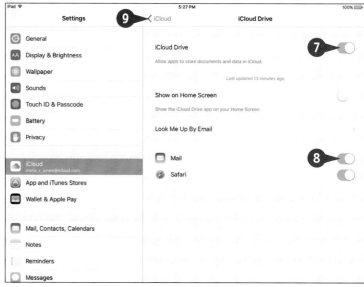

The Photos screen appears.

**11** Set the **iCloud Photo Library** switch to On (⬤) if you want to store all your photos in iCloud.

**12** Set the **My Photo Stream** switch to On (⬤) if you want to make your photos available to all your iOS devices and your computer.

**13** Set the **iCloud Photo Sharing** switch to On (⬤) if you want to share albums with others via iCloud.

**14** Tap **iCloud** (〈).

The iCloud screen appears.

**Note:** If you need to check your available storage, tap **Storage** on the iCloud screen. On the Storage screen, you can tap **Manage Storage** to manage your existing storage or tap **Buy More Storage** to pay for more storage.

**15** Tap **Backup** (🔄).

The Backup screen appears.

**16** Set the **iCloud Backup** switch to On (⬤).

**Ⓐ** The Last Backup readout shows when you last backed up your iPad to iCloud.

**17** If you want to back up your iPad now, tap **Back Up Now**.

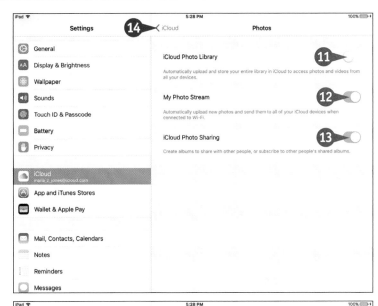

---

**TIP**

**How do I restore my iPad from its iCloud backup?**
First, reset the iPad to its factory settings, as explained in the section "Restore Your iPad to Factory Settings," later in this chapter. To do this, you must first turn off Find My iPad. When the iPad restarts and displays its setup screens, choose your language and country. On the Apps & Data screen, tap **Restore from iCloud Backup**, and then tap **Next**. On the Apple ID screen, enter your Apple ID, and then tap **Next**. On the Choose Backup screen, tap the backup you want to use — normally, the most recent backup — and then tap **Restore**.

# Restore the Operating System Using iTunes

If your iPad's operating system becomes corrupted, you can restore it by connecting the tablet to your computer and using iTunes. Restoring the iPad erases all its contents, so use this troubleshooting move only after other moves have failed.

When restoring the iPad, iTunes checks for an updated version of its software. If a new version is available, iTunes downloads and installs it automatically. The download may take minutes or hours, depending on the speed of your Internet connection.

## Restore the Operating System Using iTunes

**1** Connect your iPad to your computer via the USB cable.

**2** Click **iPad** (☐) on the navigation bar.

The iPad-management screen appears.

**3** Click **Summary**.

The Summary screen appears.

**4** Click **Restore iPad**.

**Note:** If a message appears saying *Find My iPad must be turned off before* iPad *can be restored*, tap **Settings** (⚙) on your iPad, tap **iCloud** (☁), tap **Find My iPad** (◉), and set the **Find My iPad** switch to Off (◯).

iTunes displays a message prompting you to back up the settings for the iPad before restoring.

**5** Click **Back Up**.

**Note:** If you have backed up the iPad very recently, you may prefer to click **Don't Back Up**.

iTunes displays a message confirming that you want to restore the iPad to its factory settings.

**6** Click **Restore**.

iTunes backs up the iPad if you chose to do so.

iTunes restores the iPad software.

Your iPad restarts and completes the restoration.

The Welcome to Your New iPad screen appears.

**7** Click **Restore from this backup** (○ changes to ⦿).

**8** Click the pop-up menu (◧) and choose the iPad backup to restore.

**9** Click **Continue**.

iTunes restores the data in the backup to your iPad.

## TIP

**Can I restore the iPad software to an earlier version?**

Yes, if you have the software file. iTunes stores the current version in the ~/Library/iTunes/iPad Software Updates folder on the Mac or the \Users\*username*\AppData\Roaming\Apple Computer\iTunes\iPad Software Updates\ folder on a Windows PC's system drive, such as C:. Each time iTunes downloads a new version, it deletes the old version, so copy the current version to a folder of your own if you want to keep it.

To choose which file to use, press Option+click **Restore iPad** on a Mac. In Windows, press Shift+click **Restore iPad**. In the dialog that opens, click the file.

# Restore Your iPad to Factory Settings

I f your iPad starts malfunctioning and iTunes will not recognize it, you can restore the iPad to its factory settings. Restoring the iPad to factory settings deletes all the media and data the tablet contains and returns all the settings to their default values, wiping out your accounts and customizations.

Normally, you restore your iPad to factory settings only when it is suffering severe problems that you cannot resolve otherwise or before you sell or give away your iPad.

## Restore Your iPad to Factory Settings

**1** Press **Home**.

The Home screen appears.

**2** Tap **Settings** (⚙).

The Settings screen appears.

**Note:** If your iPad is not responding to the Home button or your taps, press and hold **Sleep/Wake** and **Home** for about 15 seconds to reset the iPad.

**Note:** If you are restoring factory settings in preparation for selling or giving away your iPad, tap **iCloud** (☁), tap **Find My iPad** (🌐), and then set the **Find My iPad** switch to Off (⬤ changes to ○ ).

**3** Tap **General** (⚙).

The General screen appears.

**4** Tap **Reset**.

The Reset screen appears.

**5** Tap **Erase All Content and Settings**.

The first Erase iPad dialog opens.

**6** Tap **Erase**.

**Note:** If you have secured your iPad with Touch ID or a passcode, you must type the passcode after tapping Reset All Settings.

The second Erase iPad dialog opens, double-checking you are sure you want to erase all settings.

**7** Tap **Erase**.

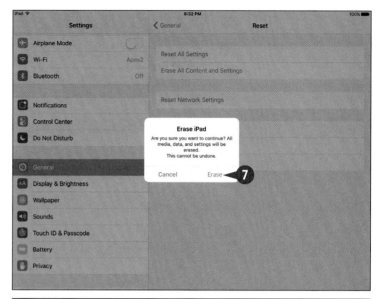

The Apple ID Password dialog opens.

**8** Type your Apple ID password.

**9** Tap **Erase**.

The iPad erases all your content and settings and restores itself to the factory settings. This takes several minutes.

When the operation is complete, the Hello screen appears, and you can set up your iPad as explained in Chapter 1.

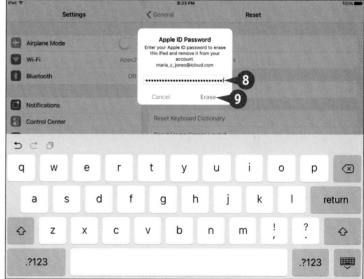

## TIP

**What does the Reset All Settings command on the Reset screen do?**

The Reset All Settings command restores all the iPad settings to their defaults, but it does not erase your data. Use this command when the iPad settings have become confused and you cannot correct them manually. After using this command, you will need to set the iPad settings again, either by restoring them using iTunes or by setting them manually, in order to get the iPad working the way you prefer.

The other commands on the Reset screen enable you to reset your iPad's network settings, the keyboard dictionary, the Home screen layout, and the Location and Privacy settings.

# Troubleshoot Wi-Fi Connections

Normally, your iPad automatically reconnects to Wi-Fi networks to which you have previously connected it, and maintains those connections without problems. But you may sometimes need to request the network address for your iPad again, a process called renewing the lease on the IP address. You may also need to tell your iPad to forget a network and then rejoin the network manually, providing the password again.

## Troubleshoot Wi-Fi Connections

### Renew the Lease on the IP Address of Your iPad

**1** Press **Home**.

The Home screen appears.

**2** Tap **Settings** (⚙).

The Settings screen appears.

**3** Tap **Wi-Fi** (📶).

The Wi-Fi screen appears.

**4** Tap **Information** (ⓘ) to the right of the network for which you want to renew the lease.

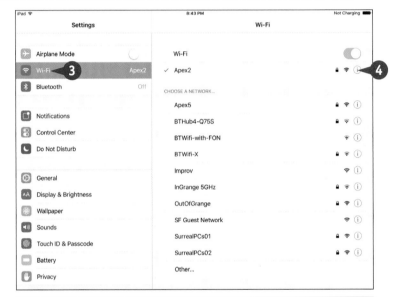

The network's screen appears.

**5** Tap **Renew Lease**.

The Renew Lease? dialog opens.

**6** Tap **Renew**.

**7** Tap **Wi-Fi** (‹).

The Wi-Fi screen appears.

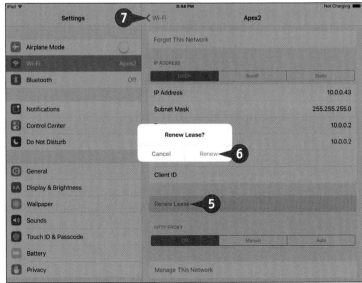

## Forget a Network and Then Rejoin It

**1** On the Wi-Fi screen, tap **Information** (ⓘ) to the right of the network.

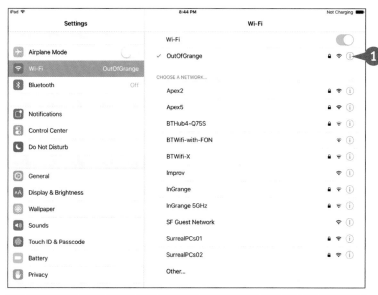

The network's screen appears.

**2** Tap **Forget This Network**.

The Forget Wi-Fi Network dialog opens.

**3** Tap **Forget**.

The iPad removes the network's details.

**4** Tap **Wi-Fi** (<).

The Wi-Fi screen appears.

**5** Tap the network's name.

The password screen appears.

**6** Type the password for the network.

**7** Tap **Join**.

The iPad joins the network.

---

## TIP

**What else can I do to reestablish my Wi-Fi network connections?**

If you are unable to fix your Wi-Fi network connections by renewing the IP address lease or by forgetting and rejoining the network, as described in this section, try restarting your iPad. If that does not work, open the Settings app, tap **General** (⚙), and tap **Reset** to display the Reset screen. Tap **Reset Network Settings**, type your passcode if prompted, and then tap **Reset** in the Reset Network Settings dialog. After this, you will need to set up each connection again manually.

# Locate Your iPad with Find My iPad

You can use the Find My iPad feature in iCloud to locate your iPad when it has been lost or stolen. You can also display a message on the iPad or remotely erase the data on the iPad. To use Find My iPad, you must first set up your iCloud account on your iPad and then enable the Find My iPad feature.

You can use Find My iPad in a web browser on a computer or a non-iOS phone or tablet. On iOS, use the Find My iPhone app instead.

## Locate Your iPad with Find My iPad

### Turn On the Find My iPad Feature

1. Set up your iCloud account on your iPad as discussed the section "Set Up and Configure iCloud" in Chapter 2.

2. Press **Home**.

   The Home screen appears.

3. Tap **Settings** (⚙).

   The Settings screen appears.

4. Tap **iCloud** (☁).

   The iCloud screen appears.

5. Tap **Find My iPad** (◉).

   The Find My iPad screen appears.

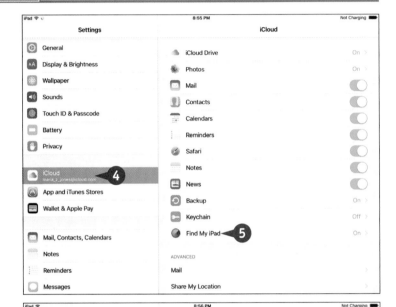

6. Set the **Find My iPad** switch to On (○).

**Note:** If a confirmation dialog appears, tap **Allow**.

   iCloud turns on the Find My iPad feature.

7. Set the **Send Last Location** switch to On (○) if you want your iPad to send its location to Apple when the battery runs critically low.

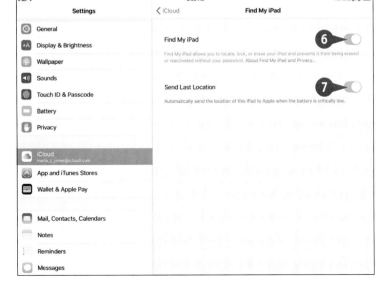

## Locate Your iPad Using Find My iPad

1 On a computer or non-Apple mobile device, open a web browser, such as Chrome, Firefox, Internet Explorer, Microsoft Edge, or Safari.

2 Click the Address box.

3 Type www.icloud.com, and press `Enter` in Windows or `Return` on a Mac.

The Sign in to iCloud web page appears.

4 Type your username.

5 Type your password.

6 Click **Sign In** (➔).

The iCloud apps screen appears.

**Note:** If iCloud displays the page you last used, click **iCloud** to display the iCloud apps screen.

7 Click **Find My iPhone**.

**Note:** You can use the iCloud feature called Find My iPhone to find the iPad and iPod touch as well as the iPhone. The iPad itself refers to this feature as Find My iPad.

**Note:** If iCloud prompts you to sign in again to use Find My iPhone, type your password and click **Sign In**.

---

**TIP**

**Is it worth displaying a message on my iPad, or should I simply wipe it?**
Almost always, it is definitely worth displaying a message on your iPad. If you have lost your iPad, and someone has found it, that person may be trying to return it to you. The chances are good that the finder is honest, even if he has not discovered that you have locked the iPad with a passcode. That said, if you are certain someone has stolen your iPad, you may prefer simply to wipe it, using the technique explained next.

continued ▶

If Find My iPad reveals that someone has taken your iPad, you can wipe its contents to prevent whoever has taken it from hacking into your data. Be clear that wiping your iPad prevents you from locating the iPad again — ever — except by chance. Wipe your iPad only when you have lost it, you have no hope of recovering it, and you must destroy the data on it.

## Locate Your iPad with Find My iPad (continued)

The iCloud Find My iPhone screen appears.

**8** Click **All Devices**.

The All Devices list appears.

**9** Click your iPad.

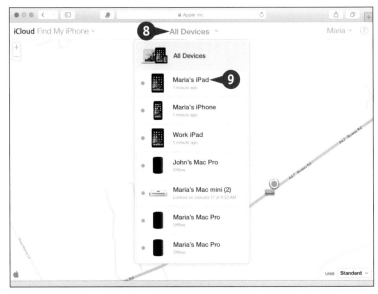

The Info dialog appears, showing the location of your iPad.

**10** If you want to play a sound on the iPad, click **Play Sound** (🔊). This feature is helpful for locating your iPad if you have mislaid it somewhere nearby.

**A** A message indicates that the iPad has played the sound.

### Use Lost Mode

**1** Click **Lost Mode** (🔒) in the Info dialog.

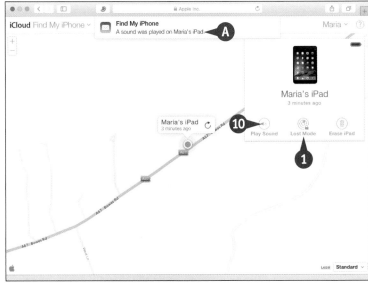

The Lost Mode dialog appears, prompting you to enter a phone number where you can be reached.

2 Optionally, click **Number** and type the number.

3 Click **Next**.

The Lost Mode dialog prompts you to enter a message.

4 Type a message to whoever finds your iPad.

5 Click **Done**.

iCloud sends the Lost Mode command to the iPad, which displays the phone number and message.

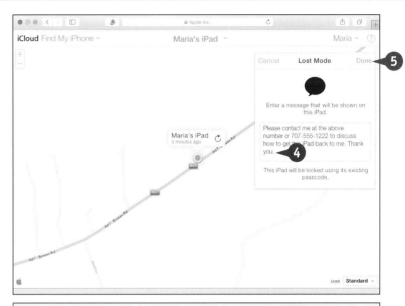

### Remotely Erase the iPad

1 Click **Erase iPad** (⊙) in the Info dialog.

The Erase This iPad? dialog opens.

2 Click **Erase**.

The Enter Your Apple ID Password dialog appears.

3 Type your password.

4 Click **Erase**.

iCloud sends the erase command to the iPad, which erases its data.

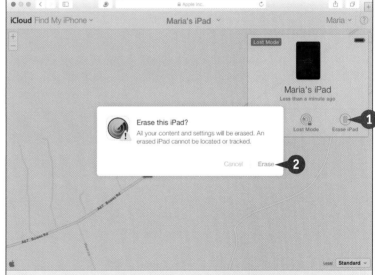

---

## TIP

**Can I remotely wipe the data on my iPad if I do not have an iCloud account?**

Yes. You can set a passcode for the iPad as discussed in the section "Secure Your iPad with Touch ID or a Passcode" in Chapter 2, and then set the **Erase Data** switch on the Touch ID & Passcode screen to On (◯). This setting makes the iPad automatically erase its data after ten successive failed attempts to enter the passcode. After five failed attempts, the iPad enforces a delay before the next attempt; further failures increase the delay.

# Index